DATE DUE

PRINTED IN U.S.A.

Studies in Body and Religion

Series Editors:
Richard M. Carp, Saint Mary's College of California
and Rebecca Sachs Norris, Merrimack College

Studies in Body and Religion publishes contemporary research and theory that addresses body as a fundamental category of analysis in the study of religion. Embodied humans conceive of, study, transmit, receive, and practice religion, with and through their bodies and bodily capacities. Volumes in this series will include diverse examples and perspectives on the roles and understandings of body in religion, as well as the influence and importance of religion for body. They will also move conversation on body and religion forward by problematizing "body,' which, like "religion," is a contested concept. We do not know exactly what religion is, nor do we know exactly what body is, either; much less do we understand their mutual interpenetrations. This series aims to address this by bringing multiple understandings of body into an arena of conversation.

Titles in the Series

Early Daoist Dietary Practices, by Shawn Arthur
Dancing Culture Religion, by Sam Gill
Risky Marriage, by Melissa Browning

Risky Marriage

HIV and Intimate Relationships in Tanzania

Melissa Browning

LEXINGTON BOOKS
Lanham • Boulder • New York • Toronto • Plymouth, UK

Published by Lexington Books
A wholly owned subsidiary of The Rowman & Littlefield Publishing Group, Inc.
4501 Forbes Boulevard, Suite 200, Lanham, Maryland 20706
www.rowman.com

10 Thornbury Road, Plymouth PL6 7PP, United Kingdom

Copyright © 2014 by Lexington Books

British Library Cataloguing in Publication Information Available

Library of Congress Cataloging-in-Publication Data

Browning, Melissa, 1977-
Risky marriage : the impact of Christian marriage on the prevalence of HIV/AIDS in Tanzania / Melissa Browning.
pages cm. — (Studies in body and religion)
Includes bibliographical references.
ISBN 978-0-7391-7660-3 (cloth : alk. paper) — ISBN 978-0-7391-7661-0 (pbk. : alk. paper) — ISBN 978-0-7391-7662-7 (ebook)
1. AIDS (Disease)—Tanzania. 2. Marriage—Religious aspects—Christianity—Tanzania. I. Title.
RA643.86.T34B76 2014
362.19697'92009678—dc23
2013023695

Printed in the United States of America

For Wes, my partner in the journey

Contents

Acknowledgments

First and foremost, I would like to thank the women and men who participated in this study. They not only showed an eagerness to be part of the project but also welcomed me as a member of their community. I am especially grateful for Pauline Gasabile who served as my mentor and research advocate in Mwanza, Tanzania. Also, I am grateful to the Diocese of Victoria Nyanza HIV and AIDS Support Group and for the women who gave of their time and experience to participate in the PAR portion of this study. Agnes, Christine, Domina, Esther, Grace, Jane, Jesca, Joan, Joyce, Maria, Scholastica, and Veronica—you have been my teachers, and I thank God for each of you. I am also grateful for others who helped facilitate or participated in my fieldwork: Bishop Boniface Kwangu and the Diocese of Victoria Nyanza, Fr. Aidan Msifiri of Saint Augustine College of Tanzania, Shalom HIV/AIDS Support Groups, Catholic Relief Services of Mwanza, the Africa Inland Church (AIC) Clinic of Mwanza, the Mwanza Missionary Fellowship group, and my field assistants, Hellen, Immanuella, and Mwaooc. I would also like to thank the International Languages Training Centre (ILTC) in Mwanza who translated and transcribed the fieldwork for this research.

I am especially grateful to those who have read my work and mentored me in this process, particularly Susan A. Ross, Aana Marie Vigen, and Patricia Beattie Jung, who provided invaluable insights during both my fieldwork and writing. I would also like to thank my editors, Rebecca Sachs Norris and Richard Carp (Body and Religion series), as well as Eric Wrona at Lexington Books. I am immensely grateful for their suggestions and support in the development of this book. I am also grateful for Marissa Carpenter who worked diligently to complete the book's index and helped with editing. Luiana Foibe Makundi generously created an amazing piece of artwork for the cover of this book and named it "Risky Marriage," honoring the stories that are found in these pages. I am grateful for her artistic vision and her passion in using art to create social change.

I would also like to thank colleagues and friends who were willing to give advice on the project, read the project proposal or portions of this dissertation, and listen while I talked about the results. Among these people are Michael Schuck, Jacob Myers, Abby Myers, Jeanine Viau, Amber Unruh, Damaris Parsitau, Emily Reimer-Barry, Elisabeth Vasko, Eunice Kamaara, Edith Kayeli, Musa Muneja, Amanda Robertson, Andrea

Hollingsworth, Josh Smith, Caroline Smith, Katy Annanasi, James Calcagno, and Japonica Brown-Saracino and Jenny Trinitapoli. I am also grateful for individuals who gave donations of supplies to help facilitate my fieldwork: Amber Unruh and Jeanine Viau, Laura Seay, Amanda Robertson and Dan Robertson, Christina Whitehouse-Suggs, Don Brown, Elaine Brown, and Mary Stephens.

This project would also not have been possible without funding. Loyola University Chicago provided a grant for fieldwork supplies through the Graduate/Undergraduate Research Mentorship Program and also funded my fieldwork through the Advanced Doctoral Fellowship and the Authur J. Schmitt Dissertation Fellowship. I would also like to thank the Religious Research Society who awarded me the Constant H. Jacquet Research Award, which funded part of the fieldwork in this project. I would also like to thank the American Association of University Women who funded the writing of this book through an American Fellowship. Loyola University Chicago and the Institute of Pastoral Studies also provided funding for indexing and for commissioning artwork for the cover through their manuscript assistance grant.

I could not be more grateful for my family who helped at every stage of this process. My sweet soulmate, Wes Browning, packed his bags and lived in Tanzania for a year while I collected data. Without his constant support, this project would have never come to fruition. I'm also grateful to my daughter, Olivia, who patiently played with others to give her mom time to write. I would also like to thank my parents, Don Brown and Elaine Brown, and my brother, Ryan Brown, and my sister-in-law, Laura Brown, who always found ways to encourage me.

I'm also grateful to those who created space for me to write. I'm thankful for friends and family who cared for Olivia: for my mom and sister-in-law, who kept Olivia during numerous writing retreats, and for Olivia's nanny, Jill Youmans. I'm also grateful for my colleagues at the Institute of Pastoral Studies at Loyola University Chicago who encouraged me to find time to write and always asked about my research. For this more, I'll always be grateful.

Introduction

When we talk about HIV and AIDS, we cannot do so without talking about bodies. For people living with HIV and AIDS, the body is a site of both pain and promise. It is where the daily struggle for human flourishing and well-being takes place. Here, thinking about the body does not come from the privileged philosophical space of the academy but from lived experiences in which care for the body is (or at least should be) all-important. For this reason, any theological discourse that seeks to address HIV and AIDS must be rooted in theologies of embodiment. In order to be relevant or realistic, these discourses must be grounded in the lived experiences of those who bear the burdens of the HIV and AIDS pandemic.

In sub-Saharan Africa, these burdens are too often women's burdens. Nearly 59 percent of those who are living with HIV and AIDS in this region are women and girls. Therefore, in responding to the sub-Saharan African pandemic, the experiences of women must guide our course. As we respond to HIV and AIDS, we must remember that pandemic itself is rooted in the particular. This book is a journey into the particular. It does not seek to represent quantitative data but rather to put qualitative experiences in dialogue with existing data on the African and global pandemics.

In the midst of places where HIV and AIDS are spreading like wild-fire, people are turning to faith to find resources for human flourishing and survival. Drawing from the lived experiences of women living with HIV and AIDS in Mwanza, Tanzania, this book takes a critical look at how Christian churches (both locally and globally) are responding to the pandemic. In arguing from women's experience that marriage is a risk factor, the book asks how Christian churches can make marriage a safer place, a place of flourishing, for all people. Since Christian churches are in the "business" of marrying people, this book argues that marriage is an appropriate and timely place for churches to create lasting change in response to this pandemic.

FIELDWORK METHODOLOGY

A book about why marriage in Africa is risky can be written in a library, its arguments supported by the latest public health statistics. But that's not what this book is. This book is deeply rooted in the lives of people living with HIV and AIDS in Mwanza, Tanzania. By basing this book on their lived experiences, I am seeking to give priority those who have experienced marriage as an HIV risk factor. While this research is rooted in the particular, many findings will resonate with communities throughout sub-Saharan Africa because of the socio-cultural similarities in this region.

The stories and data in this book come from eight months of fieldwork with members of HIV and AIDS support groups in Mwanza. The fieldwork conducted in this project includes four qualitative methodologies: open-ended interviews, participatory observation, focus groups organized around specific topics, and a participatory action research focus group.

Many of the stories in this book come from the participatory action research (PAR) phase of the research, where twelve women, 80 percent of whom contracted HIV from their marriages, spent nine three-hour sessions together over a period of three months discussing marriage, relationality, and HIV and AIDS. In between each week's meetings, the women designed and completed various activities involving drama, photography, art, and storytelling and then came back the following week to share and reflect on these activities.

In the participatory action research phase of this project, the shared goal of the group was to create a safe space where research collaborators could give voice their experiences. Beverly Haddad, a theologian and Episcopal priest in South Africa, argues that for change to happen, safe spaces for women must be created where they can speak freely about issues and solutions. In reflecting on her participatory action research and work with women in KwaZulu-Natal, she talks about the development of "infrapolitics," which is defined as a form of discourse that has one meaning in public but has an entirely different meaning in the private (hidden) realm. In creating safe spaces, Haddad sees women being given the chance to articulate these "hidden transcripts" away from the control of those in power, such as men.[1]

In many ways, the women in this study modeled the same process. Through their collaborative work participating in the research, they were able to build on each other's stories to propose creative solutions that might make marriage safe. This book is a book of stories—stories that teach us something about the complexity of the HIV and AIDS pandemic. These stories cannot be boiled down to simple categories. Too often when we read narratives of people living with HIV and AIDS we read stories and label people as "victim." This is not the case for the women in this project. While they named spaces in which they felt they had been victimized or oppressed, they simultaneously named their strengths and triumphs. In this text, I try to honor their voices by naming the various complexities of their lives as they described them. I hope to neither romanticize their struggles nor label them as victims, but I realize I may err on either side of this polarized divide. In the very act of retelling these powerful stories, I know I cannot help but fail in portraying the full, embodied complexity of the lives these women live. Perhaps this is always the case. People are not meant to be described with words but known in person.

A PROLEGOMENON TO RESEARCH: AN "INTERROGATION OF WHITENESS" IN POSTCOLONIAL SPACE

In writing this book, my attempt is to create an interdisciplinary, multivocal, and intercultural response to the HIV and AIDS pandemic. I believe deeply that if we are to respond to the deep and reaching problems in our world, then we must address these problems from multiple angles and perspectives. Global problems demand a global response.

Yet, in any research project the question must be asked as to how the researcher's social location shapes the research she hopes to accomplish.[2] It is for this reason that I pause for a prolegomenon. A common saying among foreigners who have lived in Africa opines that "Once you live in Africa, the continent is forever a part of you." It is for this reason that I felt compelled to write on HIV outside of my own cultural and geographical context. After working and studying in Kenya and knowing many people there who were living with HIV or AIDS, I wanted my research to be a response that honored their lives. And as a person living between two worlds, as an American living in Kenya, I was troubled by the responses of Western Christian churches that sent mission teams to lead abstinence crusades or preach stigmatizing sexual ethics in foreign pulpits. It was firsthand encounters with some of these sermons and crusades that made me realize that more intercultural theo-ethical work was needed on HIV and AIDS.

While I believe I have something to say, I know the words I speak come from my own experience and carry with them the baggage of my own particular culture, education, and privilege. Though East African mothers have "adopted" me and called me daughter, the place of my birth is far away from their African homes. This birthplace has given me privilege that protects me from many of the vulnerabilities that their lives are subject to each day. Because this privilege is unjust, I must confront it before a dialogue with the women in this study can have any real meaning.

Part of my own ongoing self-critical reflection and commitments to anti-racism work lead me to explore missionary movements that have imported ethical norms without understanding how they would fit within African worldviews. To illustrate, consider the example of how Western missionary churches have dealt with polygamy.[3] Early Catholic and

Protestant missionaries disapproved of and often prohibited polygamy among Christian converts. While as a feminist ethicist I believe whole-heartedly that monogamy is a better relational model for women, I am still critical of the ways in which both polygamy and the multiple "secondary" wives of men who joined missionary churches were (and still are) cast aside in the name of Christian ethical norms. Monogamy became a litmus test for male conversion without a thorough investigation of how polygamy functioned culturally and without a transformation of the cultural constructions of masculinity. As a result, many of the gendered practices associated with polygamy are still felt today as "hidden polygamy" fuels the HIV pandemic.[4] This anti-racism critique also leads me to ask why so many people affected by HIV and AIDS in this world—even in my own country—are poor, black, and female.

In short, this critique is part of my research, for an interrogation of my own culture, an "interrogation of whiteness,"[5] and an examination of Christianity's role in Africa's HIV and AIDS pandemic is long overdue. But I realize that even an anti-racism critique is not enough. I must also question the power and privilege in which I have, and still, participate. The place of my birth, my socio-economic class, my opportunity for education, all must be interrogated within my primary community of accountability, which for this book I define as the women and men who participated in this research.

I also come to this project as a person who has been married for fourteen years to a husband who is fully invested in a relationship built on mutuality and equality. In saying this, I recognize that my own experience of marriage has been very different from the experiences of the women in this study. While my experience of marriage on a personal level shaped some of the questions I brought to this project, I also sought to put this understanding aside in order to listen more closely to marriage as described by my collaborators in this project.

This point brings me to the struggle of speaking and giving space. At the American Academy of Religion meeting in 2006, I sought the advice of some wise women who have been living in this struggle. At the end of a session honoring the work of Ghanaian scholar, Mercy Amba Oduyoye, I asked the question, "As a white, Western feminist who knows Africa has become part of my life, when should I speak about Africa, and when should I stand in silent solidarity?" I received two answers. The first answer, from Mercy Oduyoye, was a caution to speak only after I've spent a long time listening. The second answer, from white, Western, feminist theologian Letty Russell, was the advice to never be silent, because silence only comes from fear. "It's better to be told you're wrong and be in dialogue," she said "than to say nothing at all."[6] Saying something requires the willingness to stand between two worlds and listen long before attempting to speak. It means embracing the paradox of never fully understanding, but understanding all too well, the struggles of my sisters in the global south. So with these wise words tucked in this prolegomenon, I will precede carefully, critically, hoping to honor, and become accountable to, the women who have called themselves my mothers, sisters, and friends during the days I have lived on East Africa's soil.

OVERVIEW OF BOOK

The aim of this book is to listen faithfully to the lived experiences of women living with HIV and AIDS and ask how their experiences can help us re-imagine Christian conceptions of marriage, sexual ethics, and health in an "HIV-positive" world. Within these pages, my hope is that this listening will point toward ways in which we as a global community can make marriage a safer space for both women and men.

I begin the book in chapter 1 by responding to one collaborator in the study who argued (in opposition to African norms) that in light of HIV and AIDS, "It's better to be single." Building on this, I examine the roles of wives and girlfriends and ask how power shapes intimate relationships in both contexts. I then focus on women and marriage in sub-Saharan Africa, turning both to the past (pre-colonial) traditions and to the present lived experiences of the women in this study.

In chapter 2, I look more deeply at the forces behind the African HIV pandemic by asking why sub-Saharan Africa is more greatly affected than the rest of the world. Here, I consider co-factors in the transmission of HIV such as traditional practices, poor health, education, and poverty. In chapter 3, I continue this discussion by looking at the taboo nature of sex in East African societies and the unique vulnerabilities of women and girls. I begin to look at some of the reasons that marriage has become an HIV and AIDS risk factor and argue that in light of this risk, the primary focus on sexual ethics (particularly abstinence and faithfulness) within faith-based programs is inadequate for prevention if women are not simultaneously empowered to choose against the religious and cultural patriarchy that disempowers them.

Chapters 4 and 5 turn to a generative theme within the fieldwork: self-sacrifice and gender. I begin in chapter 4 by looking at intercultural understandings of women's sacrifice within marriage. Here, I put my fieldwork in dialogue with feminist theories and feminist theologies to critique white, Western, feminist notions of agency and self-sacrifice. I use data from my fieldwork to talk about the risks present in intimate relationships and focus on specific issues such as polygamy and *mahari* (or bridewealth). In chapter 5 I conclude that in sub-Saharan Africa, women's sacrifice is often not voluntary or self-deprecating but instead must be understood as an alternative to their being sacrificed within patriarchal systems.

Chapters 6 and 7 continue my fieldwork analysis by focusing on another generative theme within the study: stigma. In this chapter, the theme of women's sacrifice is further explored in light of the ways in which people living with HIV and AIDS are stigmatized. My starting point is a suggestion that AIDS-related stigma and the ways in which it is experienced are likely tied to the history of colonization on the continent. I begin by drawing on intercultural interpretations of stigma, HIV and AIDS, and social systems. I then move to a postcolonial feminist interpretation of stigma where I use my fieldwork to analyze the ways in which fear, silence and secret-keeping, taboo and sin, and sacrifice function in relation to stigma. The effect of stigma on intimate relationships is explored as well as the presence of stigma in Christian churches. I conclude in chapter 7 by arguing that a postcolonial feminist interpretation of stigma demands a normative Christian ethic that turns to collective responsibility as a way of addressing the issues of HIV and AIDS in our world.

Chapter 8 focuses on intimate relationships in postcolonial space as it employs a feminist postcolonial lens to ask why marriage has become an HIV risk factor for women. By looking at marriage, not in isolation but as part of the missionary movements and colonial history that shapes the continent, a more thorough analysis of marriage is attempted, and problems within the current structures of Christian marriage in East Africa are addressed. Within this chapter, a rationale for listening to women's experience is articulated and attention is given to the balance between giving voice to all experience while creating space to speak normatively across cultures. The chapter then moves to offer a re-imagination of Christian marriage and sexual ethics. Toward this end, the second half of the chapter focuses on the importance of reframing marriage in terms of social ethics, rather than sexual ethics. I focus on particular social issues within marriage such as *mahari* (or bridewealth), marriage age, preparing for marriage and women's economic vulnerabilities. I then look at marriage through the lens of theologies of embodiment and relationality by asking what women's bodies can teach us about rethinking marriage. Pulling primarily from the generative themes articulated and the stories of lived experiences detailed throughout the book, I put my fieldwork in conversation with current theo-ethical literature in order to reconstruct a Christian sexual ethics within marriage that responds to the HIV pandemic by first listening to women.

NOTES

1. Beverley Haddad, "Faith Resources and Sites as Critical to Participatory Learning with Rural South African Women," *Journal of Feminist Studies in Religion*, vol. 22, no. 1, 2006, 135–54.

2. For more on my own critical self-reflection on the role of epistemological privilege in this project, see, Melissa Browning, "Epistemological Privilege and Collabora-

tive Research: A Reflection on Researching as an Outsider," *Practical Matters*, Issue 6, May 2013.

3. While polygyny (a relationship where one man has multiple wives) is a more accurate term to refer to polygamy in the African context, I use the term "polygamy" in this book to make the concept more accessible to readers who may be unfamiliar with other terminology.

4. Hidden polygamy is defined as a monogamous marriage with girlfriends (sometimes with girlfriends who function almost as wives) on the side. This is often practiced when men work in the city but their family is in the village. While not publicly spoken of, this often happens with the wife's knowledge.

5. In using this phrase, I am drawing on the work of Emilie Townes, *Womanist Ethics and the Cultural Production of Evil,* (Basingstoke: Palgrave Macmillan, 2006), 57–78.

6. Mercy Oduyoye, Katie Cannon, Musa Dube, Sarojini Nadar, and Letty Russell. "Women Speaking to Religion and Leadership: Honoring the Work of Mercy Oduyoye," American Academy of Religion Annual Meeting, Washington, DC, Nov. 18, 2006.

ONE

"It's Better to Be Single"

Thinking About Marriage in the Midst of a Pandemic

"It's better to be single," she said. Then she paused, as if she were waiting for the words to sink in. In Tanzania, nearly everyone thinks it's better to be married. Before I could ask her why, Christine[1] explained, "If a person is not married, you can decide to be faithful to one partner, or decide to abstain, or decide that you are always going to have protected sex, but if you're married, it is different."

Christine wasn't alone in her opinion. Later that afternoon in an interview with Jane, I heard the same sentiment. Like Christine, Jane contracted HIV from her marriage. Jane told me her husband was the only person she'd ever had sex with, but while her husband was a good man, he had an affair. Like Christine, Jane was now an HIV-positive widow. When I asked Jane if marriage was an HIV risk factor, she quickly agreed. She said that if she had not been married, she would not be HIV-positive. When I asked her why marriage was an HIV risk factor, she pinned the question back on me. Knowing that I was doing research, she pointed at me like a mother instructing a young child and said, "Indeed, there is a need for further research on this." She told me I should research this and then I could come back and let her know why marriage was so dangerous for women.

WOMEN, MARRIAGE, AND HIV AND AIDS IN SUB-SAHARAN AFRICA

In talking about the African HIV pandemic, a good place to begin is by taking a look at the numbers. How bad is HIV and AIDS prevalence in sub-Saharan Africa? As of 2011, 34 million people in our world were living with HIV and AIDS, and of these people, 22.9 million (67 percent) were in sub-Saharan Africa. Included in these numbers are 2.3 million children who are infected with the disease. Of the 16.6 million children orphaned by AIDS in our world, nearly 90 percent live in sub-Saharan Africa. Globally, 68 percent of all new adult infections and 91 percent of all new infections among children are in sub-Saharan Africa.[2]

While both new infection rates and the number of people dying from AIDS-related deaths are on the decline in sub-Saharan Africa, the region still has higher numbers in both categories than any other region in the world. There are obstacles both in curbing new infections and in procuring and distributing vital ARTs (anti-retroviral treatments) that could keep people alive. Seventy percent of the AIDS-related deaths in 2011 were in sub-Saharan Africa—1.2 million Africans died from AIDS. The sub-Saharan Africa region hosts three countries whose adult HIV prevalence has surged higher than thought possible, with Botswana at 23 percent, Lesotho at 23 percent, and Swaziland at 26 percent. This means that approximately one in four adults are living with HIV or AIDS.[3]

Though it never reached the same epidemic level as the sub-Saharan African epidemic, the spread of HIV was somewhat controlled in the West through education and pharmaceutical advances.[4] In sub-Saharan Africa, due to the size of the pandemic, curbing the spread of HIV has been a slow and arduous process. However, there have been improvements. According to statistics from 2011, new infections in sub-Saharan Africa were approximately 25 percent lower than they were in 2001. In 2011, there were 1.8 million new infections compared to 2.4 million in 2001. Due to a rollout of HIV drugs, there has been a 32 percent decline in HIV-related mortality since 2005.[5] While this is good news, the sheer numbers of those affected signal the problem will not go away any time soon.

In Africa, it is women and girls who carry the greatest burdens of the HIV pandemic. As of 2011, 58 percent of people living with HIV and AIDS in sub-Saharan Africa were women and girls.[6] Women also represent the segment of the population with the fastest growing incidence rate—almost 3,000 women are infected in sub-Saharan Africa each day. That means 57 percent of new infections in sub-Saharan Africa are among women and girls.[7] Young women ages fifteen to twenty-four are contracting HIV at three times the rate of young men in the same age group.[8] Women carry these burdens because they are more vulnerable biologically, economically, legally, socially, and relationally. Yet sub-Saharan Africa is one of the only places in our world where women have greater infection rates than men.[9] This is our first clue that something has gone horribly wrong.

In sub-Saharan Africa, HIV and AIDS have a female face. Africa's women who nurture life into existence are threatened with losing the very life-force they seek to sustain. The women who care for the sick and do not abandon the dying are being stigmatized by a disease, and their ability to protect themselves is limited by both church and society. These women also have the least access to education, the fewest resources to prevent HIV or treat AIDS, and economically, the most to lose, for poverty also has a female face. Even what many people assume to be safe spaces have become places of risk. In sub-Saharan Africa, marriage has become an HIV risk factor, particularly for women.[10]

It is women who carry the burdens of the African HIV pandemic. Yet when it comes to preventing HIV, those who are seeking solutions do not always consult women. In response to this lacuna, this book builds on eight months of qualitative fieldwork with people living with HIV and AIDS in Mwanza, Tanzania, in order to analyze the ways in which marriage has become an HIV risk factor for women. By beginning with women's experience as a hermeneutical lens, this book seeks to establish a creative space where African communities (and the global community) can imagine new alternatives to HIV prevention. Ultimately, it explores how we can re-imagine Christian marriage in ways that will promote human flourishing—the well-being and thriving of all people—and prioritize health and "abundant life" in African communities.[11]

In answering the question of why marriage is an HIV risk factor in sub-Saharan Africa, I begin with my fieldwork to suggest that one of the most fundamental obstacles in preventing HIV is inequality within marriage. This is not a new argument. African feminist/womanist theologians, aid agencies, and others working with women on the continent have pointed out that women, especially those living in rural areas, rarely feel empowered to negotiate sexual agency in intimate relationships.[12] In fact, often women are more empowered to negotiate sex outside of marriage than within a marriage. In light of economic and gender inequalities, women's bodies can become their only commodity, limiting the availability of agential decision-making. But once women are married, research collaborators in the study suggested that many women lose even the small ability to control their bodies as their bodies are often seen as the commodities of their husbands.

The women in this study reported that in many marriages in Tanzania, decisions about sex are made by men, not women. Women collaborators said that within their marriages they had little power to demand their husband's faithfulness or even to inquire about his comings and goings. They said that married women took great risks when refusing sex, as this act could lead to their being abandoned or to a loss of property, children, or livelihood. During a focus group session, one woman said that when she refused sex in her marriage, she would be "beaten first and raped later." The other women in the room agreed that this is what usually happened to them as well.

Such realities prompt me to conclude that when it comes to preventing HIV, the issue at hand is far more complex than a simple choice to be "abstinent" or "faithful."[13] This book seeks to address this complexity by putting women's experiences in dialogue with the theo-ethical literature on HIV and AIDS and Christian marriage. Specifically, in this book I argue that when advocating for abstinence and faithfulness, Christian faith-based programs often fail to reflect upon the agency and autonomy[14] required to choose abstinence or faithfulness. In any social context, when agency is limited by gender, social, economic, or other relations, teaching abstinence and faithfulness as the solution may harm women more than it helps.

While not playing the part of the victim, the women in this study did give significant examples of ways their agency has been limited by their communities. Nearly (but not all) the women in this study reported being faithful within their marriages but said that their faithfulness did not protect them.[15] Additionally, because women make up the primary membership at Christian churches across the African continent,[16] the message to be faithful is preached primarily to the faithful. When women take this instruction, they often feel compelled to be faithful to their marriages, even if their partners do not remain faithful. This makes them more vulnerable when HIV is brought into the marriage by the unfaithful spouse. Because abstinence and faithfulness require full agency, when full agency is not present, promoting and prioritizing these two practices as if they are always in reach is neither an adequate prevention strategy nor a moral option.

In order to address these concerns, I began my fieldwork design by asking two primary focus questions to guide the qualitative research and the book. First, I asked if Christian churches[17] that promote abstinence and fidelity without a critique of patriarchy do more to spread HIV than to prevent it. Or, to phrase the question another way: In the absence of gender equality and full agency, is promoting abstinence or faithfulness a viable (or moral) option to protect women? This question is paramount in light of UNAIDS focus on partnering with Christian churches throughout sub-Saharan Africa.[18] My argument in this book is that neither abstinence nor fidelity is possible without gender equality, and therefore the instruction to be "abstinent until marriage" and "faithful within marriage" could be one reason marriage is such a risk factor for women in Africa. I explore this claim within the context of African feminist theology as I argue that colonialism and Christianity have eroded traditional norms, safeguards, and taboos, especially those surrounding marriage, and therefore have contributed to the spread of HIV.[19]

Second, I asked whether or not the Christian churches are able to breathe new life into sexual ethics and into the practices of Christian marriage by listening to the experiences of women living with HIV and AIDS in sub-Saharan Africa. Could creating safe spaces for women's speech break the fatalism and stigma that surrounds HIV/AIDS? And could praxis (action and reflection) by women be the catalyst needed to curb the pandemic? If so, what constraints must be removed to give women freedom and space to empower their communities, especially communities of faith?

Here, I argue that when women are given a chance to tell their stories, a theo-ethical narrative can develop that will inform the church's sexual ethics and create new solutions to prevent HIV and AIDS. The church is in the business of marriage, and therefore talking about marriage is a good place for Christian churches and faith-based initiatives to start when thinking about HIV prevention. But the HIV pandemic points to the problems within current understandings of marriage in this region (and possibly in other regions as well). Simply put, if marriage worked, if vows were kept, if equality were present, marriage would not be an HIV risk factor. Marriage must be recreated as a safe space for women. This project asks what a space of women's flourishing would look like in the midst of this pandemic, and how a space of flourishing for women could bring the pandemic to an end.

Listening to the Present: The Situation of Women in Sub-Saharan Africa

Within both African feminist theologies and feminist economic development theories there is an urgency not only to seek out human flourishing but also to end quickly the flourishing of poverty, disease, and gender inequality. As previously mentioned, the link between patriarchy and HIV in Africa is widely recognized by both aid organizations and by African women theologians. However, even while recognizing this link, the primary focus of Christian faith-based organizations for preventing HIV has been sexual behavior change. As a result, the discussion of HIV and AIDS in sub-Saharan Africa has become a narrow conversation in behavior-focused sexual ethics, as communities in the developing world have looked for salvation in their ABCs.

The ABC campaign, which promotes *abstinence, being faithful,* and *condoms,* fails to address the social justice issues that cause the spread of the disease, such as gender inequality. While the ABCs have been said to help in some countries to lower transmission rates,[20] behavior change programs do not always work for women and can actually put them at risk, especially when men are not also targeted in these programs. Janet Fleischman, an adviser to the Global Coalition on Women and AIDS, argues for the addition of a "DEF" that would include *disclosure* of HIV status, *education* for women and girls, and *female controlled prevention methods,* such as microbicides and female condoms.[21]

For many Christian churches in Africa, focus on prevention still focuses primarily on abstinence and fidelity.[22] But what if the research is being interpreted correctly and many African women, because of patriarchal norms or economic vulnerabilities, have few viable choices when it comes to decisions about sex? What if both their survival and their demise are based in the currency of their bodies? What then can abstinence or fidelity mean to women in a society where patriarchy determines the rules and there is often a disregard for boundaries that might keep them and their sexual partners safe? Perhaps it means only blame and stigma, for if faithfulness equals salvation, contracting HIV implies sin.

While the ABC approach still has a strong following, in 2003 the *African Network of Religious Leaders Living with or Personally Affected by HIV/AIDS (ANERELA+)* developed a new approach that asked religious leaders to think differently about prevention. They proposed the acronym SAVE as an alternative to ABC, which stands for S—safer practices, A—access to treatment, V—voluntary counseling and testing, and E—empowerment.[23] This approach, rooted in the experience of people living with HIV and AIDS and those who have been affected by HIV and AIDS, more clearly identifies what is needed in terms of an effective approach to prevention.

In reflecting on these approaches, it can be argued that the primary problem with the ABC approach is that it focuses too narrowly on sexual ethics and shame. While behavior change has its merits, in the African context the responsibility for behavior change more often falls on women than on men. Prevention programs are more likely to focus on young girls who shoulder both the burden and the blame if they contract the disease.[24] Kenyan feminist theologian Constance Shishanya says that women are even blamed for their husband's infidelities.[25] In the documentary, *Epidemic: Facing AIDS,* a scene shows a town meeting in Uganda, where the community gathered to talk about AIDS. One man stood up and facing a group of women said:

> If the women folk should evolve and maintain a behavior that is so good and that at least will impress the man beyond a reasonable doubt, they will sit together and that man will remain yours and you will remain his. Let them change their behavior completely so that their men can really love them.

At this point the camera turns to one of the women, and the filmmaker asks if AIDS was their fault. Without hesitation she replies, "AIDS is not our fault." Later in the film, a couple from that same group tested positive for AIDS. As the lab technician looked at the blood work he could tell that the man had contracted the disease first. When the couple heard the news the woman was not surprised. Without ever looking at her husband she said, "You brought this to us. . . . I have been faithful."[26]

Research collaborators in this study confirmed this same complexity. They told stories of being blamed for their husband's infidelities or being blamed for an infidelity they did not commit. Almost all of the women I interviewed who were living with HIV or AIDS contracted it within their marriages. According to one study done in Nairobi, 60 to 80 percent of women interviewed who were living with HIV and AIDS had only had one sexual partner before contracting the virus.[27] Of the twelve PAR collaborators who were asked how many sexual partners they had, most cited that they had around three partners, which included second marriages. For most of the women, their first sexual partner was their husband, who ended up giving them the virus.[28]

The cry of women in Africa is "AIDS is not our fault." The world and the church must respond to African women by reassigning or removing the blame. We must learn to speak of HIV and AIDS not in terms of women's sexual morality but of patriarchy's immorality. For behavior change to work, it must apply to both women and men, which is impossible as long as patriarchy allows women to be valued as a commodity or as a means to an end.

Divining the Past: Colonialism, Christianity, and Conceptions of Marriage

In her book, *Daughters of Anowa*, Mercy Oduyoye argues that patriarchy in Africa is both indigenous and a result of the colonial project. While she sees its presence in both matrilineal and patrilineal kinship systems, she argues that traditional cultures had safeguards to lessen its effects. She sees colonialism and Western Christianity as destroying these safeguards and worsening the condition for women in African cultures.[29] While she does not point to a pristine past, she does give evidence to colonialism's reliance on men, not women, as decision makers.[30] As a Methodist, she also points to her own tradition of Christianity as bringing in the notion of the stay-at-home woman, which did not fit African culture where all people worked to contribute to the community.[31]

In understanding Africa's history, colonialism and Christianity must be seen as co-conspirators. Colonialism created systems where women were dependent on men, as work for pay became men's work, centralized in the cities. Christianity reinforced this through the concept of women's submission. Colonialism's dependence on trade also created large-scale societies dependent on moving goods and exporting resources. In the early days of HIV in Africa, the spread of the disease followed the truck routes through from Kenya to the Cape.[32] Even today, the cities across the continent are seen as places where poverty can be broken and wealth can be found. Because of the patriarchal way women and men are each valued, a family will often pull together money to send the oldest son or husband to the city to look for work. For those who are married, an environment is created where the wife will only see the husband a few times a year.

This often leads to the practice of "hidden polygamy" where a man will take a "wife" in the city, which sometimes just means sleeping with a sex worker or a girlfriend. Ironically, research shows women in polyga-

mous marriages have lower HIV transmission rates than those in monogamous marriages.[33] This could indicate a closer alignment with traditional norms, or it could point to the missionary churches' neglect of African
worldviews. Research is needed to determine what valuable taboos and
community norms might have been lost as missionary churches moved
African culture from polygamy to monogamy.

In addition to the agency required for faithfulness, it should also be
mentioned that even defining faithfulness in this context is complex. In
sub-Saharan Africa, marriage has multiple forms and meanings and
therefore what constitutes an extramarital affair is not clearly defined.
For example, in Tanzania, Christian, Muslim, and traditional marriages
are recognized in separate forms by the state. Muslims and African tradi-
tionalists may marry multiple wives while Christians cannot. Yet in reality, most people are married in both traditional and religious settings.
Traditional marriages within some communities in Tanzania permit polygamy, and in some of these communities, polygamy is the decision of
the male partner and the woman's consent is not required. This means
that what is called an extramarital affair by some could be called polygamy by others. Additionally, all marriages in Tanzania are not formal
marriages. Because *mahari* (or bridewealth) payments are expensive,
some couples will just agree to be married without going through either
religious or traditional ceremonies.[34] Several collaborators in this study
were married in this way but fully considered themselves "married"
even without the official sanctions.

Beyond the complications of polygamy and informal marriages, a va-
riety of marriage relationships are present within African traditional cultures. For example, in Africa there are not only monogamous and polygamous marriages, but other forms of marriage as well. There are *child
marriages*, where a girl child is married to an older man long before the
marriage is consummated; there is *widow inheritance*, where marriages
continue after a man's death as his brother sires children for him; there
are *ghost marriages* where a woman is married to a dead son to procreate
in his name; there are *woman-to-woman marriages* where a widow takes a
young girl who will bear children for her[35]; and in some cultures there
are *trial marriages* where the marriage is not formalized until a child is
born, while in others a broken engagement is equivalent to a broken
marriage.[36] Marriage is complex in sub-Saharan Africa, and this complexity makes the boundaries a bit messy. But in the midst of these messy
boundaries, the women in this study knew the shape they wanted their
marriages to take. Despite its shortcomings, they saw Christian marriage
as a liberative practice and believed the shortcomings were precisely
where marriage ceased to be Christian.

Economic vulnerability is another risk factor for African women and
adds an additional layer of complexity when speaking of intimate relationships. For example, this vulnerability exists for women on both sides

of the sex trade—married women are at risk when their husbands sleep with sex workers, and women who are economically vulnerable trade sex for money (or other goods) because their bodies are their only means of currency.[37] Furthermore, *both* married women and sex workers are dependent on the money that comes primarily from men. Just as a sex worker (or any woman) may see survival sex or transactional sex as the only way to feed her children, married women know their consent to sex also puts food on the table.

One collaborator in this study named Grace was married to a Luo man in what she thought would be a monogamous marriage. She married young; at fourteen she ran away from home with a man visiting her village because her parents could no longer pay her school fees. Grace and her husband had two children together, and although she married young, she valued her marriage. But then her husband took another wife without her consent. Her husband and his second wife were married in the church. Even though polygamous marriage is illegal for Christians in Tanzania, Grace said churches rarely check to see if the partners are already married. Then the *mahari* (bridewealth) was paid, and even if the churches were to protest, once the *mahari* is exchanged, tradition trumps church.

Grace didn't know what to do. She tried to live in this new polygamous relationship, but it became too much. After her husband took a third wife, she ran away to Nairobi, where she took a job as a maid. But after she left, her children were not doing well without her. Her oldest son was especially distraught. She managed to pay his school fees for his first two years of secondary school, but by his third year her situation had changed. She could no longer afford the school fees, and the father refused to help as long as the boy's mother was no longer acting as his wife.

In her job as a maid, Grace said she was constantly harassed sexually by the owner of the house. She refused to sleep with him for nearly a year, but then he found out she couldn't pay her son's school fees. Her boss offered to pay the school fees in exchange for sex. She still refused but after hearing her son had been crying for two weeks because he could not finish his education, she finally gave in. She knew her poverty made it impossible to care for all her children, but she said, "Let me fight for just this one." The only weapon Grace had for the fight was her body. As a result, she contracted HIV. In 2011, Grace's son was in his final year of college. He is smart and dedicated and cares deeply for his mother. He has no idea that she sacrificed her life so that he could live his. For women who are vulnerable, choices about sex are often less a matter of morality and more a matter of survival. As the women say in Nairobi, "who can care about a disease that will kill you later when hunger can kill you now?"[38]

NOTES

1. Each research collaborator in this study chose a first name that they wanted to use for publications. Some collaborators chose to use their own names, while some chose to use a pseudonym. For a full list of collaborators cited in this book, please see Appendix: Guide to Research Collaborators.

2. Statistics taken from UNAIDS, http://www.unaids.org/en/dataanalysis/data-tools/aidsinfo/ and Avert.org http://www.avert.org/africa-hiv-aids-statistics.htm and http://www.avert.org/worldstats.htm (accessed January 25, 2013).

3. Ibid.

4. It should be noted that HIV/AIDS is still a problem in the United States, and is now spreading most quickly among African-Americans. See: Center for Disease Control and Prevention, "HIV among African Americans," http://www.cdc.gov/hiv/topics/aa/ (accessed September 20, 2010).

5. UNAIDS Regional Fact Sheet 2012, http://www.unaids.org/en/media/unaids/contentassets/documents/epidemiology/2012/gr2012/2012_FS_regional_ssa_en.pdf (accessed January 22, 2013).

6. Ibid.

7. Linda Fuller, *African Women ' s Unique Vulnerabilities to HIV/AIDS*, (Basingstoke: Palgrave Macmillan, 2008), 3.

8. AMFAR AIDS Research, "Statistics: Women and AIDS," (November 2009), http://www.amfar.org/abouthiv/article.aspx?id=3594 (accessed September 3, 2010).

9. The only other place is the Caribbean, where the spread of HIV and AIDS in many ways parallels the sub-Saharan African epidemic.

10. As early as 1992, the UN was naming marriage as an HIV/AIDS risk factor. For more on women and HIV/AIDS in Africa, and on marriage as a risk factor, see Avert.org, "Women, HIV and AIDS," http://www.avert.org/women-hiv-aids.htm (accessed January 20, 2011).

11. The term "abundant life" comes from Christian Scriptures (John 10:10) is used in African theology and African feminist theology to describe a quest for a full, integrated life. See, Mary N. Getui and Matthew M. Theuri, ed. *Quests for Abundant Life in Africa*, (Nairobi: Acton Publishers, 2002).

12. See, for example, Constance Shishanya, "The Impact of HIV/AIDS on Women in Kenya," in *Quests for Abundant Life in Africa*, ed. Mary Getui and Matthew Theuri, (Nairobi: Acton Publishers, 2002), 45–61. See also: UNIFEM, "HIV/AIDS—A Gender Equality and Human Rights Issue," www.unifem.org/gender_issues/hiv_aids/at_a_glance.php (accessed April 30, 2010).

13. Here, I am referring to the often referenced ABC method of prevention, which stands for "abstinence, be faithful and condomize." Churches often focus exclusively on the first two—abstinence and faithfulness—without fully realizing that choices to be abstinent or faithful are being limited by gender inequality and a lack of mutuality and relationality in marriage.

14. Throughout this book, I use the terms *agency* and *autonomy* in order to reflect more fully on the complexity of the conditions necessary for moral decision-making. Agency is defined as the capacity of an agent to act. Full agency means that there are no constraints that keep a person from acting. This concept explores what is necessary—relationally, culturally, economically, socially and politically—for an actor to make a decision and carry out that decision. Autonomy, though similar, is a concept that is based more in Western philosophical thought than in African philosophy. It means that a person is acting without coercion and making a choice based on informed consent. Both concepts help us in thinking through the requirements and the obstacles for making a moral choice.

15. Only two out of twelve women in the participatory action research (PAR) group said that they had gone "outside" of their marriage. One woman said she had an affair because her husband was having multiple affairs and would not stop sleeping around. Another woman had sex outside of her marriage after separating from her husband

because he took a second wife. This woman had sex with her boss in order to pay her child's school fees. All of the women in the PAR study said their husbands (or partners) had been unfaithful. In presenting this data, I realize that self-reporting can be a highly unreliable indicator of what actually happens. However, in reporting these findings, I hope to honor the voices of the women who repeatedly named male infidelity as a primary risk factor in their contracting HIV.

16. Mercy Amba Oduyoye, *Beads and Strands: Reflections of an African Woman on Christianity in Africa*, (Maryknoll: Orbis, 2004), 99–100.

17. In this book, the words "church" and "churches" are used to designate Christian congregations, indigenous and missionary, Protestant and Catholic, who have a presence in sub-Saharan Africa. Within this book, I am critiquing churches who carry in their doctrines Western understandings of sexuality that have created a divide between African and "Christian" ways of understanding sex. I am also critical of church policies that do not recognize the extent to which patriarchy negates women's choices when it comes to abstinence and fidelity.

18. Pauline Muchina, *Roundtable Discussion on HIV/AIDS in Africa*, American Academy of Religion Annual Meeting, Nov. 18, 2006. See also, UNAIDS, "Developing strategies to work with FBOs," April 10, 2008, http://www.unaids.org/en/Resources/Press-Centre/Featurestories/2008/April/20080410DevelopingstrategiestoworkFBO/ (accessed January 22, 2011).

19. In this line of argument, I follow the thought of Mercy Oduyoye in *Daughters Of Anowa: African Women and Patriarchy*, (Maryknoll NY: Orbis Books, 1995).

20. This idea is based primarily on the success of Uganda's behavioral change program, yet Uganda used a combination of methods to achieve success. In first implementing the PEPFAR program, the US used Uganda as a model in endorsing its abstinence until marriage approach to fighting AIDS in Africa (For more see: Avert.org, "The ABC of Prevention," www.avert.org/abc-hiv.htm (accessed January 22, 2011).

21. Janet Fleischman, "Beyond 'ABC': Helping Women Fight AIDS," The Washington Post: June 29, 2004, A23.

22. For example, the Catholic Church and official Catholic aid organizations (such as Catholic Relief Services) do not promote or distribute condoms. In my fieldwork, some Baptist and Africa Inland Mission (AIC) churches approved of condoms outside of marriage as a realistic, though not ideal, preventative measure, but on the whole, very few churches in Tanzania would openly promote condom use. Most Pentecostal churches disapproved of condoms, though official positions were different with each individual church.

23. Ramadhan Rajab, "Kenya: War Against HIV/AIDS Stepped Up," *The Star*, (Nairobi), March 29, 2012, http://allafrica.com/stories/201203300124.html (accessed May 17, 2012).

24. Laura Duhan Kaplan points out inequalities in Zimbabwe and Swaziland, and I would add that these (to some extent) are present throughout the continent. See Kaplan, "HIV/AIDS Policies: Compromising the Human Rights of Women," in *Linking Visions*, ed. Rosemary Tong, Anne Donchin, and Susan Dodds, (New York: Rowman and Littlefield, 2004), 237.

25. Shishanya, "The Impact of HIV/AIDS on Women in Kenya," 58.

26. *Epidemic: Facing AIDS — Uganda, India, Brazil, Thailand, Russia*, DVD, Directed by Rory Kennedy, (Brooklyn: Moxie Firecracker Films, 2002).

27. Aylward Shorter and Edwin Onyancha, *The Church and AIDS in Africa*, (Nairobi: Paulines Publications Africa, 1998), 116.

28. One woman cited only one sexual partner (her husband); one woman cited two sexual partners; seven women cited three sexual partners. (Included in these numbers were two women who counted a rapist as a partner and two women who were married twice). One woman cited four partners, and one woman cited eight sexual partners.

29. Oduyoye notes that in traditional Akan society, women functioned as policy makers and were responsible for many religious rituals. Oduyoye cites the role of the "Queen Mother" who was the female ruler and kingmaker in the Asante political system and says that women in this role "eluded the British" colonists. She argues that colonialism introduced a system that was beneficial to Asante men when it eliminated this role and turned instead to men as political decision makers. (See Oduyoye, *Daughters Of Anowa*, 92-95). Oduyoye gives other examples of eliminating safeguards when she speaks of women filling military, economic, and religious roles in traditional Akan society. For more, see *Daughters of Anowa*, 79-108.

30. Ibid., 89–96.

31. Ibid., 104, 197–98.

32. Candice Bradley, Philip L. Kilbride, and Thomas S. Weisner, *African Families and the Crisis of Social Change*, (Westport: Bergin & Garvey Publishers, 1997), 111–14, 120.

33. While research on the subject is limited, many studies have shown that HIV rates are lower among polygamous marriages than monogamous marriages. For example, in their 1994 study of men in Nigeria, Orubuloye, Caldwell & Caldwell cited lower HIV rates among polygamous men than men in a monogamous marriage due to lower occurrences of extra-marital affairs in polygamous marriages. (See: I.O. Orubuloye, Pat Caldwell and John C. Caldwell. "Commercial sex workers in Nigeria in the shadow of AIDS," in *Sexual Networking and AIDS in Sub-Sahara Africa: Behavioral Research and the Social Context*, 1994.), 101–16. In another four-country research study in 2006, Damien De Walgue argued that polygamy did not seem to impact HIV transmission in Tanzania, Cameroon or Ghana; and that in Burkina Faso, those who were polygamous were less likely to be HIV-positive. (See: Damien De Walque, "Who Gets AIDS and How? The Determinants of HIV Infection and Sexual Behaviors in Burkina Faso, Cameroon, Ghana, Kenya, and Tanzania," *World Bank Policy Research Working Paper No. 3844*, 2006). In another study coming from Malawi, HIV rates were found to be higher in polygamous marriages but this was due to male extramarital affairs. (Georges Reniers and Rania Tfaily, "Polygamy and HIV in Malawi" *Demographic Research* Vol. 19, Art. 53, 2008.) To summarize, we could argue that polygamous marriages are risky for the same reasons that monogamous marriages are risky. Though the data does not show polygamy to be necessarily more risky than monogamy, it does show that when there is a risk, the impact is greater due to a greater number of affected partners.

34. In Kenya these are called "come-we-stay" marriages, and in Tanzania they are known as *"ndoa ya kienyeji"* or *"ndoa ya mkeka"*

35. Woman-to-woman marriages are still practiced in Kenya and made the news again in 2012. See: Muliro Telewa, "Kenya's legal same-sex marriages," BBC News, Feb. 15, 2012, http://www.bbc.co.uk/news/world-africa-16871435 (accessed May 17, 2012).

36. See Francis-Xavier S. Kyewalyanga, *Marriage Customs in East Africa*, (Hohenschaftlarn: Renner Publication, 1977). See also: John Mbiti, *Love and Marriage in Africa*, (London: Longman, 1973), 77, 196.

37. Bradley, Kilbride and Weisner cite a focus group interview where Kenyan girls were asked their reasons for having sex with men in their community and 44 percent gave money as the top reason. Another 9.6 percent cited gifts while only 9.8 percent cited "love." See Bradley, *et al.*, 118.

38. This has become a modern proverb used by women to defend their choice (or others choices) for at-risk sex. Anne Waweru quotes this in Mark Schoofs, "AIDS: The Agony of Africa - Part 5: Death and the Second Sex," *Village Voice*, December 1999, www.villagevoice.com/news/9948,schoofs,10565,1.html (accessed January 22, 2011).

TWO

Why Africa?

Forces Behind the Sub-Saharan African HIV and AIDS Pandemic

LISTENING TO A PANDEMIC

When we talk about HIV and AIDS in sub-Saharan Africa, too often we say too little. It is easy to point fingers, blaming the spread of the pandemic on one or two simple villains: unfaithful partners, truck drivers, sex workers, sugar daddies, or gender inequalities. . . . But this pandemic is far too complex, and far too particular, for simple answers. The only simple thing we can say is that there is no one reason why HIV has spread to pandemic levels in sub-Saharan Africa.

In the next two chapters I will attempt to look at the many reasons for the pandemic's spread in sub-Saharan Africa while simultaneously returning to the particular—the lived experiences of people living with HIV and AIDS in Mwanza, Tanzania. Yet even as I name these vulnerabilities and causes, it must be remembered that just as no one person can speak for an entire continent, no one reason (or set of reasons) is the cause of this entire pandemic. While quantitative research has taught us much about the pandemic and has named the generalizations we can make, we also need qualitative research, the "thick descriptions" of ethnography, if we seek to creatively end this pandemic. A return to the particular is deeply needed in places where the reasons for the spread of HIV and AIDS are many and varied.[1]

So, why Africa? Why has this virus reached pandemic levels in this place and at this time? Some theorists, such as John Iliffe, suggest that the African HIV pandemic is the worst because Africa is the place of origin for HIV. He argues that since Africa's pandemic is older, then it is necessarily worse. While Iliffe does not discount other co-factors, such as poverty or gender inequality, he argues that the history of the disease on the continent is the primary explanation for HIV and AIDS reaching pandemic levels.[2] While Iliffe makes a convincing argument, we cannot focus only on the disease's history. From a theo-ethical standpoint, the co-factors Iliffe and others name are extremely important. Poverty, gender inequality, poor health, traditional taboos and practices, lack of education, and the movement of goods and people across the continent make the perfect storm for creating a pandemic.

HIV and AIDS in Postcolonial Space

In order to understand HIV and AIDS in sub-Saharan Africa, it is helpful to situate the pandemic within postcolonial space. While we cannot point to a pristine past before colonialism, it is helpful to recognize the ways in which colonization contributed (and globalization is still contributing) to this pandemic. One way of understanding this is to look at the ways in which colonization and now globalization impact the movements of goods and peoples.

A primary aim of colonialism was to utilize valuable natural resources on the continent for the benefit of the home country. In Southern Africa, gold and diamonds were mined; in East Africa, the fertile land was used to grow sugar, coffee, and tea for export. The work required to maintain these operations meant that families were separated. In South Africa, for example, miners from South Africa and neighboring countries were (and still are) typically housed in dorm environments, unable to live with their families. This meant long periods of separation where married partners would only see each other three to four times a year. The mining camps quickly became home to sex workers who made their living off of miners who had money but whose wives were far away. On top of this, mining is dangerous work. And in the midst of this dangerous work, it is hard to be concerned with a disease that can bring death years from now when you're faced with the possibility of death every day as you go to work. With these conditions, it is no surprise that mining camps have some of the highest rates of HIV on the continent.[3]

In a similar way, in the early days of the pandemic's spread, towns that were along truck routes were the hardest hit. As truck drivers moved goods between urban centers, they brought HIV with them, and communities along the truck routes were some of the first affected. [4] One woman in this study named Veronica was married to a truck driver. At age thirteen, she was his seventh wife and she contracted HIV from her marriage. Truck drivers do not only impact communities along the road but also bring HIV home to their families. Like mining, trucking is also a dangerous profession in Africa. The roads are unsafe due to their poor conditions and the poor condition of the vehicles that travel them. And when road accidents occur, medical help is often too far away to respond. In many African countries, there are few ambulances or emergency response services, and so truck driving carries with it the same fatalism as mining or other dangerous jobs.

Colonialism and globalization also relocated work in sub-Saharan Africa to urban centers and commercial factories and farms. This relocation of work weakened familial and communal structures.[5] While in traditional societies entire families were part of the framework of community, today it is very common for a mother and children to be in the village while the father/husband is working in the city. In traditional societies, families and clans survived by sticking close together. It was unusual for a member of the family to move away from the familial land. Once colonialism introduced a monetary system and urban life, many abandoned the homestead in search of income. Families and communities would often pool their money together to send one member to the city and look for work, expecting him or her to send money back home. While this community effort helped many (at least monetarily) through hard times, it broadened the spread of HIV, and overall, it weakened communities and families.

The real danger comes into play when urban migration is coupled with the concept of polygamy or multiple partners. Before colonialism and modern Christian missionary movements, many ethnic groups in sub-Saharan Africa were polygamous, and some still are. But most Western missionaries considered polygamy sinful and many churches required that new converts have only one wife (which often meant abandoning all but the first or favorite wife).[6] Yet in this shift from polygamy to monogamy, very little was done to analyze why people practiced polygamy. As a result, polygamy did not end but only went underground. A girlfriend in the city was not considered a problem because she was just like a second wife. Polygamy, which was formerly regulated by the community and by systems of marriage, was left with little to no civil or communal regulation. The women in this study even complained of Christian pastors who did not conduct checks on men who wanted to be married and therefore conducted second and third marriages.

Mercy Oduyoye talks about the ways in which mission enterprises have not only changed traditional dynamics but have also diminished traditional safeguards women held to protect them from patriarchy.[7] While Oduyoye identifies as a Christian and has worked in both ministry and academic positions, she is still unsure as to whether or not Christianity has been beneficial to the continent.[8] She cites the hospitality of African peoples and says that when the Christian missionaries and colonizers came, Africans never expected them to be predators.[9]

Dube reinforces Oduyoye's notion of missionaries as predators by telling a story popular in Africa's oral history. In the story, the missionaries came and asked the people to pray. When they closed their eyes, the African people had the land and the Missionaries had the Bible, but when they opened their eyes again, the Missionaries had the land, and the Africans had the Bible. The story, according to Dube, makes two points. The first is that the land and resources that belonged to Africans for so long were lost through imperial and colonial movements on the continent. The second point is that for better or worse, Africans have the Bible, and despite the difficulties Christianity has brought with it, the resources of faith are still essential to African peoples.[10]

Mercy Oduyoye argues that traditional societies had some safeguards to protect women but that these safeguards have been lost in this postcolonial space.[11] Using Oduyoye's logic, we could argue that even traditional polygamy was a better system for women than hidden polygamy where men have secret multiple partners outside of marriage.

Another example that supports Oduyoye's argument comes from my fieldwork. Research collaborators reported that in East Africa, married women were formerly able to appeal to their parents, uncles, or community elders if they were treated unfairly within marriage. While this principle still applies in theory, today it rarely produces any lasting results. The women in this study believed this practice had been corrupted by the commercialization of *mahari* (or bridewealth).[12] They said the *mahari* payments were no longer simply symbolic but monetarily excessive. This meant that families who received large *mahari* payments were less likely to want the marriage to end since if it did, the *mahari* must be returned. Many of the collaborators had called on family members when they were abused or when their husband was unfaithful, but all were sent back to their husbands. While *mahari* was formerly modest—and therefore not difficult to return—the women argued that the commercialization of *mahari* has changed everything because now the *mahari* payments are simply to much to return, especially if they have already been spent.

Traditional Practices and the Spread of HIV and AIDS

While traditional African cultures had some safeguards to protect women, it also created or ignored certain practices that still make women vulnerable. Male infidelity, widow inheritance, child marriage, female circumcision, and some forms of traditional healing all find reference within traditional culture and still put women at risk today. Practices such as these are why theologians who are members of the Circle of Concerned African Women Theologians argue that African culture must be both retrieved and interrogated.[13]

Musimbi Kanyoro tells a folktale to illustrate this dilemma. She begins the story by saying there was once a hyena who smelled some meat, so he began following the path toward the delicious smell. But soon, there was a fork in the road, and the hyena did not know which way to go. So instead of choosing a path, he walked with his body split between the two paths until he eventually split into two. Kanyoro uses this story to articulate the difficulty for African feminists who walk between the two worlds of culture and religion.[14] Kanyoro, Dube, Oduyoye, and others all emphasize the importance of interrogating both culture and religion in an effort to maintain wholeness and see this as a primary aspect of doing theology. Oduyoye argues that African feminists must retrieve what can be retrieved but cannot blindly sanction their own cultures. Instead, all cultures must be interrogated as African feminists ask whether or not aspects of both culture and Christianity are life-giving to women.[15]

When it comes to interrogating culture in light of the HIV and AIDS pandemic, a key issue at hand is that of male infidelity, which is sometimes promoted and other times simply ignored within traditional cultures. Many men do not consider it wrong to have multiple partners (even if their wife is unaware) as long as they provide for their partners and children. Kenyan theologian John Mbiti, in his classic work *African Religions and Philosophy*, argues that fidelity is practiced for the sake of the community, and infidelity is only considered an evil when it is both forbidden and then disclosed. Mbiti puts it this way:

> To sleep with someone else's wife is not considered "evil" if these two are not found out by the society that forbids it; and in other societies it is in fact an expression of friendship and hospitality to let a guest spend the night with one's wife or daughter or sister. It is not the act in itself which would be "wrong" as such but the relationships involved in the act: if relationships are not hurt or damaged, and if there is no discovery of breach of custom or regulation, then the act is not "evil" or "wicked" or "bad."[16]

While Mbiti is not speaking as an ethicist but as a scholar of religion creating a descriptive analysis, I still take issue with his proposition that infidelity could occur without the relationship being hurt or damaged. The women in this study did not believe Mbiti's suggestion was possible. They were all deeply hurt by their husband's infidelities, whether or not these infidelities were ever disclosed. The women noted even though many of them had not known about their husbands' affairs, they were left with an HIV-positive status as a reminder, and this deeply impacted them.

Reporting on a fifteen-year ethnographic study of the Meru of Northern Tanzania, Liv Harem confirms Mbiti's argument, namely that it is still the discovery of the act and not the infidelity in itself that is considered immoral. Harem puts it this way:

> They [the Meru] follow a principle that regulates "illicit" sexual behavior and enables members of both sexes to manipulate a wide sexual network in a morally acceptable way. The matter at stake is not the actual number of sexual relationships, but managing those relation-

ships with "dignity" (tikisi) and "respect"—which, above all, means to
keep them secret.[17]

This secrecy is a traditional practice that protects men and harms women.
It provides a means for a double standard to function, where women are
expected to be faithful to their marriages and men are allowed freedom to
have multiple partners without it being seen as immoral. Of course, this
makes sense in light of the long-standing presence of polygamy in the
region, where men having multiple partners was not seen as immoral.
Even more, in light of the HIV pandemic, the harm is not only emotional
or relational; it quite literally endangers both women and men. Today, it
is the presence of HIV that discloses infidelity and also makes secret-
keeping ultimately impossible.

Widow inheritance and sexual cleansing are also especially problematic. Before the arrival of Christian missionaries, these practices were
common among most ethnic groups in East Africa.[18] While less common
today, these rituals are still practiced among certain groups of people,
such as the Luo in Kenya and Tanzania. Widow inheritance, or Leverite
marriage, is when a man "inherits" his dead brother's wife in order to
have children with her on behalf of the dead brother. This is particularly
dangerous because AIDS is often not listed as a cause of death, due to
stigma. As a result, when a widow is inherited after her husband has died
of AIDS, the virus can be further spread to the brother and possibly
future children.

In some communities, such as the Luo community, a "sexual cleansing" is required before the woman can be inherited.[19] The belief behind
this is that the woman is poisoned with the spirit of her dead husband
and must be purified before she can have sex with anyone else. In Western Kenya, because of the HIV pandemic, professional cleansers are being
hired for this ritual as family members of the dead husband often refuse.
Condoms are never used because in this ritual because it is the sperm of
the cleanser that causes the cleansing to take place.

Women often stand up against these practices, but because of pressure
from their communities in places where this is still practiced, they are not
always given a choice as to whether or not they will be inherited. Violet
Kimani notes that among the Luo, even if a woman runs away to avoid
inheritance or sexual cleansing, the ritual must still be done to her before
she is buried. In other words, a professional cleanser would be hired to
perform the ritual on the dead woman's body.[20] Women who refuse this
ritual are also thought to put their sons at risk, since they are not entitled
to inherit their dead father's property until the mother has been
cleansed.[21] For many women, the *mahari* (or bridewealth) paid for them
means they have no choice but to consent or leave their community.

For Luo men, a similar process of sexual cleansing is required, but this
does not have to take the form of sex. This ritual is sensory in nature and

is performed by an older woman who knew his wife. Instead of sex, the ritual is supposed to cause a wet dream. Some Luo men prefer to expedite the process and hire a sex worker instead for ritual cleansing.[22]

Child marriage is another problematic practice. While governments within the region have, in theory, prohibited child marriage, it still occurs.[23] Of the twelve women who participated in the participatory action research portion of this study, five were under eighteen when they were married. One collaborator, Veronica, said the Catholic Church where she was married forged her birth certificate so she could be married at thirteen. Other collaborators were as young as fourteen and fifteen when they married. While child marriage is on the decline, the practice of older men dating young girls (often in exchange for cell phones or school fees) is on the rise.[24]

Female circumcision is another practice that puts girls at risk. In East Africa, there are two types of female circumcision. One form involves the removal of the clitoral hood while a second, more extensive form, known as infibulation, entails the removal of all external genitalia and even part of the *labia majora*. In this invasive procedure, the girl is then stitched up, leaving only a small opening for urine or menstrual blood to pass.[25]

In her memoir, *Desert Flower*, Ethiopian writer Waris Dirie talks about how her menstrual cycle would last most of the month and a simple trip to the bathroom to urinate could take a half hour.[26] This practice increases the likelihood of contracting HIV because each time the woman has sex, there is tearing of the vaginal tissues. The procedure and any subsequent acts of sexual intercourse leave behind scarring which makes the woman more susceptible to infections. This leaves fewer natural barriers when a person is exposed to HIV and makes contraction more likely.[27]

Additionally, because circumcision for both boys and girls often takes place in traditional ceremonies, the risk of infection is present when the same razor blade is used for multiple people in the initiation ceremony or when other safety precautions are not taken.[28] It is important to note that male circumcision is an effective way to lessen the chances of contracting HIV,[29] but of course, the procedure must happen in a sterile environment.

Sex in Africa also has a ritual and communal dimension[30] that is particularly problematic in light of the HIV pandemic. John Mbiti gives examples of multiple communities in Africa who used ritual sex to seal rites of passages or other events. One example is from the Akamba in Kenya who use ritual sex during circumcision rituals. During the week-long initiation ritual, the man and woman who perform the circumcisions on the boys and girls are required to have ritual sex. The parents of the initiates are also required to have ritual sex on the third and seventh nights of the initiation.[31] Mbiti also says that the initiation ceremony itself involves "symbolic sexual acts" between the boys and girls, yet he fails to fully describe these acts. Mbiti puts it this way: "Each boy is given a special stick, which he must retain; and that evening a dance for the initiates takes place. With their special sticks the boys perform symbolic sexual acts upon the girls."[32]

Beyond the ritual dimension of sex, in many African communities, sex is seen as communal. For example, among the Maasai of Kenya and Tanzania, it is permissible for a woman to have sex with any of her husband's age-mates (the group of people who went through initiation with her husband).[33] Mbiti notes that sex is not only for procreation or religious ritual, but also used to express hospitality. Mbiti explains it this way:

> On the other hand, there is the opposite "joking relationship" in which people are free and obliged not only to mix socially but be in physical contact which may involve free or easier sexual intercourse outside the immediate husband and wife. There are areas where sex is used as an expression of hospitality. This means that when a man visits another, the custom is for the host to give his wife (or daughter or sister) to the guest so that the two can sleep together. In other societies, brothers have sexual rights to the wives of their brothers (remembering that here a person has hundreds of brothers and their wives are "potentially" his wives as well). Where the age-group system is taken seriously, like among the Maasai, members of one group who were initiated in the same batch, are entitled to have sexual relations with the wives of fellow members.[34]

Mbiti goes on to say that the Maasai use this allowance of the age-mate system to bear children for a man who is absent (perhaps due to work) and to make sure women do not go outside of the community for sex when their husband is away.[35]

In separate individual interviews, two women in this study described another disturbing use of ritual sex by traditional healers. One woman went to a healer to be cured of HIV, and another woman consulted a healer about infertility issues. In both cases, the traditional healer told the women that the "medicine" had to be inserted vaginally—with his penis. The practitioner consumed the "medicine" and then through sexual intercourse, delivered the "medicine" to the women. One woman embarrassingly admitted that she consented to the procedure, which did her no good.

Another traditional practice that is risky in light of the HIV pandemic is the extensive period of post-partum abstinence that many African women are required to observe. In some communities, it is taboo to have sex while pregnant or breastfeeding. The belief behind this taboo is that the seminal fluids will contaminate the breast milk and cause diarrhea.[36] During this time of abstinence for women, men are not expected to practice the same restraint. Several of the women in this study noted that their husband did not "go outside" the marriage until after the birth of their first child.

A final traditional practice that is also problematic is the use of "dry sex." In this traditional practice, women will attempt to dry their vaginas in order to please their male sexual partners. Often the women will sit in saltwater or bleach or will insert twigs, grass, tobacco or fertilizer into their vaginas to reduce lubrication. While some men find this more pleasurable, it makes sex painful for women and also increases the likelihood of vaginal tearing, therefore it likely increases the risk of contracting HIV. This is just another example of a situation where men's pleasure is valued over women's well-being and flourishing.[37]

Poor Health as an HIV Risk Factor

One HIV risk factor that is often overlooked is the overall health of the individual. From poor nutrition to concurrent infections, if the body is weak when it is exposed to HIV, the ability to fight against the disease is lessened. One common myth that I discovered in my fieldwork was that most of the women believed that if you have sex with a person who is HIV-positive, then you'll automatically contract HIV. Yet, people who are healthy and do not have concurrent infections could be exposed to the virus without contracting it, especially if they are exposed when the virus is not in its most contagious form.[38] For a person who is healthy, contracting HIV is more like Russian roulette than like playing with a fully loaded gun. The body has natural barriers to fight off all infections, but when the immune system is compromised, then the body becomes more vulnerable.

Concurrent infections are especially problematic risk factors for women. These include the presence of other STDs, which increase vaginal discharge and weaken the vaginal walls, making women more susceptible. Another less explored concurrent infection is vaginal bilharzia. This illness is caused by the presence of schistosomiasis, a bacteria carried by snails, which is prevalent in the lake regions of Africa. In Mwanza, situated along Lake Victoria, bilharzia is a big problem.

Eileen Stillwaggon argues that health co-factors such as bilharzia have been completely overlooked in studies on HIV and AIDS prevalence in the lake regions of Africa. Stillwaggon argues that it is no accident that the locations with the highest HIV prevalence also have the highest prevalence of schistosomiasis. She gives the example of KwaZulu-Natal, South Africa, where the prevalence exceeds 60 percent.

According to Stillwaggon, while prevalence alone does not prove causation, there are several known mechanisms of infection that link the two, such as the genital inflammation and lesions caused by bilharzia and lowered immune functioning due to repeat infections.[39]

Stillwaggon also notes that in many parts of the world schistosomiasis has been eliminated but says that this is not the case in Africa because "African health budgets cannot cover the necessary diagnostic and therapeutic measures to eradicate the disease."[40] Stillwaggon sums up her argument by saying, "The HIV/AIDS epidemic in sub-Saharan Africa is not an isolated phenomenon. It is a predictable outcome of an environment of poverty, worsening nutrition, chronic parasite infection, and limited access to medical care."[41] Stillwaggon rightly argues that we might pay more attention to these and other co-factors if the focus on HIV as a sexually transmitted disease did not obscure our focus.[42]

Like Stillwaggon, Paul Farmer also emphasizes the importance of not underestimating co-factors of emerging diseases. Farmer argues, "Even in cases of microbial mutations, however, we often find signs that human actions have played a large role in enhancing pathogenicity or increasing resistance to antimicrobial agents."[43] Throughout his writings, Farmer recognizes poverty and poor health as HIV co-factors. Farmer puts these co-factors within the realm of structural violence. In thinking through structural violence, Farmer takes his cue from liberation theologians. He defines structural violence by saying:

> Structural violence is violence exerted systematically—that is, indirectly—by everyone who belongs to a certain social order: hence the discomfort these ideas provoke in a moral economy still geared to pinning praise or blame on individual actors. In short, the concept of structural violence is intended to inform the study of the social machinery of oppression.[44]

Farmer illustrates this through his work in developing countries, such as Haiti and Rwanda, where extreme poverty puts health out of reach. Farmer makes the point that infectious diseases are more likely to kill the poor than the rich.[45] Speaking about HIV and AIDS, Farmer argues, "The most well demonstrated co-factors are social inequalities, which structure not only the contours of the AIDS epidemic but also the nature of outcomes once an individual is sick with complications of an HIV infection."[46] According to Farmer, structural violence not only causes inequalities that make room for sickness but also prevents public health solutions from becoming readily available. Farmer says, "We live in a world where infections pass easily across borders—social and geographic—while resources, including cumulative scientific knowledge, are blocked at customs."[47]

In sub-Saharan Africa, poor health is a problem not only due to a lack of global spending on health but also due to lack of local resources. Low government spending on healthcare, widespread poverty, and environmental degradation are all co-factors in the spread of HIV. Preventative healthcare is simply not a priority (or a possibility) for many governments in sub-Saharan Africa. In 2001, at a meeting on the Millennium Development Goals (MDG's)[48] in Abuja, an agreement was made by African governments to spend 15 percent of their budgets on health. Yet as of 2010, only six sub-Saharan African countries have been able to keep this commitment.[49] On average, Africa's fifty-three governments spend about fourteen dollars or less per person on health. Some spend as little as one dollar per person per year. In the latest data from 2005, Tanzania was improving but still only spending seventeen dollars per person.[50] In order to reach the MDGs by 2015, the World Health Organization recommends that governments spend at least forty dollars per person. Sub-Saharan Africa has on average only 1.15 health workers per 1,000 people and 50 percent of all Africans are not able to access lifesaving medications.[51] Illnesses that should be preventable or curable continue to take far too many lives.

While one of the Millennium Development Goals is combating HIV, each of the goals represents a deficiency that has allowed the virus to spread. Poverty, lack of education, gender inequality, a lack of child and maternal health, environmental degradation, and lack of global collaboration have all been factors in driving the virus to pandemic levels. When we look at the African pandemic, there is no one reason the virus has spread but more reasons than we can manage to count.

Poverty as an HIV Risk Factor

According to UNICEF, 89 percent of Tanzanians live below the international poverty line. In other words, they make less than the Tanzania shilling equivalent of $1.25 a day.[52] Liberation theologian Gustiavo Gutiérrez defines poverty in Latin America as structural violence that results in hunger, sickness, death, and oppression.[53] As Gutierrez makes this claim, he argues that structural violence is structural sin. When we participate in or benefit from structural violence, we are morally culpable for its effects. The same realities that Gutierrez speaks of in Latin America are present in Tanzania and much of sub-Saharan Africa. Structural violence is present, and it brings poverty, which brings a person closer to death. If we are to seek out human flourishing in the midst of structural violence, then we must collectively take responsibility for the violence in our midst as we seek to dismantle it.

This closeness to death creates a fatalism that makes HIV one possible problem among many. Simply put, you cannot care about whether or not you contract HIV when there are so many imminent threats to your life. Hunger will kill you more quickly than AIDS. And even if you could care—even if you chose to get tested—the needed medicines might still be out of reach. Poverty means that a person or a family cannot give much thought to education or preventative healthcare. When a poor person is sick, they will delay going to a doctor because of the financial costs of lost work or lack of money to pay for medical services or transportation. Malnutrition and poor health, which result from poverty, also weaken the immune system and make a person more susceptible to HIV.

For families who are not already poor, HIV and AIDS cause poverty. It strikes people in their prime working and childbearing years, crippling labor forces across Africa. Families not only lose a person who generates income but an additional person who must care for the sick family member. Often this means an older child will be forced to drop out of school to care for a sick parent, and the cycle of poverty is never broken. And when the family is pushed into poverty because of HIV or AIDS, the person who is sick only gets worse, as food security is compromised by the lack of income. Because traditional support systems are breaking down, poverty due to HIV or AIDS is not temporary. There are fewer extended family members to help carry the weight, because entire communities are over-burdened. Africa now has a generation of grandmothers raising grandchildren after their parents have died from AIDS. [54]

Education and Risky Behavior

In sub-Saharan Africa, when poverty is present, education quickly becomes a luxury rather than a necessity. Even when primary school education is provided by the government, the small cost of buying a uniform or school supplies can keep children out of school. This can also further the spread of HIV if children are not exposed to prevention programs when they are part of the educational process. More importantly, young people who are not in school are less optimistic about their future and more likely to participate in risky behaviors. While it does not solve all our problems, general education plays a significant role in ending this pandemic. Simply put, if we want to end this pandemic, we need to spend time helping children learn how to read and write and do math. We need to teach valuable trades and skills that will give people economic options for their lives. This general education is as important (or perhaps more important) than sex education because it gives young people opportunity to choose against risky behaviors. But even more importantly, education gives women more life options, which can become options for prevention.

Formal education in sub-Saharan Africa is not without problems. Most classrooms are overcrowded and books and other educational resources are scarce due to inadequate educational budgets. Teachers are also among those who are greatly affected by the HIV pandemic. Many have become too sick to teach, which exacerbates the teacher shortage in sub-Saharan Africa. [55] Additionally, many schools use educational models that are based on the systems imported by colonial governments. Learning is rote memorization, and children are not encouraged to think for themselves or question their teachers. Teachers in sub-Saharan Africa are seen as authority figures who give out information rather than as co-learners in an educational process.

Also based on the colonial model, many of the better secondary schools (or high schools) are boarding schools. This means that parents who want their children to get into college are forced to send the children away to school and are often only allowed to visit every few months. Most boarding schools in East Africa have strict rules on visitation and on whether or not the child can leave the campus. This separation means that as a child is coming into adolescence and beginning to think about or experiment with sex, they are away from family and community members who could give valuable advice. While there might be cultural taboos against talking to parents about sex, being away from the wider community of grandparents, aunts, and uncles as well as a parent's watchful eye could impact the decisions a young adolescent might make.

Even with these shortcomings, for the women in this study, education was all-important. One woman in the study named Maria was never able to go to school. When she was a child, she was forced to stay home and take care of her family. Her days were filled with fetching water, caring for grandparents, and cleaning the house. Then she was married young, and soon she was a mother. Not only did she not receive education, but she lost her childhood as well. When she told her story during one of our PAR sessions, the room grew quiet for a moment out of respect for her loss. Then other women started telling their stories, of how their education was ended by forces out of their control. Only two of the twelve women in the PAR group were able to finish high school.

Irish Jesuit theologian Michael Kelly argues that education is crucial in any HIV and AIDS response. Kelly says, "Every legitimate response to the disease starts out from education." Kelly goes on to argue that educational systems must respond because it is the young who are greatly affected by HIV and AIDS.[56] Vandemoortele and Delamonica call education a "social vaccine" and put great faith in its ability to prevent HIV.[57] The collaborators in this study would agree. While I was conducting fieldwork in Mwanza, Tanzania's second largest city, most of the collaborators (like residents in most of Africa's cities) originally had come to Mwanza from rural areas outside of the city. The collaborators in the research were very concerned about the lack of knowledge about HIV and AIDS in the rural areas.

When it comes to HIV, education can contribute to ending the pandemic in two ways. First, formal education gives people options. If the women in this study had received more education, they might have had more choices about their future. Even within traditional structures, a woman who has more education brings in a greater *mahari* (or bride-wealth) and therefore can be matched with a more educated husband. Since education can lead to greater equality, this can work in a woman's favor and give her greater autonomy.[58] More importantly, formal education can give women confidence and a set of skills they can use to generate their own income.

Beyond formal schooling, education functions at a second level as it facilitates correct knowledge about HIV and AIDS and eliminates myths. For example, many people in sub-Saharan Africa believe that if a person looks healthy, then they could not be HIV-positive. Some collaborators in this study reported that because they did not look sick, people did not believe them when they disclosed their status. Because many places in sub-Saharan Africa lack an infrastructure to effectively disseminate information, and because it is often taboo to speak of AIDS, many are left with more fiction than fact.

One collaborator named Agnes knew she was living with HIV and tried to dissuade men from being interested in her. One man pursued her constantly, even after she disclosed her status. He finally convinced her to start a relationship by saying that there are many ways a person can get HIV—including getting HIV from witchcraft—so sex was not that risky. She consented but said she later regretted it. She said she was concerned for his health, so she ended up dissolving the relationship.

During that same interview, I asked Agnes a specific question to hear her wisdom for creating change. I asked: "If you were in charge of a prevention program, what one thing would you do to stop the spread of HIV?" She answered by pointing to education and giving an example of how she tries to educate others:

> I would sensitize the girls that they should go check their health . . . and when they check and see they have been infected they should not see that as the end of the world. They should figure out ways to keep living until God has decided to take them—just like the drivers who get accidents and die. . . . But (these girls) should figure out what could they do to reach their dreams and make them come true. . . .
>
> For example like me, I always tell my young sister that not everyone you see walking on the road is beautiful, even if he gives you a hundred thousand or a million shillings. Try and think, why did he give you that million and what does he mean? I do not want you become hurt like me, because if we all get hurt who will help the other? So I always try to keep her aware. I love telling the women and men—especially the men because they are the ones who are ignorant—you might find that you agree with him to have sex using a condom and after two months, he will tell you that you are human and that if you knew that HIV was being spread—whatever—let it be. So we as women find ourselves being mostly infected due to the speed of having sex that kills us a lot, not like the others who go slowly but we go in a high speed.

Agnes, like many other women in the study, believed that education was the answer that gave women options. It kept them from crashing into love at "high speed." The women in the study who were public about their status considered their going public a sacrifice they made to educate others. They felt as though they had been blindsided—like a driver in an auto accident—and they wanted others to avoid the same fate.

Yet it must be acknowledged that while education can help dispel myths and give correct information, it will not always lead to changed behavior. In order for behavior to change, we must begin to dismantle the fatalism that comes with poverty. In the interview excerpt above, the male character in Agnes' scenario names the risk as being human. The man convinces the woman to stop using condoms come what may. In other words, life is risky so one more risk doesn't matter. If a person could die of hunger, poor health, a road accident, or dangerous work conditions, then dying from sex doesn't seem so scary. Education will not reach its full potential for ending the HIV pandemic until it is able to deconstruct fatalism and give space for realizing hope and dreams.

NOTES

1. For more on a return to the particular in HIV and AIDS research, see *Journal of Feminist Studies in Religion Roundtable: HIV Gender and Religion.* Introductory article by Sarojini Nadar and Isabel Phiri, "Charting the Paradigm Shifts in HIV Research: The Contribution of Gender and Religion Studies," *Feminist Studies in Religion,* Vol. 28, No. 2 (2012). Also in this roundtable, see responses by Nyambura J. Njoroge, Melissa Browning, Margaret A. Farley, Ezra Chitando, and Dora Rudo Mbuwayesango.

2. John Iliffe, *The African Aids Epidemic: A History,* (Athens: Ohio University Press, 2006), 1–2.

3. Catherine Campbell, *Letting Them Die: Why HIV/AIDS Prevention Programmes Fail,* (Bloomington: Indiana University Press, 2004), 23–35.

4. Iliffe, 24–25, 40–45.

5. It is important to note that when we are talking about family in sub-Saharan Africa, we are never talking about a "nuclear family" in the way that we talk about family in the West. In sub-Saharan Africa, a family is never only a married couple and their children. Families always include extended family—both living and dead. In many cases, aunts, uncles, grandparents and even neighbors have the same authority as a child's parent. Likewise, tasks such as farming, caring for livestock, and raising children are often distributed among those in an extended family rather than just a nuclear family. For this reason, when I speak of family, I am speaking of the extended family, which I argue has been weakened by colonialism and globalization.

6. For more on the shift from polygamy to monogamy and the early missionary movement in Tanzania, see Derek Peterson, "Morality Plays: Marriage, Church Courts, and Colonial Agency in Central Tanganyika, ca, 1876–1928," *American Historical Review,* October 2006, 983–1010.

7. Oduyoye, *Daughters of Anowa,* 3.

8. Ibid., 183.

9. Oduyoye, *Beads and Strands,* 51.

10. See Musa Dube, *Postcolonial Feminist Interpretation of the Bible,* (St Louis: Chalice Press, 2000), 3–4. In my own fieldwork, when certain topics were considered taboo, collaborators would often refer to their memory of either a biblical text or traditional wisdom to navigate the subject at hand. For example, some women were not yet willing to talk about how the church stigmatized HIV-positive people, but they would speak of scriptures that showed Jesus' openness to the sick. The passages where Jesus healed the woman with the issue of blood (Luke 8) and Jesus' healing those with leprosy were frequently mentioned. In the same way, the women were not quite willing to say women should not obey their husbands, but they frequently cited the

scripture that said a husband should love a wife the way Christ loves the church (Ephesians 5:25). In this way, sacred texts were being re-read in ways that were applicable to the women's lives and in ways that subverted patriarchal and colonial readings of these and other texts.

11. Mercy Oduyoye, *Daughters Of Anowa*, 106.

12. As previously mentioned, *mahari* is the Kiswahili word that can be loosely translated as "bridewealth" or "dowry." Throughout this book, I will use the word *mahari* in order to stay true to the word's specific meaning in East Africa.

13. Isabel Apawo Phiri and Saronjini Nadar, "Introdution: 'Treading Softly but Firmly,'" in *African Women, Religion and Health: Essays in Honor of Mercy Oduyoye*, 1–18.

14. Musimbi R.A. Kanyoro, "Engendered Communal Theology: African Women's Contribution to Theology in the 21st Century," in *Talitha cum! Theologies of African Women*, ed. Nyambura J. Njoroge and Musa W. Dube, (Pietermaritzburg, South Africa: Cluster Publications, 2001), 158.

15. Oduyoye, *Beads and Strands* , 90-100; See also, Isabel Apawo Phiri and Sarojini Nadar, "Treading Softly but Firmly," in *African Women, Religion and Health*, ed. Isabel Apawo Phiri and Sarojini Nadar, (Maryknoll, NY: Orbis, 2007), 1–13.

16. Mbiti, *African Religions and Philosophy*, (Nairobi: East African Educational Publishers, 1969) 213.

17. Liv Haram, "Eyes Have No Curtains": The Moral Economy of Secrecy in Managing Love Affairs among Adolescents in Northern Tanzania in the Time of AIDS," *Africa Today*, Vol. 51, No. 4, 57–73, (Summer 2005), 60. Later in the same article, Harem expounds on this point by saying, "What is at stake is how it is done. If you want to "steal" (iiva) sex, a term often used when referring to "illicit" sexual relationships, you must do so with dignity and respect, or, as the Meru put it, *kuve nrango, anderunda mboni ta utondo* "It is necessary to use one's brains or sense." In other words, one should hide such behavior, particularly from those who may be provoked by it. Hence, as long as "illicit" sex is not boasted or talked about in the open, but carried out discreetly, it seems to be silently accepted. Neither the sexual activity itself, nor the actual number of sexual relationships, is what counts; rather, the important thing is the manner in which the "illicit" sexual relations are practiced." (p. 66).

18. Violet Nyambura Kimani, "Human Sexuality," *Ecumenical Review* 56, no. 4: 404–21, (2004), 408.

19. Ibid.

20. Ibid., 409.

21. Ibid., 419.

22. Ibid., 411.

23. See UNFPA, *State of the World Population 2005*, esp. Chapter Five, "The Unmapped Journey: Adolescents, Poverty and Gender," http://www.unfpa.org/swp/2005/english/ch5/chap5_page3.htm (accessed September 20, 2010).

24. For more on the sugar daddy syndrome, see Fuller, 95–104. For prevalence on girls ages fifteen to twenty-four see AMFAR AIDS Research, http://www.amfar.org/abouthiv/article.aspx?id=3594 (accessed Sept. 3, 2010).

25. For more on female circumcision see: Mary Nyangweso Wangila, *Female Circumcision: The Interplay of Religion, Culture and Gender in Kenya*, (Maryknoll, NY: Orbis Books, 2007) and Ephigenia W. Gachiri, IBVM, *Female Circumcision*, (Nairobi: Paulines, 2000).

26. Waris Dirie, *Desert Flower*, (New York: Harper Perennial, 1999), 141–44.

27. Margaret Brady, "Female Genital Mutilation: Complications and Risk of HIV Transmission," *AIDS Patient Care and STDs*, Vol 13, No 12, 709–16, December 1999.

28. Ibid.

29. CDC, "Male Circumcision and Risk for HIV Transmission and Other Health Conditions: Implications for the United States" http://www.cdc.gov/hiv/resources/factsheets/circumcision.htm (accessed September 20, 2010).

30. See John Mbiti, *African Religions and Philosophy*, (Nairobi: East African Educational Publishers, 1969), 146–48 and Kimani, 404–21.

31. Mbiti, *African Religions and Philosophy*, 124–25.

32. Ibid, 124.

33. Kimani, 413.

34. Mbiti, *African Religions and Philosophy*, 147.

35. Ibid.

36. Ruth Muthei James, "The Promotion of the 'ABC' of Sex in The Prevention of HIV/AIDS in Africa: Implications for Women," In *People of Faith and the Challenge of HIV/AIDS*, edited by Mercy Amba Oduyoye and Elizabeth Amoah, (Ibadan, Nigeria: Sefer, 2004), 159. It should be noted that this practice is not present among all communities in sub-Saharan Africa. For example, according to Susan Allen, the Director of the Rwanda Zambia HIV Research Group and faculty member at Emory's Rollins School of Public Health, women in Rwanda see sex during pregnancy as a way to give the child "vitamins" and have a very short post-partum abstinence period. (Conversation with the author, December 6, 2010).

37. For more on dry sex see Ambasa C.R. Shisanya, "Socio-cultural Vulnerability of Women to HIV/AIDS: A Theological Strategy to Transform Power," in *People of Faith and the Challenge of HIV/AIDS*, 246. See also Fuller, 31, 74–75.

38. The virus is in its most contagious form a few days or a few weeks after the virus is contracted. This is called "Acute HIV Infection." For more see: The Body, "Acute HIV Infection," October 14, 2009, http://www.thebody.com/content/art5998.html (accessed September 20, 2010).

39. Eileen Stillwaggon, *AIDS and the Ecology of Poverty*, (New York: Oxford, 2006), 74–77.

40. Ibid., 75

41. Ibid., 69.

42. Ibid., 79–80.

43. Paul Farmer, Infections and Inequalities , (Berkeley: University of California Press, 1999), 40.

44. Paul Farmer, Haun Saussy, and Tracy Kidder, ed. *Partner to the Poor: A Paul Farmer Reader*, (Berkeley: University of California Press, 2010). 369–70.

45. Farmer, Infections and Inequalities , 42.

46. Ibid., 52.

47. Ibid., 54.

48. In September of 2000, world leaders gathered at the United Nations in New York to adopt the "United Nations Millennium Declaration" which included the following eight goals: End poverty and hunger, Universal education, Gender equality, Child health, Maternal health, Combat HIV/AIDS, Environmental sustainability, and Global partnership. For more on the Millennium Development Goals, see http://www.un.org/millenniumgoals (accessed September 20, 2010).

49. The countries meeting this commitment include Rwanda, Botswana, Niger, Malawi, Zambia, and Burkina Faso. See: PMNCH/Africa Public Health Alliance & 15% Campaign, Press Release: "Countdown to 2015: Small investment could save 11 million African lives," (July 21, 2010), http://www.who.int/pmnch/media/membernews/2010/20100721_africanunion_pr/en/index.html (accessed September 20, 2010).

50. World Health Organization (WHO), "World Health Statistics 2008," http://www.who.int/whosis/whostat/EN_WHS08_Full.pdf (accessed September 20, 2010).

51. PMNCH/Africa Public Health Alliance & 15% Campaign, "Countdown to 2015: Small investment could save 11 million African lives."

52. UNICEF, "Statistics by Country: Tanzania," http://www.unicef.org/infobycountry/tanzania_statistics.html (accessed September 3, 2010).

53. Gustavo Gutierrez, *We Drink from our Own Wells: The Spiritual Journey of a People*, (Maryknoll: Orbis Books, 1992), 9–10.

54. David Smith, "Grandmothers' summit to put spotlight on Africa's 'forgotten victims' of Aids," *The Guardian*, May 3, 2010, http://www.guardian.co.uk/world/2010/may/03/grandmothers-summit-aids-africa (accessed January 23, 2011).

55. Michael J. Kelly, *Education: For An Africa Without AIDS,* (Nairobi: Paulines, 2008), 76–80.

56. Ibid., 75.

57. Jan Vandemoortele and Enrique Delamonica, "The `education vaccine' against HIV," *Current issues in comparative education,* Vol. 3, No. 1, (2000), www.tc.edu/cice/Issues/03.01/31vandemoortele_delamonica.pdf (accessed September 20, 2010).

58. I am not suggesting here that *mahari* is not problematic for women, but simply making a point that even in the traditional marriage selection process, education can give women more options. However, it should be noted that this could also backfire as men who pay higher dowries for their wives will sometimes demand more; justifying their demands by reminding their wives of the high dowries they paid.

THREE

"Let's Talk About Trust, Baby"

HIV/AIDS Vulnerabilities and Intimate Relationships

"LET'S TALK ABOUT TRUST"

When I first lived in East Africa in 1998, condoms were not nearly as widespread as they are today. Because most people did not use them, public health organizations such as PSI[1] began marketing condoms to the general public in hopes of curbing the HIV pandemic. In 1998 the locally subsidized condom brand, "Trust condoms,"[2] had a series of radio commercials that used the song, "Let's talk about sex, baby" by the then popular group Salt 'n Peppa and turned it into a condom jingle that sang, "Let's talk about trust." It was a clever marketing strategy, primarily because sex is taboo in East Africa. Even if you use condoms, you do not "talk about sex." But because Salt 'n Peppa did get airtime on the hip rock stations, young people got the point when the word "trust" was substituted for "sex." The most interesting aspect of these radio commercials was that they all started with a dialogue where two people met for the first time, and within the fifteen- to thirty-second commercial time slot, decided to have sex. The cheery "let's talk about trust" jingle at the end promoted the message that individuals could engage in casual sex with little to no consequences, as long as they used a condom called "trust."

In 2013 in East Africa, Trust condoms are still being sold. And while they no longer sport the same jingle, the message is much the same. In a more recent TV commercial, a young man and woman meet while crossing the street during a rain shower. As they are waiting at the crosswalk it is raining, but as soon as they cross the street the rain stops. As the woman is closing her umbrella, the umbrella sleeve blows away. In response, the man stops in the crosswalk and seductively pulls a condom out of his pocket, opens it, and uses it to close her umbrella. In another ad, a young man appears at a train station and uses a condom to fix a leak in young girl's water bottle.[3] In both commercials, the "sexual encounter" was between strangers, suggesting that condoms are for casual sex. The commercials end with the slogan, *"Maisha iko sawa na Trust"* — "Life is ok with Trust."

While the message is somewhat problematic,[4] the condom advertisers may be onto something. In East Africa, casual sex is far less dangerous than married sex or sex in steady relationships. In casual sex, single women (and men) can negotiate for condom use, ask their partners to take an HIV test, or leave an unfaithful partner with little economic or personal impact. In this way, girlfriends are more powerful than wives. Within marriages, there are few protections for women. The fidelity that is presumed by conjugal *trust* is too often absent, and other protections against STD's are off limits. In this study, women living with HIV and AIDS in Mwanza said over and over again that if a woman wants to protect herself from HIV, then it is better to be single.

In this chapter, I take seriously their claim that being single is safer as I begin to ask why marriage is an HIV risk factor in East Africa. I start by looking at the current climate and the taboo nature of sex and sexuality in this region. I then give an overview of the ways in women in sub-Saharan Africa are particularly vulnerable to HIV and AIDS. I end the chapter by looking at the complex nature of agency and autonomy within intimate relationships. Here, I use stories from research collaborators in the research to introduce the idea of relational vulnerability, which I argue is the key in understanding why marriage has become an HIV risk factor.

LET'S NOT TALK ABOUT SEX: THE TABOO NATURE OF SEX IN SUB-SAHARAN AFRICAN SOCIETIES

As I sat down to interview the head nurse at the Africa Inland Church HIV/AIDS clinic in Mwanza, I noticed several objects on her desk were covered with thick lace handkerchiefs. I assumed that these objects were being protected from the dust, like so many other things covered in lace handkerchiefs and tablecloths throughout East Africa. Mid-way through the interview, I asked the nurse if the taboo nature of sex presented an obstacle in her conversations with clients. She said it was a big problem, and then she removed the lace handkerchiefs to reveal two anatomical models—one of a penis and one of a vagina. As the look of surprise spread across my face the nurse told me not to worry. She said that most people are shocked when she removes the handkerchiefs.

You can't begin to talk about HIV and AIDS in Africa until you understand how much AIDS (and sex) are not talked about. The Yoruba have a proverb that says, *"A ki fi gbogbo enuu soro"* which is translated, "We don't speak with the whole mouth."[5] In African cultures, some subjects and actions are set aside and protected by taboo. Augustine Asaah points out that "taboo subjects in Africa include frightful phenomena such as death, abnormalities such as madness and incest, and sacred issues such as sex."[6] Other taboos center around blood and bodily fluids. When it comes to HIV and AIDS, multiple taboos are at play: sex, death, blood, bodily fluids and even "madness" (the term many Africans have used for late stage HIV-associated dementia).

In traditional African societies, talking about sex was (and still is) often considered taboo. Cross-generational and cross-gender talk about sex is almost always taboo. Men generally do not talk to women about sex, and parents do not talk to children about sex. Conversation between parents and children about sex is considered taboo, even when the talk is informative in nature.[7] While children have become more mobile and able to get information about sex from other sources, the relationship between parents and children is still a very formal relationship.[8] Among some ethnic groups, there is an exception where talk about sex can come from the grandparents, but this is still considered rare.[9]

One popular writer puts it this way:

> To talk about sex in some African cultures can be equated with cursing at the church. Sex is simply not discussed. It is believed that good families do not discuss this issue. In fact, to discuss sex with older adults is considered a sign of promiscuity. Childhood sexual curiosity and questions are learned from one's peers.[10]

But when parents are not the ones who educate their children about sex, myths abound. Adolescent youth might believe sex is a necessary rite of passage to ensure future virility. One example comes from another popular writer who says that a teenage boy might believe that if he does not "have live sex with a girl in the bush, his penis will not develop to the desired size or even the boy may fail to father children."[11] In some places such as Tanzania, in order to avoid talking about sex, euphemisms are often used. One euphemism that is used in Mwanza is *"kitendo cha ndoa"* which refers to sex as "an act of marriage."[12]

In some African cultures, sexual pleasure for women has also been considered taboo.[13] In East Africa, when a woman seems to know too much about sex or shows too much pleasure, she is thought to be sleeping around. For some ethnic groups in sub-Saharan Africa, a primary motivation for female circumcision was to eliminate women's pleasure and, therefore, keep women faithful. Yet this is complex, because even in places where women's sexual pleasure is considered taboo, it is also celebrated through rituals where women learn how to gain pleasure from sex.[14] This complexity could be linked to the idea present among some ethnic groups that suggests women have an even greater capacity for sexual pleasure than men. Within some expressions of Islam in Africa, women are thought to have a capacity for sexual pleasure that is nine times higher than that of men. Yet within this same line of thought, women are thought to be passive and seen as the source of sexual immorality.[15]

Even when sexuality is taboo, women's power within the sexual encounter is often both respected and feared. One example of this power within marriage comes from the Delta area of Nigeria. Patience Turtoe-Sanders tells the story of the *Egweya,* a group of the oldest women in the community who are responsible for keeping the husbands in line. If a husband was abusive or neglectful of his family, the wife could ask the *Egweya* for help. If the *Egweya* found the husband guilty, they would gather at his compound, completely naked, and begin to sing of the wrongs the husband has committed. Turtoe-Sanders says that the women would then point to their vagina and say, "We have come to open our *toto* (vagina) to you. . . . It is through this *toto* that you were formed. It is through this *toto* that you came into this world, and it is this *toto* that will kill you." Through their singing and dancing, these women evoke a warning and summon the ancestors to act. If the husband does not reform his ways, the oldest woman of the group will call on the ancestors to curse him. Turtoe-Sanders calls the *toto* a "weapon" that can "unmake a man" and says that when a woman curses a man through her *toto,* the curse is irreversible.[16]

Coming into this study, I was worried the taboo nature of sex would keep us from getting to the real issues. Surprisingly, I found the opposite was true. As the twelve women met together each week, a safe space was created where women's speech was welcomed. The collaborators began to see that others in the room had similar experiences, and as a result, they opened up more each week. By the time we got to the topic of sex on week five, I had volunteers offering to create skits to show me exactly what they were talking about. So in one sense, while these subjects are taboo, there is always a possibility for pulling them from the realm of taboo into common speech once safe spaces are created.[17]

THE PARTICULAR VULNERABILITIES OF WOMEN AND GIRLS

The taboo nature of sex is likely one reason for the pandemic's spread in sub-Saharan Africa, but there are other important factors as well. Women in sub-Saharan Africa are among those most vulnerable to HIV biologically, economically, legally, socially, and relationally. But in Tanzania, the burdens women carry are hidden. None of the women in this research even knew that the virus was more prevalent among women than men. They knew there were more women in their HIV support groups, but they rightly guessed only the partial reason, that men were less likely to get tested and know their status.

During the time I lived in Mwanza, I was often asked to speak at churches or to introduce myself when I visited a church. I learned quickly that I should say I was researching "HIV and the Church" rather than "HIV and Women." When I said my research focused on women, the men wanted to know why and the women felt blamed. Often it seemed that both men and women blamed women for the disease, not recognizing the particular vulnerabilities women in sub-Saharan Africa face each day.

In order to speak more specifically about women's vulnerabilities, I will pull directly from my fieldwork with women in Tanzania and from the written work of other feminist theorists and theologians in Africa. As a white, feminist theologian from the West who is a beneficiary of freedoms won by the women's movement, I do not want to take my definition of equality and impose it in an African space. For this reason, I seek to retell the experiences of the women in this study in solidarity with the vulnerabilities that they have named as realities. As I begin to talk about these vulnerabilities I do not want to paint a picture of African women as weak or as victims. The women in this study showed strength and resiliency in the face of insurmountable obstacles. However, it must also be acknowledged that many have experienced great unfairness and injustice. Sadly, their situation is not unique but is true to the experiences of many women throughout sub-Saharan Africa.

Biological Vulnerabilities

The first unique vulnerability of women lies with their biology. When it comes to contracting HIV women's bodies can be their greatest enemies. In a heterosexual encounter, women are at least two times more likely to contract HIV from men than men are from women.[18] Seminal fluids are more abundant than vaginal secretions, and women's vaginas have a greater surface area with which to contract the virus.[19] The virus targets immune cells, which are plentiful in the mucous membranes of the vagina. While skin is an effective barrier against HIV, mucous membranes allow the virus to enter, and the presence of immune cells facilitates infection.[20] Many of these cells are CD4+ cells, the cells that the HI virus most easily infects.[21] A woman's cervix and uterine walls also provide easy entry for the virus because of their thin mucous membranes, which are often only one cell-layer thick.[22] This is especially problematic for young women who have even thinner mucous membranes and an immature outer cervix.[23] As cited earlier, women's vaginal health is also a factor in their contracting HIV. Sexually transmitted infections and a decrease in good bacteria in the vaginal tract can make an unhealthy woman two and a half times more likely to contract HIV than a woman who is healthy.[24]

Only a few of the women in this study were aware that biology played a role in the likeliness of their being infected with HIV. During one PAR session, the topic came up as we were talking about why women had higher HIV and AIDS prevalence than men. When one woman in the group mentioned biology, several laughed in disbelief while a few others chimed in and agreed with her point. There was little consensus in the group as to whether or not biological factors were at play in women's vulnerability. None of the women could give any specifics, but some had heard that it was easier for women to contract HIV than men. Because the PAR method allows for teaching moments, we as a group shifted the conversation to talk briefly about anatomy, using hand-drawn diagrams to explain the differences in male and female vulnerabilities. By tying sex to science, this teaching moment allowed us to overcome speech taboos and create room for more honest conversation about sex.

Economic Vulnerabilities

The second vulnerability women face is an economic vulnerability. One example of this is land ownership. Throughout much of sub-Saharan Africa women are not allowed to inherit land. This increases a woman's vulnerability to HIV because the very land she lives on is often tied to a husband or male relative.[25] For families who live off subsistence agriculture, land means life. Owning land means access to food, shelter and sometimes water. In the midst of the HIV pandemic, land grabbing has become a common problem. In these cases, (usually) a husband dies and the extended family of the husband will force the woman and her children off the land, sometimes accusing the woman of using witchcraft or poison to kill her husband. Other times the property is taken from orphaned children after their parents die.

Women in this study also reported being kicked out of their houses when they disclosed their status. And because women often have no rights to the land, there is little legal recourse. One collaborator, Scholastica, contracted HIV within her marriage and discovered her status while she was pregnant. As she was beginning her second trimester, she was terribly sick but her husband would not let her visit the doctor. Eventually, she saved up her own money and went by herself. When she went to the doctor, she learned she was HIV-positive and disclosed this to her husband. The following week, after returning from her aunt's funeral, she found her house cleared out and her husband gone. He had sold all of their belongings and left with the cash, leaving her pregnant with an empty rental house and no money to pay the rent.

Beyond issues of land ownership, women are more economically vulnerable because they have less education and fewer marketable skills. In East Africa, when families cannot send all of their children to school, usually a boy is chosen to attend school over a girl. One woman in this study ran away and married early because she was not able to continue school. Later in her marriage, she had two children, a boy and a girl. Because she was also poor, like her parents, she said she chose to send the boy to school over the girl. Her son was able to make it to university while her daughter had not been able to finish secondary school.

In this study, only three of the twelve women in the PAR project worked in professional jobs. One was a counselor/receptionist, another worked in a women's NGO she helped to found, and a third worked in education. The rest of the women worked informally by selling vegetables, fish or used clothes, or by sewing. The women said that in Tanzania, when a woman is married she is often not allowed to work outside the home. In these instances, women are financially dependent on their husbands. This is one of the reasons women are not able to refuse sex with unfaithful partners. It could mean economic suicide. Collaborators reported that some men who pay *mahari* (or bridewealth) or pay for a woman's daily expenses expect sex in return, no matter what.

Worldwide, the feminization of poverty is also on the rise. About 70 percent of those who are poor in our world are women.[26] When women work outside the home, they also get paid less for their work. The global wage gap in 2008 showed there was a difference of 17 percent in men and women's pay in favor of men.[27]

Because women have less education, fewer resources, and are economically dependent on men, when they need to make money, they have fewer resources at their disposal. Even those who want to start a small business—such as selling vegetables at the market—often lack the small capital needed to get the business started. For these women, a small microloan (often the equivalent of twenty or thirty dollars) to launch or build a business could mean the difference between survival and flourishing. When interventions or resources are out of reach, some women turn to sex work or participate in other forms of transactional sex. Some of the women in this study said that they had sex with someone in order to pay their children's school fees or had entered a sexual relationship because it provided economic security. These decisions were motivated by survival. When all things are not equal, love and relationality will never be the only motives for sex.

Legal Vulnerabilities

Women are also vulnerable to HIV because they are not given legal protections that could ensure basic human rights. Some of the most serious legal vulnerabilities women face are within the realm of marriage. In citing examples of this, I will focus primarily on marriage laws in Tanzania.

Tanzania, like most African countries, does not recognize marital rape as a crime.[28] As of 2009, only six of the fifteen states that make up the

SADC (Southern Africa Development Community) had created policy statements against marital rape.[29] Even with these statements, marital rape was not necessarily criminalized. In Tanzania, marital rape is only criminalized if the couple is separated at the time of the rape, and in Zimbabwe marital rape is illegal but cannot be brought to court without the authorization of the Attorney General.[30] Each of the twelve women in the PAR study said that they had either been forcefully raped or had been a victim of non-consensual sex within their marriage.[31] Many of the women said that in these situations, their partner's unfaithfulness was their main reason for refusing sex. In sub-Saharan Africa, marital rape is not only a violation of women's rights but also a death sentence when contracting HIV is the result.

The non-recognition of marital rape is even more severe in light of marriage and divorce laws in the region, which also limit women's autonomy. In Tanzania, the official marriage age is eighteen, but with the consent of her father (or mother if the father is dead), a girl can be married as young as fifteen. If the girl is younger than fourteen, a marriage can still take place if the courts approve it first. Girls under twelve years can be married for religious reasons as long as the marriage is not consummated before the age of twelve.[32] While women's advocacy groups are pushing for an older marriage age in Tanzania, customary law still tends to win over common law and child marriages continue to take place.[33]

Four types of marriages are recognized by the Marriage Act of Tanzania: monogamous Christian marriages, polygamous Muslim marriages, and civil and traditional/customary marriages, both of which can be potentially polygamous.[34] According to the law, a marriage must be declared polygamous or monogamous when it is validated and cannot be changed without consent of both parties. However, women in this study said that this consent is rarely required. Nearly all of the women feared that their husbands—Christian, Muslim, or African traditionalist—would bring home a second wife. Polygamy is only allowed for men in Tanzania. Women may not marry multiple partners. This double standard echoes the double standard for marital fidelity where men are given license to cheat while women are expected to be faithful.

Laws on divorce also create vulnerabilities for women. According to the Marriage Act, a couple can only be divorced in Tanzania if they have been married for more than two years. Additionally, the couple has to attempt to reconcile the marriage with the church where they were married or with a reconciliation board before applying for divorce. Collaborators in this study said that Christian couples were required to obtain consent from their church before they could take the case to court, and some churches refused to give consent.

The research advocate for this project, Pauline Gasabile, who works for the Anglican Diocese in Mwanza, serves on marriage reconciliation boards for the church. She said that while churches try to help, they often recognize that little can be done and will give approval for the divorce. She also said that when the case goes to court, the process is long and costly and sometimes more trouble than it is worth. In order for the court to grant a divorce, they must be convinced the marriage is "of irreparable breakdown." Accepted reasons are listed in the marriage act and include: adultery, brutality, desertion, separation (for more than three years), sodomy, irresponsibility, and imprisonment (for more than five years).[35]

Conditions set forth for *mahari* (or bridewealth) must be met for a marriage to be valid in Tanzania. Because *mahari* payments are so expensive, many couples will decide to marry informally. In these cases, women are vulnerable because they do not have any of the protections afforded to legally married couples. While Tanzania recognizes "a presumption of marriage" for couples that have lived together for more than two years, this is sometimes difficult to prove when seeking protections from the court.[36]

Domestic violence is another significant vulnerability that women face where few legal protections are provided and enforced. While according to the Marriage Act, corporal punishment against a spouse is not permitted; there are no corresponding laws in Tanzania's Penal Code to enforce this.[37] Though the government of Tanzania has enacted campaigns to end violence against women, it is still a widespread problem in the country. In 2007, *The Guardian* newspaper in Tanzania published the findings of WiLDAF (Women in Law and Development) that showed over 50 percent of women in five regions in Tanzania regions were beaten daily by their partners.[38]

Socio-cultural Vulnerabilities

One of the greatest HIV vulnerabilities women in sub-Saharan Africa face is their identity and status as women in relation to patriarchal structures within states, religions, communities, and families. These socio-cultural vulnerabilities provide an explanation for women's economic and legal vulnerabilities as well. Throughout sub-Saharan Africa, boys are generally more valued than girls, especially within patrilineal groups in the region. A woman is praised if she has many sons but not praised as much if she has many girls. Baby girls are not as celebrated as boys, especially if they are born before boys. From the time a girl is young, she learns how to serve others, especially the men in her life. She even serves her male siblings.[39] When the time comes to go to school, girls only go if there is extra money after the boys' school fees have been paid. And if a parent or grandparent falls ill, it is often the young girls who are required to stay home and care for them.

As previously mentioned, throughout a girl's life, there are various rites of passages (such as female circumcision) that put girls at risk.[40]

When women are married the *mahari* payments can be a cause of risk when it is perceived as the purchase price for a wife. Once married, a woman's freedom and autonomy can be severely limited by her husband. While this is not universally true, a loss of autonomy in marriage is common throughout the region. Women in this study cited having to get permission from their husbands to visit doctors, travel to see family, or work outside the home.

Wherever patriarchy is found, women will be oppressed. While African women have unique vulnerabilities, they are still vulnerabilities that are primarily caused by patriarchy. No matter the context, when women have education, economic security, and autonomy to negotiate safe sexual practices in their relationships, they will be much less vulnerable to HIV.

Global Vulnerabilities

An additional level of vulnerability exists for women at a global level. When we look at statistics from around the world we find multiple inequalities that affect women. The feminization of poverty and the global wage gap between genders have already been mentioned. Women's health is also an area of global concern as we look at high rates of maternal mortality and inadequate nutrition for women, especially those who are pregnant and breastfeeding. We should also be concerned when women's bodies are regulated through making abortions illegal or through forced sterilizations.[41]

When it comes to HIV, a hermeneutic of suspicion is warranted when we realize the mass availability of male condoms compared to the limited availability of barrier devices for women, such as the female condom. Perhaps an even greater hermeneutic of suspicion comes into play when one realizes how difficult a female condom is to use in comparison with to male condoms! While various microbicides were currently in clinical trials at the time of writing, no prevention methods currently exists that can be totally controlled by women and undetected by men.[42] Until a female controlled prevention method is available, women will not be able to fully protect themselves from HIV.

New female-controlled prevention methods are currently unavailable because research in this area is still underfunded. In her book, *Theological Bioethics,* US Catholic theologian Lisa Sowle Cahill rightly argues that while diseases that primarily affect the poor are not researched, money is continually being directed toward curing diseases that generally affect the affluent. In making this argument, Cahill uses statistics to show that diseases such as malaria, pneumonia, diarrhea, and tuberculosis carry 20 percent of the world's disease burden but receive less than 1 percent of research funds. According to Cahill, this research focuses on a bottom line of profit rather than on the common good.

Cahill extends this argument to look at drug companies who are more likely to benefit when their research is out of reach or provided at a cost.[43] Providing women-controlled prevention methods would certainly change the course of this pandemic. Yet, because the resulting prevention methods would be used primarily by poor women in the developing world, this research is not market-driven but donor-driven, meaning less money is available.

Globally, women's issues are underfunded, and HIV and AIDS is no exception. When they are funded, there are often strings attached that limit women's autonomy. For example, when the PEPFAR (President's Emergency Plan For AIDS Relief) was launched in 2003, organizations receiving money were required to spend two-thirds of all prevention funding on abstinence and faithfulness education.[44] Another example of this is the Global Gag Rule (or the Mexico City Policy), which was in place 1984–1993 and 2001–2009. This policy prohibited non-profits outside the United States from promoting or performing abortions, even if they did not use US funding for these activities. The effect of this policy was a decrease in services to women as women's health clinics were closed. The policy also made safe abortions less available, forcing women to turn to unsafe procedures, which often cost them their lives. Of course, the US policy represents a double standard, as abortions are legal in the United States, but not in countries who are dependent on USAID for funding.[45]

Global underfunding of HIV prevention programs not only creates vulnerabilities for women but also points to a deeper issue at play. In order for women in sub-Saharan Africa to have a real shot at eliminating gendered vulnerabilities to HIV, true global solidarity is needed. But before we jump to solidarity, we have to question whether or not it is even possible. The women who I walked alongside of for eight months in Mwanza have lives that are drastically different from my own. I would be naïve to think I could ever fully understand the obstacles and joys of their lives. Yet there is space for friendship and listening, and in this space, we can seek an imperfect solidarity.

Mujerista[46] theologian Ada María Isasi-Díaz argues that "solidarity is the appropriate present-day expression of the gospel demand that we love our neighbor."[47] She says solidarity consists of two interdependent elements: mutuality and praxis.[48] Like Musa Dube and Kwok Pui-Lan, Isasi-Díaz argues that the oppressed have an epistemological priority[49] but that the oppressors (or former oppressors) also have a role to play as "friends" of the oppressed. In creating this friendship, the former oppressors must renounce the oppressive structures in which they have participated in order to stand in a new space of solidarity with the oppressed.[50] She goes on to say that the "friends" have important work to do, for they "are able to demystify the world of the oppressors from within, to expose its weakness and incoherence, to point out its lies."[51] In the face of injustice and crushing vulnerabilities, the global community must stand in solidarity with the women who are affected by this pandemic.

Relational Vulnerabilities

The women in this study also exhibited another vulnerability that I am naming relational vulnerability. I am defining this as a lack of mutuality and equality within intimate relationships that leads to an impoverished relational state where individuals are impacted emotionally, spiritually, bodily, and physically. Relational vulnerabilities create an imbalance of power where one (or more) individuals in the relationship is deprived of full agency and lives within forced choices to cope or survive within the relationship. When relational vulnerabilities are present, equality, mutuality, trust, and compassion are not present, or not present in equal measures, between partners in the relationship. In African contexts, relational vulnerability means the absence of *"I am because we are, and since we are, therefore I am."*[52] It pushes an individual to the periphery rather than allowing that person to participate fully in community and family life.

In this study, almost every woman I interviewed had experienced or was experiencing some degree of relational vulnerability. Most of these women had contracted HIV within their marriage when their husband had been unfaithful. Then, upon discovering their status—usually through prenatal testing—they told their spouses and then were blamed for bringing the disease home and thrown out of the house.

In the introduction to her book on African women and HIV and AIDS, Linda Fuller argues that:

> Throughout Africa, infected women are certainly not limited to those involved as sex workers; rather, most are mothers from every social strata and geographic area, with those living along trade routes being especially at risk. If the truth be known, though, nearly all women are at risk, including—actually, especially—those who have had only their husband as a sexual partner.[53]

Fuller makes the point that women in this study knew all too well—their marriages made them vulnerable. "It's better to be single." A single woman is much more powerful than her married sisters. Girlfriends can ask for condoms or demand an HIV test, but wives often feel they cannot.

The women collaborators in this study frequently spoke of women staying "inside" the home and men "going out." This phrasing applied not only to descriptions of women's work vs. men's work but to their description of their husband's social lives as well. The women said that within marriage, the symbolic space for women was inside the home, (even though most women do work outside the home). While men moved freely between their responsibilities in the home and responsibilities and involvement outside the home, women's first priority was caring for the home and the children.

In my fieldwork, when we talked about marriage becoming a safe space, the women frequently mentioned the divide between what happens outside the marriage and what happens inside. We could not talk about marriage as a safe space without talking about the importance of a safe space for women outside of marriage. In reflecting on this, I came to the conclusion that there is a strong connection between the exclusivity of intimate relationships and the importance of exclusive/inclusive individual space outside of intimate partnerships. In other words, you can't have one without the other. If in any given community women are not given space for education, personal growth, and agential decision-making, then they will also not be able to carve out the needed space for health and well-being in their intimate relationships. And until women are given equal space with men in their communities and relationships, they will continue to be vulnerable to diseases such as HIV.

BETTER TO BE SINGLE?: AGENCY, AUTONOMY, AND TRUST IN INTIMATE RELATIONSHIPS

When aid organizations begin to talk about women and HIV in sub-Saharan Africa, there is often talk about the need for women to be "empowered." This is true, but I wonder if the concept of empowerment can really articulate all that is relationally wrong when intense vulnerabilities are present. Women need to be empowered, but when there are relational vulnerabilities, a "disempowering" of the dominant partner is also needed to restore a "balance of power." As a feminist theologian, I also wonder if the concept of "power" can even help us reach mutuality. Women should be "empowered" to direct their own lives in relation with others. But this does not necessarily solve the problem of patriarchy, which is an active oppression.

In the midst of patriarchy, women's autonomy and agency is limited by patriarchal structures. Within marriage, this not only means a limitation of freedom in terms of women's ability to make decisions, but it also means a limitation of trust. When there is an imbalance of power, the only trust that can exist in a relationship would be akin to the trust between a parent and a child. This level of trust is inappropriate for an intimate relationship between two adults, and therefore it causes problems. When women are not seen as equal partners in a marriage, there is little reason for men to be faithful.

Perhaps the best way to reflect on agency and autonomy in intimate relationships is by listening to the lived experience of a collaborator in this research. Veronica's story gives us a good example. Veronica was married young—she was only thirteen years old. The priest who married her and her husband forged her birth certificate to make the marriage legal. When Veronica left her home in Tabora, she never dreamed she was leaving to get married. She thought she was going to be a domestic worker for a truck driver. She stayed in this man's house for about six months while he made trips to and from Dar es Salaam. Each time, when he came home, she did what was expected—she washed his clothes and cooked his food.

The fourth time he returned home, she awoke in the middle of the night to cook him food, but afterwards she was not allowed to return to her bed. Instead, she was told to come into his room, and he locked the door behind her. Veronica was told that she had been the maid, but now it was time for her to become the wife. Veronica said she didn't know what was happening to her. There were no mothers or aunties to prepare her for her informal "wedding night." At thirteen years and seven months, Veronica was not even old enough to menstruate, much less become someone's wife.

Before Veronica turned fifteen, she was pregnant with her first child. She heard the neighbors talk about how many women her new husband had been with, they said he had been with six wives before her, but she said she got used to it. Veronica and her husband had four children together. By the time her third child was born, her husband used to stay out drinking every night. But no matter what time he came in, Veronica was expected to wake up, give him a bath, and cook him food.

One night he came in at three AM, and Veronica had had enough. She challenged him—she asked her husband why he needed to stay out all night when all his needs were provided for at home. She said that she didn't go out of the house and wanted to know why he stayed out every night. She appealed to his emotion—she said she was lonely and missed him when he was away. But Veronica's husband became angry with her and went outside and picked up the family's dog. He went into their bedroom and pulled back the covers and put the dog in the bed. He told Veronica that if she was lonely she could have sex with the dog. Then he pushed Veronica into the bed with the dog.[54]

That night Veronica went to her sister's house, but her sister talked her into going back home. If you press charges, she said, if you lose your husband, then what would you have? Veronica's husband won her back by buying her a new dress, but her problems did not end. Not long after this event, the family was out of money, and Veronica asked her husband for money to buy food for their children. He looked at her and said, "You have your vagina, go and sell it to make money. Why should you ask me for money when you have a vagina you can sell?"

Veronica was devastated but took him seriously—after three days with no food for the family, she thought prostitution might be her only option, so she said she took a shower and went out with intentions to trade sex for food. Before she got to the gate she turned back. She couldn't do it. She had always been faithful to her marriage and she wasn't willing to give that up.

Veronica's husband continued to stay out late, and soon he began to get sick. She had seen people with HIV and AIDS on TV so she began to look for the symptoms. Veronica would listen outside of the toilet to see if he had diarrhea. She asked her husband about the rashes on his body, but he said it was just from the long journeys driving his truck. Veronica asked him to take an HIV test, but he refused. Soon, he became so sick that he finally consented to an HIV test. A friend talked him into it. Veronica and her husband went for the test together, and after testing, Veronica told the nurse that they wanted to receive their results together. The nurse looked at her and replied, "Ma, you are already infected."

Veronica said that in that moment she was angry and full of rage. She said that even though she was robbed of her childhood by being married at thirteen years old, she had been a good and faithful wife. Her husband was her only sexual partner. In that moment, Veronica was so overcome with anger that she grabbed her husband by the neck of his shirt, pulled him up, and slapped him—an action that is unheard of for a Tanzanian woman. In Tanzania, the opposite is expected—men hit women but women rarely hit men. Her husband responded by asking for her forgiveness, but Veronica was not yet willing to forgive.

Veronica was still in disbelief. The next day, she went back to the doctor again and asked him to test her other arm, in case she only had HIV in one arm, hoping the rest of her body might be spared. When the second test came back positive, Veronica believed death was near. She gave away all her clothes. She gave one set of dresses to her sister-in-law and then left in tears after being scolded her for giving away her clothes. Her sister-in-law said that if she gave away her clothes, they wouldn't have anything to use to clean up her diarrhea.

Yet Veronica's story is a story of survival. She cared for her husband until he died of AIDS. Then she began to rebuild her life. She said she did forgive her husband, and she forgave those who stigmatized her, but the forgiveness did not change the fact that her life was ruined. When she spoke her story, she mourned the loss of her childhood. She lamented that she had no parents to protect her. She blamed her brothers for taking *mahari* and throwing her away to be married before she was grown. She blamed her church for forging her birth certificate, for not seeing her as a person but only as a thing to be given away.

Veronica's story is also a story of relational vulnerability. In her story, we find an unequal relationship, a relationship that lacked honesty and faithfulness, a relationship that lacked trust and freedom, a relationship that lacked love. The consequences of this relational vulnerability were a loss of health, of prosperity, and even life. Unfortunately, Veronica's story resonated with too many women in the group. They too had experienced similar relational vulnerabilities that had exposed them to HIV.

Intimate Relationships: Why Abstinence and Faithfulness Aren't Enough

In light of Veronica's story and the stories of the other women in this study, I can argue confidently that promoting abstinence and faithfulness are rarely sufficient responses to HIV and AIDS. Yet, within the religious literature on HIV prevention, there is a single-minded, almost blind reliance on abstinence and faithfulness as the solution to the HIV pandemic. Abstinence and faithfulness are preached while the patriarchal underpinnings of Christian marriage and intimate relationships are rarely challenged. When relational and other vulnerabilities are present, when both partners in a relationship do not have full or equal agency, neither abstinence nor faithfulness is a real possibility. For abstinence or faithfulness to be a moral choice, a relational foundation must be present that encourages agency, choice, and mutuality. When relationality is not present, the relational poor can live only in a context of forced choices. Free choice and full agency can only be realized within a community of persons where personhood and mutuality are recognized and respected.

To say this a different way, we can give an example. If a person can chose to abstain from sex until marriage but then they are raped, that choice is taken from them. Many of the vulnerabilities described in this chapter can be compared to rape in that they rob an individual of free choice and full agency. A girl who has to choose between dropping out of school and selling her body to pay school fees is in the same situation as a person who is raped. Any choice she has is a forced choice, limited by the poverties that surround her life.

The women in this fieldwork knew relational vulnerability well, but they were unclear as to the solutions. They were not optimistic that marriage could be changed. They did believe that remaining single, or waiting until you were at least thirty to get married, was one way to protect yourself from contracting HIV/AIDS. Single women, they said, could control their bodies; they could protect themselves. According to the women in this study, a married woman gave up control of her body — she could not ask her husband to wear a condom, she could not refuse sex. For the women in this study, marriage represented a loss of bodily integrity, autonomy, and agency.

Yet even in the midst of these reflections, even in admitting that they had been mistreated, the women in this study were still were not willing to say that women should hold an equal voice to men within intimate relationships. Within their churches and society, there were no real models of marital equality. It was still an abstract idea. These women were simply hoping to live in a marriage where they were not abused. But the problem is, the two are connected. Relational vulnerability means an inequality of power is present, and when an inequality of power is present, intimate relationships can rarely be fair or just. They will always inflict harm—quietly or blatantly—and the one who is harmed is most often the partner with the least power, which is usually the woman.

It is no coincidence that there is a feminization of poverty in our world. This is a result of relational poverty—of unequal relationships. The relationality—or lack thereof—that we see in marriages is mirrored in other relationships of power—such as in the state, in the church, in the community, in the family. So how is it that on a continent where community is valued above all, such intense relational vulnerabilities exists?

As a westerner I have to admit that when I talk about community in Africa, I have to be careful not to romanticize the concept. I come from a place where we say, "I think therefore I am," or maybe in the words of a younger generation, "I am—whether you like it or not." I come from a place that could use a little more, *"I am because we are . . . "* Community is a hallmark of African cultures and societies, but we have to admit that communities can also isolate and alienate. For every *"I am because we are . . . "* there are one or two who are told they "are not" because we don't think you are.

In the face of death and risk, those who are vulnerable often compensate for these risks with their bodies. The feminization of HIV and AIDS is written on the bodies of women. Yet, even in the midst of these vulnerabilities, the women in this study reached out for relationality and mutuality. This was best seen in the ways in which they cared for their children and even their sick husbands. Grace, whose story was in chapter 1, literally gave away years of her life by submitting to a forced choice that would pay her son's school fees. Veronica forgave and cared for a husband who gave her a death sentence. These women reached for relationality and rejected the vulnerabilities of their lives. They risked life, so that life could go on. The problem with this is that we cannot romanticize their struggles. We must find space to say that while we see strength and life in the choices these women make to care and to forgive, their situations are unjust on multiple levels.

LET'S TALK ABOUT TRUST (AGAIN): WHAT CONDOM ADVERTISING CAN TEACH US ABOUT HIV AND AIDS IN AFRICA

I began this chapter with an illustration about Trust condoms that described the brand's marketing strategies in East Africa. As previously mentioned, in these commercials, sensual encounters between strangers are used to promote the brand. This marketing strategy has much to teach us about HIV and AIDS in sub-Saharan Africa. In paying attention to these commercials,[55] we can learn something about sex and intimate relationships that will help us better understand the particular vulnerabilities women face.

Of the five commercials surveyed, four involved encounters between complete strangers. In the fifth commercial, it is unclear whether the two actors have just met or are in a relationship. This tells us something about the nature of condom use in East Africa. Generally speaking, condoms are used in casual relationships or beginning relationships. *The Daily Nation* reports that as relationships progress, condoms are used less.[56] This is problematic within intimate relationships because collaborators in this research said that as the relationship became more established, the male partner was more likely to cheat.

Each commercial ends with the slogan, *"Maisha iko sawa na Trust"* — Life is ok with Trust. In reflecting on this slogan, it seems as if the condom metaphorically replaces the "trust" that is expected in intimate relationships. When you cannot "trust" your partner, you can "trust" a condom. This slogan also speaks against those who say that condoms do not work and cannot be trusted.

The overall idea in these commercials is that condoms are for people you don't know, perhaps because it's believed that you can trust people you do know. They also reinforce a theme that surfaced in my fieldwork—girlfriends have more power than wives because they can negotiate for condom use. In these commercials, the actors are portrayed as equals. They are dressed similarly, appear to be of the same socio-economic class, and are equally interested in sex. Yet it is always the man in the commercial who pulls the condom out of his pocket and saves the day by using it to fix a leaky radiator or water bottle, retrieve jewelry lost from the side of a boat, or close an umbrella. While this may be effective in convincing men who are hesitant to use condoms of the product's general sex appeal, it furthers the point that the decision to use a condom in too often left to men. In one commercial, the woman whispers something in a man's ear, which prompts him to buy a condom, but even in this commercial the decision to buy the condom rests on him.

The commercials also represent a masterful balance between breaking and observing taboos. Sex is never spoken of or portrayed, but sensuality is abundant. In this sexually charged atmosphere, the actors barely touch or even speak and never kiss. The settings for the commercials are often public spaces—streets, train stops, a roadside garage, or a crowded beach. In one commercial, a Nairobi street turns into a Garden of Eden-like paradise when two lovers buy a condom.

My point in this analysis is not necessarily to criticize the condom commercials. While I would like to see a broader social message promoted that includes women, I do recognize the importance of targeting men, since it is men who often refuse to use condoms based on conceptions of masculinity. The primary issue I hope to raise is the metaphor of trust within these commercials. By positioning condoms as the "trust" within casual relationships, it is assumed that in long-term relationships, condoms are not needed because trust is present.

Characteristics for Loving Relationships

During the first PAR session, I asked the women collaborators to name the most important characteristics of loving relationships or good relationships. The women named understanding between partners, love, transparency, peace, honesty, and trust as key characteristics of loving relationships.[57] We reflected further on these characteristics by speaking about the ways they functioned. The women agreed that these key traits could be compared to a fence around a family's homestead. They protected the marriage and allowed it to grow, defending it against threats from "outside." As the conversation moved from the theoretical to the concrete, the women began telling stories about their own marriages, many of which began with these characteristics before turning into something completely different.

One woman named Agnes started the conversation by telling the story of her marriage:

In the beginning my husband and I were so much in love. Whenever he received his salary he would bring it home and we discussed how to use it. He gave me anything I wanted. We were even on par, thoughtwise. He would not go to a place or even eat elsewhere without me. If he had any contact with any women even in terms of his work he would inform me. That time there was a lot of peace and trust between us. I was also free to tell him anything. This later changed especially when I had continuous miscarriages. I miscarried three times and he even went so far as to get a doctor to remove my womb. I refused and that was the beginning of my problems. He even began being unfaithful to me. We moved from Mwanza to Bukoba, and later on I found out that he had a mistress in Bukoba and he had even rented a house for her and was supporting her. When things got worse, we separated. While we were separated I went to stay at my grandmother's place and there I discovered I had conceived. I carried the pregnancy successfully to term and gave birth to a baby boy. He denied being the father of my son claiming that I must have been unfaithful. I struggled to bring up our son on my own in the village. Unfortunately at the age of two years my son passed away. Then he blamed me for killing his son. I told him that he actually had contributed to our son dying as he had neglected us both. I suspect at that time I was already infected with HIV as this child was always sickly. I also underwent so many challenges raising him as I had no source of income and therefore he had a troubled upbringing. My husband continued to abuse me saying that I had slept with many men.

Christine echoed Agnes' story and described her situation this way:

For me, when my husband and I got married we trusted one another so much. We were always together and even went to places together. This love went on when I gave birth to our first, and second child. After the birth of my third child, one day unexpectedly my husband did not sleep at home. He had never done that ever since I knew him and even since I got married to him. That was a great shock to me. I could not believe my eyes on that day.

In these stories, trust is a key component at the beginning of the relationship that decreases as the relationship continues. When the trust disintegrates, it makes the relationship vulnerable to HIV. Yet in these spaces, when husbands began to be unfaithful, the women in this study gave numerous examples of families, pastors and priests encouraging them to go back home. This left the women increasingly vulnerable. For some, reconciling their marriages shortened their lives.

NOTES

1. PSI (which stands for Population Services International) was founded in the 1970s to use marketing to promote health globally. PSI handled the initial marketing for the Trust brand condoms, which are the most popular (and most affordable) condoms in Kenya. See: www.psi.org for more info.

2. Trust condoms are manufactured abroad and imported but are marketed locally for East African audiences. The Kenya government highly subsidizes this brand, which, in 2010, was selling for ten shillings (about eight cents, USD) for a pack of three. Unlike most imported condoms that use near naked female models to advertise their brands, Trust condoms often use a silhouetted couple standing face to face in its advertisements.

3. At the time of writing, both of these commercials were available on YouTube and could be found by searching for "trust condom ad." For additional media clips and video related to this book, see the author's website: www.melissabrowning.com/marriage

4. I say this message is problematic not because condoms do not work but because condoms do not guarantee "safe" sex and they certainly don't create trust. As I have argued previously, within the sexual encounter there is more at play than just "biological" safety. While condoms can protect someone from contracting HIV, there are other factors as play (spiritual, emotional, physical) that can make sex unsafe. For more on this argument, see: Melissa D. Browning, "HIV/AIDS Prevention and Sexed Bodies: Rethinking Abstinence in Light of the African AIDS Epidemic," *Theology and Sexuality*, Vol. 15.1, (2009): 27–46.

5. Augustine H. Asaah, "To Speak or Not to Speak with the Whole Mouth: Textualization of Taboo Subjects in Europhone African Literature," *Journal of Black Studies*, Vol. 36, No. 4, (2006), 497–514.

6. Ibid., 498.

7. Daniel Wight, *et al.* "Contradictory sexual norms and expectations for young people in rural Northern Tanzania," *Social Science & Medicine* 62, (2006), 987–97, 991.

8. Ibid., 989.

9. This is true among certain ethnic groups in East Africa, such as the Kisii in Kenya. See: Norbert Brockman, *et al.* "Kenya" in *The Continuum Complete International Encyclopedia of Sexuality*, ed. Robert T. Francoeur and Ramond J. Noonan, (2004), http://www.iub.edu/~kinsey/ccies/ke.php (accessed September 20, 2010).

10. Chinazo Echezona-Johnson, "Sexual taboos and HIV/AIDS in Africa," Opinion piece published at helium.com, http://www.helium.com/items/805050-sexual-taboos-and-hivaids-in-africa (accessed September 20, 2010).

11. Joan Kigozi, "Sexual taboos and HIV/AIDS in Africa," Opinion piece published at helium.com, http://www.helium.com/items/425552-sexual-taboos-and-hivaids-in-africa (accessed September 20, 2010).

12. Wight, *et al.*, 991.

13. See Assitan Diallo, "Paradoxes of female sexuality in Mali. On the practices of Magnonmaka and Bolokoli-kela," in *Re-thinking sexualities in Africa*, ed. Signe Arnfred, (Uppsala: Nordic Africa Institute: 2004), 173–94. See also, Ruth Muthei James, "The Promotion of the 'ABC' of Sex in The Prevention of HIV/AIDS in Africa: Implications for Women," in *People of Faith and the Challenge of HIV/AIDS*, ed. Mercy Amba Oduyoye and Elizabeth Amoah, (Ibadan, Nigeria: Sefer, 2004), 155.

14. Ibid.

15. Chi-Chi Undie and Kabwe Benaya, "The State of Knowledge on Sexuality in sub-Saharan Africa: A Synthesis of the Literature," *JENDA: A Journal of Culture and African Women Studies*, Issue 8, (2006), http://www.africaresource.com/jenda/issue8/undie-benaya.html (accessed September 20, 2010).

16. Patience Turtoe-Sanders, *African Tradition in Marriage*, (Brooklyn Park, MN: Turtoe-Sanders Communications, 1998), 61–63. Lloyda Fanusie also talks about the importance of the genitals in African thought. See, Fanusie, "Sexuality and Women in African Culture," in *The Will to Arise*, ed. Mercy Amba Oduyoye and Musimbi R.A. Kanyoro, (Maryknoll, New York: Orbis Books, 1992), 142–51.

17. Beverley Haddad, "Faith Resources and Sites as Critical to Participatory Learning with Rural South African Women," 135–54.

18. AMFAR, "Basic Facts About HIV," http://www.amfar.org/abouthiv/article.aspx?id=3352 (accessed September 7, 2010).

19. CATIE (Canadian AIDS Treatment Info Exchange), "Women and the Biology of HIV Transmission," http://www.catie.ca/eng/PreventingHIV/fact-sheets/Women-Biology.shtml (accessed September 7, 2010).

20. CATIE "HIV Transmission: An Overview," http://www.catie.ca/eng/PreventingHIV/fact-sheets/transmission-overview.shtml (accessed September 7, 2010).

21. CATIE, "Women and the Biology of HIV Transmission."

22. Ibid.

23. Ibid.

24. Ibid.

25. UNAIDS, "Greater action needed to protect women's inheritance and property rights in the face of HIV," (March 13, 2009) http://www.unaids.org/en/KnowledgeCentre/Resources/FeatureStories/archive/2009/20090313_Propertyright.asp (accessed September 7, 2010).

26. UNIFEM, "Women, Poverty and Economics," http://www.unifem.org/gender_issues/women_poverty_economics/ (accessed September 9, 2010).

27. Ibid.

28. Marital rape is also known as spousal rape (a more common term in the US context). It is worth noting that even in the United States, while spousal rape is outlawed in all fifty states, in thirty states the burden of proof in the case is still on the victim. For more on spousal rape in the United States see, Jennifer McMahon-Howard, Jody Clay-Warner and Linda Renzulli, "Criminalizing Spousal Rape: The Diffusion of Legal Reforms." *Sociological Perspectives*, Vol. 52, No. 4 (Winter, 2009), pp. 505–31.

29. Pamela Mhlanga, "Southern Africa: Justice for survivors of marital rape, how far has SADC come?" Pambazuka News, Issue 332, (Dec. 14, 2007) http://pambazuka.org/en/category/16days/45014 (accessed September 7, 2010). Additional note: At the time of writing, Kenya, Ghana and Malawi were also in conversation about criminalizing marital rape. See: Sally Armstrong, "Marital Rape in Africa: The right to say no," *The Globe and Mail*, June 11, 2010.

30. Karen Stefiszyn, "A Brief Overview of Sexual Offences Legislation in Southern Africa," Prepared for: Expert Group Meeting on good practices in legislation on violence against women, Geneva: UN Office on Drugs and Crime, UN Division for the Advancement of Women, (May 26–28, 2008), 4.

31. While I would call all instances of non-consensual sex rape, here I am attempting to honor the voices of the women who participated in this study. While each PAR collaborator said they had been forced into sex at one time or another by their hus-

bands/partners, most of the women did not call this rape. (Again, the definition of rape in Tanzania still does not include marital rape.) The most striking statement about forced sex was first mentioned in m One, where a collaborator said that refusing sex meant you would be "beaten first and raped later." All of the women in the PAR group agreed with this woman's statement and said that they had been in similar situations.

32. *The Law of Marriage Act*, 1971, United Republic of Tanzania www.tanzanet.org/.../laws/the_law_of_marriage_act_1971_(5_1971).pdf (accessed September 7, 2010).

33. Customary laws are unwritten laws or regulations that are based in tradition and carry legal weight because of their long-standing use. For example, before the Marriage Act of 1971, marriages in Tanzania were carried out through either customary law or Islamic law. Customary law, which is localized, heavily influences formal law in sub-Saharan Africa and often causes formal laws not to be enforced. For more on law in Tanzania, see: *Legalbrief Africa*, "Customary & Islamic Law and its Future Development in Tanzania," Issue 107, (Nov. 28, 2004) http://www.legalbrief.co.za/article.php?story=20041128143334824 (accessed September 7, 2010).

34. Ibid. and *The Law of Marriage Act, 1971.*

35. See *The Law of Marriage Act, 1971.*

36. Ibid.

37. Immigration and Refugee Board of Canada, "Tanzania: Situation of women victims of domestic violence, including legislation and the availability of protection and support services," (July 15, 2008), TZA102862.E, http://www.unhcr.org/refworld/docid/48d2237a23.html (accessed September 7, 2010).

38. The regions named were Singida, Mtwara, Shinyanga, Iringa and Ruvuma. The study showed that male reactions to their wives' increases in income were the primary reason for the increase in abuse. For more see: Lusekelo Philemon, "Rise in Women's Incomes has Perpetuated Soaring Domestic Violence," *The Guardian*, Dar es Salaam, (Nov. 23, 2007), http://216.69.164.44/ipp/guardian/2007/11/23/102986.html (accessed September 9, 2010).

39. Shisanya, "Socio-cultural Vulnerability of Women to HIV/AIDS: A Theological Strategy to Transform Power," 245.

40. For more on traditional practices that make women vulnerable, see previous section in chapter 2 on "Traditional Practices and the Spread of HIV/AIDS."

41. See Karen L. Baird, "Globalizing Reproductive Control: Consequences of the 'Global Gag Rule'" as well as K. Shanthi, "Feminist Bioethics and Reproductive Rights of Women in India: Myth and Reality," both in *Linking Visions: Feminist Bioethics, Human Rights, and the Developing World,* ed. Rosemarie Tong, Anne Donchin and Susan Dodds, (New York: Rowman and Littlefield Publishers, Inc, 2004).

42. While the female condom is the closest barrier method designed for women, it is not a method that can be hidden from a partner, and therefore cannot be used by women who fear repercussions from using (or asking for) condoms within their marriage.

43. Lisa Cahill, *Theological Bioethics: Participation, Justice, Change,* (Washington DC: Georgetown University Press, 2005), 217.

44. This restriction was repealed during the Obama presidency. For a history of PEPFAR see: PEPFAR Watch, "PEPFAR's Past: 2003-2008," http://www.pepfarwatch.org/about_pepfar/pepfars_past/ (accessed September 20, 2010).

45. For more on the history and ethical implications of the Global Gag Rule, see Baird, 133–46.

46. According to its founder, Ada María Isasi-Díaz, *mujerista* theology "brings together elements of feminist theology, Latin American liberation theology and cultural theology" in reflecting on the lived experiences of Latina women. See Ada Maria Isasi-Diaz, "Mujeristas: A Name of Our Own," *Christian Century*, May 24–31, 1989, 560.

47. Isasi-Díaz, "Solidarity: Love of Neighbor in the 1980's," in *Lift Every Voice: Constructing Christian Theologies from the Underside,* ed. Susan Brooks Thistlethwaite and Mary Potter Engel, (San Francisco: Harper Collins, 1990), 32.

48. Ibid., 33.

49. Isasi-Diaz articulates this concept by saying: "Mutuality of the oppressor with the oppressed also starts with conscientization. To become aware that one is an oppressor does not stop with individual illumination but requires the oppressor to establish dialogue and mutuality with the oppressed. The first word in the dialogue that can bring awareness to the oppressor is uttered by the oppressed." (Ibid., 36).

50. Ibid., 37.

51. Ibid., 38.

52. This is a popular African philosophical maxim. See Mbiti, *African Religions and Philosophy*, 108–9.

53. Fuller, 16.

54. It should be noted that in most African cultures, dogs are not inside animals. Most Tanzanians fear dogs and would never think of putting them in the bed or on furniture. This action was a tremendous insult, and when Veronica told her story, the women in the room gasped in disbelief.

55. This brief analysis relies primarily on five Trust condom commercials that were available on YouTube. At the time of writing, most of these commercials could be accessed on YouTube by searching for "Trust condom" or "Kenya condom ad." The five commercials analyzed for this chapter include the umbrella/crosswalk ad, water bottle ad, car repair ad, boat ad, and garden ad.

56. Chris Hart, "Why condom use is an uneasy affair," *The Daily Nation*, Nairobi, (March 27, 2010).

57. In Kiswahili the women named *maelewano kati ya mume na mke* (harmony or understanding between husband and wife), *upendo* (love), *uwazi* (transparency), *amani* (peace), and *ukweli na uaminifu* (honesty and trust).

FOUR

Agency, Risk, and Relationality

An Intercultural Dialogue on Women and Self-Sacrifice

Throughout African histories and cultures, women have always been seen as life-givers. In many African creation myths, women play a direct role as co-creators of humankind. Yet in some of these myths, women are also blamed for severing the connection between the people and God.[1] The dichotomy present in Africa's mythology also exists in everyday understandings of African women who are both revered for procreation and blamed when life does not flourish. The women who give life also bear the burden for sustaining life. When harvests are abundant and children live, African women are praised. Yet when food is hard to find and resources are scarce, it is often the women who will endure the greatest sacrifices to protect their families and sustain their communities.

It could be said that within all cultures, self-sacrifice is an action that takes place when a person is compelled to give of one's self. This compulsion can come from internal or external sources. Self-sacrifice can be an act of agency or a measure of self-abnegation. It can be a response of love, an obligation or duty, or a fulfillment of culturally prescribed roles. For women around the world, sacrifice is too often related to gender, to whom women see themselves to be or to whom others want them to become. And when sacrifice is related to gender, it is rarely voluntary and therefore cannot be considered a moral good.

This chapter will focus on self-sacrifice in relation to love and intimate relationships among African women, particularly in relation to the stories of the women living with HIV and AIDS who participated in this study. Western feminist theology[2] will be used as a dialogue partner to create a postcolonial, intercultural reflection that will help us understand how women's sacrifice is related to the African HIV pandemic. Through understanding the differing conceptions of love and relationality each group participates in, new possibilities for mutuality rooted in community will be proposed that take seriously the effects of colonialism and the legacy of patriarchy that has been intensified in its wake.

Drawing on understandings of gender, love, and community within African theology, I will argue that for African women, love as self-sacrifice is often less of a "temptation"[3] based on pre-defined gender roles and more of a means of survival in a postcolonial and patriarchal system. I will examine how love and sacrifice differ in individualistic and communal contexts and explore how love within marriage is understood in contemporary African contexts. Throughout the chapter, I will share the reflections of the women who participated in this fieldwork and ask what their experiences can teach about living in a world where marriage has become an HIV risk factor for African women.

AGAPE, CHRISTIAN TRADITION, AND WESTERN FEMINIST THEOLOGY

For all its many strengths, Western feminist theology has been criticized for universalizing the concerns of mainly white, middle-class, Western women as the concerns of all women.[4] The lesson learned from this criticism is that as women, we each must speak from our own social location and experience while listening to the experiences of others. Womanist theologian Mariana Ortega critiques white feminists who use womanist theology for their own ends by calling them "lovingly, knowingly ignorant." Ortega says that women of color don't need their words legitimized through white women speaking for them. Drawing from Marilyn Frye's work, Ortega proposes a process of "looking, listening, checking and questioning" for feminists as they explore differences in women's experience. Ortega goes on to propose María Lugones' concept of "world traveling" as a way of knowing others in their differences by being open to our own roles as both oppressors and oppressed.[5] If we hope to dialogue interculturally on issues that are pertinent to women's flourishing, we must begin by recognizing not only what we have learned from each other but also how we have failed one another.

The first failure that comes to mind is the patriarchal legacy of colonialism. While one cannot point to a pristine past in African history in relation to gender, Mercy Oduyoye argues that colonialism and Christianity diminished safeguards within African culture that curbed patriarchy.[6] In the same way, Beverly Lacayo argues that the African woman has always been a "strong partner" who supported the family. Lacayo suggests that the introduction of currency and wages has undermined women's strength and marginalized them within society.[7] Any patriarchy that was present in Africa was certainly fortified by the male-rule model of colonialism.

With an understanding of the dynamics of patriarchy, it becomes apparent that women's self-sacrifice is part of the reason for its continuation. Christian practice throughout the world has provided a flawed theological rationale for self-sacrifice based on imitation of the cross of Christ.[8] Even within this study, some women spoke of their own sufferings and then dismissed them in the next breath, referencing the cross and how much Jesus suffered for them. Yet at the same time, the cross was also redemptive for these women. A favorite verse of the women in this study was that a husband should love their wife like Christ loved the church.[9] Yet, as the women held up their end of the bargain, as they sacrificed for and obeyed their husbands, their sacrifices were rarely met in kind. Very few women in the study said they knew of examples of husbands who "loved their wives like Christ loved the church."

With the exportation of Christianity to Africa through missionary movements, this same teaching of Christian love as self-sacrifice may have also contributed to diminishing the safeguards of which Oduyoye speaks.[10] The women in this study said that their pastors and churches encouraged them to sacrifice themselves because this was their Christian duty. While the Christian life certainly calls us to a mutuality that loves the neighbor and compels us to give of ourselves, self-sacrifice becomes dangerous when those who sacrifice the most are women.

In her classic 1960 article, "The Human Situation: A Feminine View," theologian Valerie Saiving Goldstein argued that the "sin" of women was not the temptation of pride but of triviality and a poor self-image. Goldstein stated that women surrendered too much of themselves, and this temptation toward sacrifice would not be helped with a theological elevation of agape and a devaluing of self-love.[11] Judith Plaskow expanded on Goldstein's work by naming sensuality as the sin of women. Reflecting on some shortcomings of Reinhold Niebuhr's theology, she defined sensuality as a failure to rebel against society.[12] Both Goldstein and Plaskow criticized theologians such as Niebuhr and Anders Nygren who saw pride and self-love as obstacles to true Christian love.[13] Beverly Wildung Harrison also rejected sacrifice as a central moral virtue in favor of "radical acts of love" based in activity rather than passivity.[14] Harrison described sensuality as a source of knowledge, arguing that all knowledge is "body-mediated knowledge . . . rooted in our sensuality."[15] For these early feminist theologians, love as completely disinterested and altruistic left little room for the self-assertion necessary to face women's struggles.

Since the articulation of Goldstein's "feminine view," feminist theologians have written widely on the shortcomings of agape as the supreme model of Christian love. It has been critiqued, reinterpreted, and even reclaimed by feminist theology. Rather than rearticulate these views here, this chapter will seek to use the work that has been done by early feminist theologians on agape as a contrast point for the ways in which African women understand love and self-sacrifice. In attempting to create this intercultural dialogue, some broad strokes from feminist theology can be noted to help us chart a course for comparison.

The first point that can be mentioned comes from Goldstein's original article where she speaks of the "temptation" of women toward self-abnegation. Her use of the word "temptation" is revelatory for her context. Goldstein's primary argument suggests that the differing natures of men and women also mean that the ideals of their love and the sources of their "sin" are not the same. Goldstein pulls from cultural anthropology to argue that gender differentiation is a universal norm.[16] For Goldstein, these differences or inclinations between men and women provide a starting point for a theology that is not one-size-fits-all.[17] Giving attention to our intercultural dialogue, we must ask if a tendency toward self-sacrifice comes out of a "temptation" to play into a certain nature or if self-sacrifice has a different origin in the African context. Following Goldstein's example of paying attention to women in a global context, we can also look to African women to see what we can learn of love and sacrifice within our distinct contexts as we seek to embrace the commonality of women's experience(s) while not sacrificing the particularity of their epistemologies.

A second applicable theme that can be isolated in the feminist literature on agape is found in an understanding of self-sacrifice in relation to community. Barbara Hikert Andolsen, in her summary on feminist theology and agape, pointed out that Reinhold Niebuhr takes the divide between the private realm and the public realm for granted.[18] While he believes agape is a possible model for interpersonal relationships, he does not see it as a possibility within history for states or groups who are motivated by self-interest. Because of this, Niebuhr still gives priority to self-sacrificial love but calls it an "impossible possibility."[19] In the African context, the division between the public and the private is not found in traditional thought but exists as a result of colonialism. In response to this, we can ask what form love and sacrifice take when the divide between the public and the private is not present. This raises the question of whether differing interpretations of self-sacrifice might be based on the way we organize ourselves in both intimate relationships and communal/political groups. Here, we can compare understandings of the self in relation to others as a way of understanding both self-sacrifice and love.

This brings us to a third theme of mutuality, which has been proposed to counter agape as self-sacrifice. Mutuality has become a normative principle in feminist theology and ethics.[20] Feminist theologians such as Beverly Harrison, Barbara Andolsen, and Margaret Farley see mutuality as an essential component to love.[21] This understanding of mutuality within love can allow an understanding of sacrifice that promotes love of neighbor rather than women's self-abnegation. In the African context, mutuality can also provide a new model that stems from the spirit of community and sisterhood that is already present. In addition, understanding what mutuality could become in the context of African community could also inform the way mutuality is understood as a form of intimate love and genuine friendship in the West. These three themes, though they do not cover all of what has been written on agape in Western feminist thought, do provide a starting point for intercultural dialogue. In putting Western and African understandings of self-sacrifice in conversation, I hope to give voice to both similarities and difference in a way that teaches us how to stand in solidarity with one another.

AFRICAN WOMEN AND SELF-SACRIFICE IN INTERCULTURAL PERSPECTIVE

In attempting to navigate an understanding of self-sacrifice in relation to love among African women, it is important first to understand the lives and experiences of African women, placing them as the subject in our dialogue. Toward this end, the experiences of the women in this study form the primary reference point for this chapter. To understand the lives of African women we also must speak against the forces that silence them. African women live in a world where oppression cannot be singled out from one source. Religion, patriarchy, colonialism, racism, and classism have all played and still play their role as oppressors. In addition, poverty, disease, and the breakdown of traditional structures have all diminished the power and resources traditionally available to women. While the women in this study acknowledged these forces of oppression, they also argued rightly that African women should never be thought of as weak or understood only through the lens of victimization. Although they are often oppressed by both external and internal forces, they are still resilient and determined, seeking always to sustain and create life and promote flourishing within their communities.

Mercy Oduyoye encourages African women by saying, "be a woman and Africa will be strong."[22] Oduyoye argues that Western scholarship on African women has rarely seen them as a subject of study in their own right, but has only studied them within systems of marriage or population. She points out that the generalizations of African women against the background of a "normative" Western culture has led to inaccurate representations. As a Methodist, Oduyoye points to her own tradition of Christianity as bringing in the notion of the "stay-at-home" woman, which did not fit the African conception where all adults work both in and outside the home to contribute to the community.[23]

Temptation or Survival?

Drawing on Oduyoye's critique, we can turn to Goldstein's argument and ask whether or not the self-sacrifice that can be attributed to African women is a result of a "temptation" toward self-abnegation. Goldstein's own argument and social location might give us a partial answer. Goldstein speaks with optimism of the possibility that "those endless housewifely tasks . . . may virtually be eliminated" in her time.[24] But as fast food and TV dinners replaced long hours in US kitchens in the 1960s, many African nations were just winning their independence from colonial rule. The elimination of "endless housewifely tasks," to borrow Goldstein's term, is still not on the horizon for many African women who walk miles to find potable water. While Goldstein sees women as having a choice between participation at home or in the outside world, she speaks of a possibility that would be foreign to many African women.

During one participatory action exercise, I asked the women in this study to use digital cameras to take pictures of "women's work." Some of the women used the cameras to take pictures of themselves going about their daily tasks. Veronica took this approach and brought in a slideshow of fifty pictures showing the chores she completed each morning. Washing clothes by hand, hanging them out to dry, pounding sorghum, cooking food, caring for children—the list was endless. Other women in the group took pictures of women in Mwanza cleaning streets, digging ditches, working in gardens, cooking food, sewing clothes, and carrying children. The women reminded each other that these days, women not only had their own work, but they did the work of men as well.

In response to the differences present between women in Africa and women in the West, I would argue that self-sacrifice is not a "temptation" for African women but rather a means of survival in cultures that have become oppressive patriarchies. Mercy Oduyoye makes the distinction between women's self-sacrifice and women being sacrificed.[25] In light of this distinction, it can be argued that African women are more likely to navigate gender in reference to taboos or survival rather than in response to essentialized notions of being female.

Taboos, which in the African context can be defined as actions or speech that are prohibited by cultural groups, often center on women.[26] Many taboos fall into Oduyoye's category of "sacrificing" women. Cultural taboos apply to women in their roles as mothers, wives, and elders, and some taboos are become less important as women grow older. Taboos are effective because they garner the power of both superstition and blame. No one wants to be seen as the one who causes another's death or impotence because a taboo action was committed. Certain subjects, such as sex, are also considered taboo. Taboos that control speech and action are powerful forces in the lives of women because the woman who dares to speak against them risks losing the resources for her survival. During the fieldwork, research collaborators told stories of women who demanded condoms or questioned their husbands about affairs only to be divorced with no means of support.[27]

While taboo is formative in determining the actions of African women, survival and immortality may be even more pressing. African women understand their lives in relation to the community, both living and dead. Procreation is of primary importance within African communities. Both women and men believe immortality is reached through the children who are born to them. In African culture, you are not dead until you are forgotten. Therefore, to have children who will carry on your name and remember you as an ancestor is to ensure your immortality.[28]

When the women in this study talked about sacrifice, they often talked about what they do for their children. Maria said that she had to sacrifice herself when her husband left her. "I sacrificed myself at the time when my husband deserted me, he ran away from me. I gave myself to serve my family only, to serve my children so that they should study because I did not study. Until now I struggle for them only." The women agreed that not all women sacrificed themselves for their children, but good women—good mothers—always did.

Mama Gasabile gave the example of the street children who attend the feeding program at the diocese twice a week. She said that she counsels each of these children, and over and over again she hears stories of a mother's absence. Some women have left the home, leaving the children with their fathers, while other mothers have died. In either case, the child's life becomes particularly hard when the mother is not present. Mama Gasabile ended her story by quoting the biblical proverb "A foolish woman destroys her house . . ." and everyone in the group chimed into finish the proverb, "with her own hands."[29] In this way, the women in the group saw a woman's hands as capable of building or destroying a house through her efforts or lack of effort. Unfortunately, they didn't see the father's hands as useful one way or another. Veronica continued this line of thought by echoing the biblical proverb with a traditional proverb. "If a child hurts himself he must say MAMA! He can't say Father!" Everyone laughed, realizing it was true. It is the mothers, not the fathers, who care for children and build the house.[30]

Mama Gasabile used childbirth as an example and said that for women in Africa, "giving birth is to give yourself." She elaborated by saying, "You give birth to a child; you know you are going to die, but at that very moment you get relief." Even the act of giving birth is terribly dangerous in places like Tanzania, where maternal mortality claims the lives of one in twenty-four women.[31] The risk of having a child involves a willingness to sacrifice, and this sacrifice seems endless once the child enters the world.

This push toward procreation can be both beautiful and destructive. While children are always welcomed, a woman who cannot have chil-

dren is not. An impotent man can have a brother take his role in procreation, but a woman is often divorced, or the marriage becomes polygamous.[32] Even when children are born, poverty and disease often give
women few options beyond self-sacrifice if their children are to live. As
the Ashanti proverb says, "When a woman is hungry, she says, 'Roast
something for the children that they may eat.'"[33] Choosing self-concern
or self-love over self-sacrifice implies a choice is present. For many
African women, the pressures of both taboo and survival tie the pursuit
of immortality to an unavoidable self-sacrifice.

Dividing the Public and Private

Even under the pressures of patriarchal taboo and the forces that
threaten survival, African women should be praised for their pursuit of a
holistic, integrated means of living. For African women, and especially
for those in traditional rural settings, the divide between public and private, work and home, or sacred and secular are as foreign as the colonists
who created their divisions. Life is not compartmentalized but is understood as an ever-flowing source that they must tap into through their
actions. This can be described as a search for abundant life or, to borrow
the language of feminist theologies, a search for human flourishing.

In seeking to shape life into an integrated whole, sacrifice traditionally
could be understood as everyone sacrificing, regardless of gender, for the
sake of the community. Oduyoye notes that sacrifice as a religious practice has always been central in African traditional religions. Reflecting on
Christianity, she holds up women's sacrifice as a model for Christian
churches to follow. Oduyoye sees this model of sacrifice where everyone
gives for the sake of the common good as more true to both African
tradition and Christianity.[34]

Oduyoye's model must be understood in the context of African
thought. African philosophy responds to the Cartesian maxim "I think
therefore I am," by saying that in Africa, *"I am because we are, and since we
are, I am."*[35] Every action, be it self-less or selfish, is evaluated in terms of
community. But traditional understandings of community cannot be ro-
mantically embraced in cultures where some women are no longer part
of the collective "I am." Sacrifice based on gender, not on a contribution
to community, looks strangely similar to the colonial patriarchy of male-
ruled states. With the division between the public and private being non-
existent in traditional Africa, it could be suggested that men have learned
to run their households like a patriarchal state.

The stories of the women in this study certainly support this argument. The women described their own marriages as spaces where their
autonomy was limited. It was for this reason that many women argued it
was better to be single, because when you are married, you don't even

have control over your own body. Jesca saw women's sacrifice as necessitated by men's unwillingness to sacrifice. She put it this way:

> The way I see it, women sacrifice because first of all we have mercy, second because the families depend on us. When you decide to sacrifice, like when you go to be tested (for HIV), you think you should sacrifice so at least you can push your family ahead and you can rule it. Men don't feel for their family because today a man can leave the children inside and go even a whole week without leaving food for them. He hasn't left anything and he doesn't know what the children are eating, but the mother, you cannot leave the children. First of all when I leave home I am thinking of my children. There is no maize flour inside, now today will my children eat? What will they eat after school? But when a man leaves, he has left. He thinks, after all, their mother is there! We women show mercy. In all families we are the major foundation.

Jesca reemphasized a recurring theme that surfaced in the study. Women are connected with the home; they are "inside" while men go "outside" not only to work, but also to find relationships and father children. This reflects the patriarchal division of men who ruled the state and women who cared for the home.

Yoruba feminist scholar Oyeronke Oyewumi argues that gender was an invention of the colonialist state, as she shows how relationality in Yoruba society was traditionally based on seniority. She uses language to show that references to individuals are not gendered, as there are no words in Yoruba to differentiate between male and female siblings or children.[36] In the same way, the Kiswahili language of East Africa does not have gendered pronouns, and often when Kiswahili speakers speak English, words like "he" or "she" are used "incorrectly" in reference to the gender of the referent.

Though the arguments made by Oyewumi and Oduyoye are not the same, both point to the impact of colonialism and Christianity on African understandings of gender. A recognition of the patriarchy that was exported to Africa is essential if we are to pursue an understanding of flourishing that does not mean sacrifice for women. While African women carry the life of the community, they carry far more than their fair share of its burden when life is hard. To re-interpret the old proverb, women may hold up *more* than half the sky. While patriarchy and gender roles are at play, the sheer weight of external pressures, such as communities devastated by HIV and AIDS and poverty, often leave women without the privilege of choice. This does not mean that women cannot rise up from these circumstances, for indeed, they do every day. But it does mean that if women in the West wish to stand in solidarity with women in African countries, we must first work together to relieve the pressure put on women by disease, poverty, and underdevelopment.

African women, as Oduyoye has suggested, need the space to *"be* women," so "Africa will be strong."[37]

AFRICAN WOMEN AND AGENCY

This argument brings us to a discussion of women's agency in Africa. In the midst of a patriarchy that disempowers, we can look to proverbs and folklore that remind of the potential power African women have. A Fulani proverb from Senegal says, "Woman is fire. If you have to, take a little." While some proverbs point to women's role as mothers and caregivers, most seem to imply women are dangerous, like fire.[38] It can be argued that these disempowering proverbs have been coined in response to women exhibiting both agency and voice. In this way, proverbs like these are not only disempowering, but also empowering as they warn of women's strength.

While patriarchy in any context will limit the choices available to women and therefore limit women's agency, a form of agency can still be seen in the way women work around and within these structures. While these ways of existing and seeking out life within patriarchy may not necessarily be equated with human flourishing or abundant life, the actions of women should be evaluated in terms of the holistic life they seek.

South African theologian Denise Ackermann makes the distinction between "tenacious endurance" and "mere existence" when speaking of women living with AIDS in South Africa. Ackermann says that "tenacious endurance, in contrast to mere existence, promises some opportunity, and I repeat some, for human beings to take control of their lives, even in dire circumstances."[39] The distinction Ackermann makes gives space for acts of agency even in a culture that suppresses women's agency.

If agency is defined as making autonomous decisions or relying solely on one's own judgment, then African women might not be given status as moral agents. Yet with this definition, African men might not be given that status either due to a heavy reliance on community in moral decision-making throughout the continent. In order to understand agency in the African context, it must be conceptualized in terms of community rather than individual autonomy. For this reason, words such as empowerment, self-determination, or communal agency[40] might be more fitting within the African context. For the purpose of this chapter, I will use these terms interchangeably to emphasize the different aspects of agency for African women.

Western feminist theory has created space for a sense of communal agency through a differentiation between agency and autonomy. Susan Sherwin separates the two concepts by saying agency is making decisions about one's own life, whereas autonomy, interpreted as relational autonomy, allows a person to be seen as an agent even when choices are limited due to oppression or pressure from external forces. For full autonomy to be present, these oppressive structures must be removed.[41] In a similar sway, Diana Meyers builds on feminist voice theory to interpret agency and autonomy within patriarchal cultures. Feminist voice theory focuses on the ability of women narrate their own lives through self-discovery, naming, and self-determination. Meyers suggests that even within the context of patriarchy, women exercise some agentic skills.[42] Arguing that the categories of "free agents, incompetent dependents, or helpless victims" are not helpful in understanding women's experience, Meyers goes a step further to define autonomous people as those who have "well-developed, well-coordinated repertoires of agentic skills and call on them routinely as they reflect on themselves and their lives and as they reach decisions about how best to go on."[43]

In reflecting on Meyers' definition, we could ask if these "well-developed, well-coordinated repertoires" could in fact exist not only in individual self-determination but also in communal self-determination. With this possibility, women can still be understood as self-determined or empowered when they make decisions in consensus within community, when they are speaking within or against patriarchal structures of oppression and expressing their own voice. While feminist theory helps in creating an intercultural understanding of agency, empowerment, and self-determination, these concepts cannot be measured for African women by only exporting definitions of these terms from the West. Instead, a fuller understanding can be found through examples of African women finding their voice in the midst of a patriarchal culture.

One example of voice-finding comes from the Fiote people of Central Africa. On a normal day, a woman would prepare food for her husband and place it in a pot covered with a banana leaf. But if the woman became frustrated with her husband, she would cover the food with a special pot-lid that was sculpted in relief with images that represented a proverb. Since a child, and not the woman, was responsible for delivering the food, the message created a safe distance for the woman while still publicly demanding dialogue. The husband was called to respond to the message as he sought advice from other men, and if he did not understand it, he would have to rely on a specialist to decode the message. This example shows that self-determination and voice exist for some women even within patriarchal contexts.[44]

In a more contemporary example, Isabel Apawo Phiri tells of an HIV and AIDS essay competition in the KwaZulu-Natal province of South Africa that was advertised as only for males but received thirty-five of its eighty-six entries from teenage girls. Phiri analyzed the girls' entries and found evidence of both patriarchal beliefs and self-determination as they named injustice and proposed creative solutions. Most of the girls spoke as if they were men in order to follow the rules of the competition, but by not disguising their names, Phiri suggests that they wanted their identity as females to be known. When the essays moved to issues such as gender violence or virginity testing, the girls resumed their own voices, speaking as a female. According to Phiri, the girls' entries exemplified voices that were both self-reflective and seeking change.[45]

In my own research, I found example after example of women exhibiting agency by working around patriarchal structures. Here is one. A particular patriarchal issue that women in Tanzania have to deal with is the possibility of their not being believed. The women in this study said that because they looked healthy, very few people believed that they were HIV-positive, and some thought they were just seeking attention rather than being truthful about their status. This happened to Agnes. On two occasions she had men pursue her who would not believe that she was HIV-positive. During a PAR session, Agnes told a powerful story about how she disclosed her status to a fiancé.

Like many of the women in the study, Agnes looked healthy, young and vibrant. The antiretroviral drugs she was taking were working, and no one could tell she was living with HIV. But she was in a new relationship, so she was worried. She said, "If I make my status a secret, I shall finish many." So Agnes came up with a plan to disclose her status. She said she wanted she and her partner to both be tested, so they went to the clinic together. When the doctor returned with the results, Agnes insisted that he give them their results together, not separately. When the doctor told Agnes she was HIV-positive, her boyfriend began to shake. She said he was dumbfounded and could not believe she was actually HIV-positive, even though she had tried to tell him. She said she chose to disclose her status this way in order to protect him, so she could end the relationship if necessary. After the doctor broke the news, Agnes told her fiancé and the doctor that she had known her status for three years and was on medication. For Agnes, this disclosure and the eventual loss of a fiancé represented a great sacrifice on her part. Her fiancé was willing to ignore or disbelieve her status, but Agnes would not let him, and in this way she showed both love and agency within the relationship.

In response to Agnes' story and other examples, I would argue that an understanding of African women should not first interpret them as victims without agency but as determined communal agents who constantly seek out life. Understanding women's sacrifice in the African context must meet women where they are through a search for examples of communal agency, empowerment, and self-determination that can be built upon to tear down structures of oppression.

NOTES

1. This is similar to the creation narrative in the Hebrew Bible and in other stories of origins in sacred texts throughout the world. For more on African creation myths, see John Mbiti, "The Role of Women in African Traditional Religion," *Cahiers des Religions Africaines* 22 (1988): 69–82. See also, Stephen Belcher, African Myths of Origin, (Harmondsworth, England: Penguin, 2005).

2. Feminist theologies used in this book are many and varied. However, in this chapter, the primary dialogue partners are white, feminist theologians who were writing early in the history of feminist theology. While feminist/womanist/mujerista thought on self-sacrifice has expanded far beyond these initial works, the goal of this chapter is not to survey the literature on self-sacrifice but to provide dialogue partners that will illustrate the differing conceptions of self-sacrifice across and between cultures. For this reason, the primary emphasis on feminist theology in the West comes from the work of Valarie Saiving Goldstein and other feminist theologians who expounded on her thought.

3. Here, I am using the language of Valarie Saiving Goldstein, whose work will be examined in the following sections of this chapter. In this article, Goldstein argues that women are not tempted by the sin of pride but of self-abnegation. Goldstein describes women's "temptations" by saying: "For the temptations of woman as woman are not the same as the temptations of man as man, and the specifically feminine forms of sin—feminine, not because they are confined to women or because women are incapable of sinning in other ways but because they are outgrowths of the basic feminine character structure-have a quality which can never be encompassed by such terms as 'pride' and 'will-to-power.' They are better suggested by such items as triviality, distractibility, and diffuseness; lack of an organizing center or focus; dependence on others for one's own self-definition; tolerance at the expense of standards of excellence; inability to respect the boundaries of privacy; sentimentality, gossipy sociability, and mistrust of reason-in short, underdevelopment or negation of the self." (See Goldstein, 108–9). See Valarie Saiving Goldstein, "The Human Situation: A Feminine View," *Journal of Religion* 40:2, (1960): 100–112.

4. See, for example, Audre Lorde, "An Open Letter to Mary Daly," in *Sister Outsider*, (Trumansburg, New York: The Crossing Press Feminist Series, 1984), 66–71.

5. In this metaphor, "world traveling" should not be confused with voyeurism or cultural tourism, which would be critiqued by Ortega. Rather, the metaphor suggests a sense of awareness beyond one's one cultural and social location. For more see, Mariana Ortega, "Being Lovingly, Knowingly Ignorant: White Feminism and Women of Color." *Hypatia*, 21:3 (Summer 2006): 56–74.

6. Oduyoye, *Daughters Of Anowa*, 79–108.

7. Beverly Lacayo, MSOLA, "Sisterhoods and Empowerment of Women in Central and East Africa," *SEDOS Bulletin*, 26, (1994): 270–75.

8. For more on this and for feminist responses to reading the cross as self-sacrifice, see Joanna Dewey, "Let Them Renounce Themselves and Take Up Their Cross': A Feminist Reading of Mark 8:34 in Mark's Social and Narrative World," in Amy-Jill Levine, ed. *A Feminist Companion to Mark*, (Sheffield, England: Sheffield Academic Press, 2001), 23–36.

9. Ephesians 5:25

10. While feminist/womanist theology has contributed much to the discussion of women's self-sacrifice in relation to the cross, African feminist theology has had fewer negative things to say about the cross specifically. Sacrifice within Christianity is critiqued from other perspectives. Anne Nasimiyu-Wasike, for example, argues that African women identify with Jesus' suffering and see Christ as the liberator, encouraging them not to accept their suffering fatalistically. See Anne Nasimiyu-Wasike, "Christology and an African Woman's Experience," in *Faces of Jesus in Africa*, ed. Robert J. Schreiter, (Maryknoll, New York: Orbis, 2005), 70–81.

11. Goldstein, 100–112.

12. Judith Plaskow, *Sex, Sin and Grace: Women's Experience and the Theologies of Reinhold Niebuhr and Paul Tillich.* (New York, University Press of America: 1980), 87–89.

13. See Reinhold Niebuhr, *Moral Man and Immoral Society: a Study of Ethics and Politics,* (Louisville: Westminster John Knox Press, 2002) and *An Interpretation of Christian Ethics,* (Cleveland: Meridian Books, 1963). See also, Anders Nygren. *Agape and Eros,* (Philadelphia: Westminster Press, 1953). It is also helpful to mention here that Rebekah Miles makes a convincing case for a retrieval of Niebuhr as a source for feminist theology in her book, *The Bonds of Freedom.* She points out the similarities between Niebuhr's thought and feminist theologies in that they both take power structures and their transformation seriously, understand sin within the social context, and use experience as a starting point. Miles goes on to argue for a feminist modification of Niebuhr, which she says is possible because the method of Niebuhr's own work leaves it open to critique. By stating that feminism and Christian realism are not necessarily at odds, Miles advocates for a feminist Christian realism where Niebuhr is used critically as a source for feminist theology. See Miles, *The Bonds of Freedom,* (Oxford Oxfordshire: Oxford University Press, 2001), 6–10, 24.

14. Harrison articulates this view by saying, "Sacrifice, I submit, is not a central moral goal or virtue in the Christian life. Radical acts of love—expressing human solidarity and bringing mutual relationship to life—are the central virtues of the Christian moral life. That we have turned sacrifice into a moral virtue has deeply confused the Christian moral tradition." See Beverly Wildung Harrison, "The Power of Anger and the Work of Love: Christian Ethics for Women and Other Strangers," in *Making the Connections: Essays in Feminist Social Ethics,* Carol S. Robb, ed. (Boston: Beacon Press, 1985), 18.

15. Ibid., 13.

16. Goldstein, 102–4.

17. It should be noted that most feminists today would disagree with Goldstein's focus on gender as a universal arising from nature. This disagreement is present for both African and Western feminists. For the Western context, see, Susan A. Ross and Mary Catherine Hilkert, "Feminist Theology: A Review of Literature," *Theological Studies* 56: 2, (1995): 327–52. For the African context see Oyeronke Oyewumi, *The Invention of Women,* (Minneapolis: University of Minnesota Press, 1997).

18. Barbara Hilkert Andolsen, "Agape in Feminist Ethics" *Journal of Religious Ethics* 9 (1981), 70.

19. Niebuhr, *An Interpretation of Christian Ethics,* 104.

20. Ross and Hilkert, 327–52.

21. See Andolsen, "Agape in Feminist Ethics"; See also Beverly Wildung Harrison and Carol S. Robb, ed, *Making the Connections: Essays in Feminist Social Ethics,* (Boston: Beacon Press, 1985); and Margaret A. Farley, *Just Love: A Framework for Christian Sexual Ethics* (New York: Continuum, 2006). Alternatively, Karen Lebacqz argues that in heterosexual ethics, we must not ignore the concrete realities that have shaped men and women. For this reason, Lebacqz responds to experiences of rape and violence against women by proposing a sexual ethics that is based on "love of enemies" that recognizes the history and current existence of male domination in male/female relationships. Lebacqz says, "To recognize the one whom one loves as 'enemy' is to accept the implications of the social construction of sexuality and to understand that the task is not simply to create a private haven into which one can retreat, but to work for a new social construction of sexuality that will undo the injustices that permeate the present culture." See: Karen Lebacqz, "Love Your Enemy: Sex, Power, and Christian Ethics," *Annual of the Society of Christian Ethics,* 10.01, 1990, p. 3–23.

22. Oduyoye, "Be a Woman and Africa Will Be Strong," in *Inheriting our Mothers' Gardens: Feminist Theology in Third World Perspective,* ed. Letty Russell *et al.,* (Philadelphia: Westminster Press, 1988), 35–53.

23. Ibid., *Daughters of Anowa,* 106–8.

24. Goldstein, 110.

25. Oduyoye, "Church-Women and the Church's Mission in Contemporary Times," *Bulletin de Théologie Africaine*, 6, no. 12, (1984): 259–72.

26. Examples include taboos that say women cannot speak when a man is talking, or that a woman is unclean during her menstrual cycle, or that she cannot have sex while she is breastfeeding. Because taboo is often tied to purity laws, women are free from some taboos (and in some cultures even allowed to speak and hold male roles) after menopause. For an explanation of some taboos and their possible sources, see Fanusie, 142–51.

27. For additional case studies see, Arit Oku-Egbas, "Peering Through the Keyhole: Marriage, HIV/AIDS and the Implications for Women's Sexual Health," *Sexuality in Africa Magazine*, 2:3, (2006).

28. For more on immortality and procreation see John Mbiti, *Love and Marriage in Africa*, (London: Longman Group, 1973). For a critique of the importance on procreation within marriage, see Mercy Oduyoye, "A Coming Home to Myself: The Childless Woman in the West African Space," in *Liberating Eschatology: Essays in Honor of Letty Russell*, ed. Margaret A. Farley and Serene Jones, (Louisville, Kentucky: Westminister John Knox Press, 1999), p.105–20; and Mercy Oduyoye, "A Critique of Mbiti's View on Love and Marriage in Africa," in *Religious Plurality in Africa: Essays in Honor of John S. Mbiti*, ed. Jacob K. Olupona and Sulayman S. Nyang, (New York: Mouton de Gruyter, 1993), 341–65.

29. Proverbs 14:1.

30. It is also worth noting that in many African societies, women not only build the house metaphorically, but literally. For example, among groups such as the Maasai of East Africa, women are responsible for building their houses (usually made of wood, mud and dung) before they are married. Even in Mwanza, a more urban setting, the women in my fieldwork told stories of overseeing the building of their houses, or making or overseeing repairs to their houses.

31. See UNICEF, Tanzania Country Report, accessed October 13, 2010 at: http://www.unicef.org/infobycountry/tanzania_statistics.html

32. Mbiti, *Love and Marriage*, 117–19.

33. Yvonnecris Smith Veal, MD, "Women: Choose Your Role," *Journal of the National Medical Association*, vol. 88, no. 3, 1996, 143.

34. Oduyoye, "Church-Women and the Church's Mission in Contemporary Times."

35. Mbiti, *African Religions and Philosophies*, 108–9.

36. Oyewumi, 42–43.

37. Oduyoye, "Be a Woman and Africa Will Be Strong," 35.

38. Mineke Schipper explains this proverb by quoting a source who says, "To make fire, the housewife usually goes to a neighbour to ask for some live coals, which she takes home on a potsherd. She picks them up by hand from the neighbour's fire and so takes tiny bits at a time. One must practice the same caution towards women, dangerous creatures." See Schipper, 25.

39. Denise Ackermann, "From Mere Existence to Tenacious Endurance," in *African Women, Religion and Health*, ed. Isabel Apawo Phiri and Sarojini Nadar, (Maryknoll, New York: Orbis Books, 2006), 221–41.

40. I am using the term communal agency to describe a form of decision-making that exhibits both self-concern and concern for the community. At its best, this can be understood as decision-making in solidarity with others. Communal agency would cease to be agency when the voice of the agent is suppressed attempt to maintain hegemony.

41. Susan Sherwin, "A Relational Approach to Autonomy in Healthcare," in Susan Sherwin, ed., The Feminist Health Care Ethics Research Network's *The Politics of Women's Health: Exploring Agency and Autonomy*, (Philadelphia: Temple University Press, 1998).

42. Diana Tietjens Meyers, *Gender in the Mirror: Cultural Imagery and Women's Agency* (New York: Oxford University Press, 2002), 5.

43. Ibid., 21.

44. Schipper, 9.

45. Isabel Apawo Phiri, "A Theological Analysis of the Voices of Teenage Girls on 'Men's Role in the Fight Against HIV/AIDS' in KwaZulu-Natal, South Africa," *Journal of Theology for Southern Africa*, 120, (November 2004): 34–45.

FIVE

Marriage and Women's Bodies

The Boundaries of Self and Conceptions of Love

With an understanding of African women acting as agents even in the midst of patriarchy and oppression, we can now turn to the daily lives of women as we seek to conceptualize both love and sacrifice in the African context. In response to some Western feminists writing on agape, I have argued that love as self-sacrifice might be less of a "temptation" for African women and more the daily work of survival. This does not suggest that women do not fall into gendered roles but rather that taboo and survival are more formative than gender in women's decision-making. I have also argued, with Oduyoye, that a distinction between self-sacrifice and women being sacrificed is essential to understanding the everyday lives of African women.

While feminist literature on agape argues rightly that many women in the West have a choice as to whether or not to sacrifice themselves, this is not yet a reality for all African women. Coming to a place of choice, be it communal or individual, first requires a process of conscientization that can lead to speaking against both neo-colonial and Christian structures that continue to destroy women's safeguards and diminish women's agency. Any self-sacrifice of women must be understood against the background of the way women are sacrificed or discarded when they show public self-determination outside of approved structures.

Yet even with an understanding of the relationship between self-sacrifice and survival, we cannot say that there is not also a link between self-sacrifice and love. Oduyoye points out that when a sacrifice is required by a traditional healer, women are the first to bring the sacrifice because they are the ones who constantly seek out the reconciliation of holistic life.[1] The primary recipients of this self-sacrifice are the family and the clan (or community). More specifically, women are known for the sacrifices they make to feed and shelter their children, as African women are often responsible for both building the house and cultivating the food.[2]

While love is apparent in self-sacrifice of this sort, a less-noticed motive of self-love could also exist for African women. When children are understood in terms of ensuring their parents' immortality, making sure that children live also ensures one's own life, even after death. In this way, self-sacrifice with the goal of immortality (by living on through one's children) could be considered a form of self-love.

Joyce believed women's sacrifice was a benefit not only to their families, but also to the entire community. She said, "I think the sacrifice of a woman is a great advantage to the society." She went on to give an example of a family she knew who was very wealthy, but once the wife died and the husband remarried, the children were forced to sleep outside and were not cared for by their father or the new wife. Joyce reflected on the story saying, "This story has already disturbed me a lot. I said ok, if God has already decided one has to go, he should remove the man and the woman should remain." Joyce went on to talk about this new wife, who was not a "mother." She said:

> Really my soul was pained—I was sharing with others in the group saying, if God has to take one, God should take the father. I have already seen very many families; I move among many people. If you analyze the problems in families without mothers, there are many problems no matter how rich they are. For the children it is different— for those who were left with a mother, it is completely different. The mother will even break stones, she will look for labor carrying water, but either way the children have eaten. The father may even go to a hotel, but mother cannot.

In this story, Joyce contrasts the unconditional love of a mother for her children with what she sees as an incomplete or inadequate love between a husband and wife. The husband in this case chooses to marry a woman who does not love or care for his children. This love, to him, is more important than his love for the children. In the same way, Joyce says, the husband may sleep outside, at a hotel, but the mother cannot.

A similar thing happened to Jesca when she was a young child. Her father divorced her mother, and the children remained with their father. This scenario is fairly common throughout Tanzania. Children over seven years old normally remain with the father, and the mother is rarely given custody or even visitation rights. Even when children under seven are allowed to stay with the mother, they often must be returned to the father once they are older. For Jesca and her younger siblings, things were alright for a few years because her grandfather forbade her father from remarrying. He said that he knew that a new wife would torture his grandchildren, so he did not allow his son to remarry.

A few years later, while Jesca was still in primary school, in standard four (or fourth grade), her father told her she was a big girl now and said, "If I bring a woman, anything bad she does to you, you will understand, won't you?" Jesca wasn't really given a chance to agree, but she was being told that her life would soon change. After her father remarried, her fears and the fears of her grandfather came true. The woman beat Jesca for no reason. Jesca said that once the woman hid her exercise book and pen, and then when her father arrived, she blamed her for losing it and beat her. Jesca ended up marrying early and soon she took in her younger siblings as well. Jesca knew she was sacrificing for her family but was proud of her sacrifice and said that "a woman is a great pillar" and this is why she sacrifices herself. Like Joyce, she saw her own sacrifice as an act of love as compared to her father's selfish decision to take a wife who would not care for her and her siblings.

But beyond love, it must be said that there is also a fatalistic aspect to the ways African women give of themselves.[3] In relation to this, a proverb comes to mind: "Better the devil you know than the angel you don't." When I was working in Kenya with a new program to move children from informal education at our facility to public schools, I heard this proverb from the lips of parents over and over again. Even though public education would provide more opportunities for their children, they were worried that the change could bring unexpected problems. Many African women view self-determination or seeking to change their situation the same way. In addition, because the concerns of daily living are so overwhelming, women often find no time to think abstractly about how to change the situation in regard to the discrimination they may experience.

Beverley Haddad argues that "safe sites" must be created in order for women's discourse to develop. Taking on the role of an "activist-intellectual," Haddad sees her primary responsibility as giving women room to create hidden discourses, which will with time become public discourses that create change.[4] In Haddad's model, communities of women recreate what African community has always intended to provide.

Within this fieldwork project, Haddad's argument rang true. The space where collaborators came together each week became a sacred space where the women shared deeply and were challenged to rethink the ways they viewed gender and their own relationships. The women said that talking together let them know that they were not alone in the struggles they experienced. They said that they drew strength from knowing other women had experienced similar things. This was especially true when it came to discussions of marriage. Several of the women said that they had always blamed themselves for their marriages ending badly, but after hearing others' stories, they were encouraged and stopped blaming themselves.

LOVE, MARRIAGE, AND SEXUALITY

In Africa, "marriage" has never been a union only between the individuals who are married but has always been about the wider community. Sobonfu Somé from Burkina Faso remembers that in her village someone would often say that they were getting married the next weekend, when the wedding was not theirs but perhaps the wedding of a family member or close friend. At Somé's own wedding, her husband (whom she had not yet met) was not present because he was living in the United States at the time. Somé makes the point that his presence was not required because marriage is more than just an agreement between two individuals.[5]

Western interpretations of arranged marriages, such as Somé's, have assumed that love between the individuals is not a priority. This is based on the belief that romantic love is unique to Euro-American culture.[6] But African myths, folktales, and proverbs tell a different story. Within this literature are stories of individuals who defy family or refuse marriage partners based on love for another.[7] The Yoruba of Nigeria have a proverb that says, "Not even God is ripe enough to catch a woman in love."[8]

Even in cultures that do not recognize romantic love or do not make it a priority, it can be argued that love as companionship or friendship is still a key component to marriage. The families who arrange or give consent to the marriage make sure the individuals will be compatible because they want the marriage to last. John Mbiti argues that the goal of African marriage is not only the creative potential present in procreation but also the creative potential for the individuals not to become one but to create a third identity through what they give to the marriage. For Mbiti, this creative potential is part of the love that grows within the marriage.[9]

The women in this study spoke frequently about the importance of love within marriage. As they told their own stories, the women talked about the ways their own marriages began, and many said at the beginning they were very much in love with their husbands. They also said that during this time, their husbands offered them equality. When their marriages were good the women saw themselves as valuable advisors and full partners in decision-making. Yet, when asked the reason for marriage, most did not mention love but children as the primary reason to marry.

During this conversation, Mama Gasabile pushed the women to think of other reasons for marriage. She said that she had her last child in 1984, and asked the group if she and her husband should get divorced now since they were finished having children. The women laughed and said that this would not be necessary, and then they began to cite other reasons such as companionship and support as key reasons for marriage.

Polygamy and Relationality

Within marital relationships, love as companionship and as romantic love were valued by the women in the study. As the women articulated these ideals, they echoed Mbiti's idea of "creative potential" in marriage, both in procreation and in the partnership. However, the partnership aspect of creative potential was an ideal, but not a reality for most of the women. One possible reason for this disconnect can be found in Mbiti's own understanding of marriage. Though sympathetic toward polygamy, Mbiti holds monogamy as the ideal and makes a concession for a polygamous marriage in the case of a woman who is unable to have children.[10] Here, in his concession, we see how the creative potential of procreation can be detrimental when women are valued only in terms of reproduction.

Polygamous marriages have been justified by saying that multiple wives are needed to produce more children. In addition, taboos centered around sex during pregnancy or breastfeeding also created the need for more wives to keep the man satisfied during the periods of time when his wife was unable to have sex. This created an atmosphere where different wives were needed for different purposes. The younger wife might be valued for sex while the older wife might be valued for her cooking or for the sons she brought to the family. But with the coming of Christianity and colonialism to Africa, monogamy began to be at least nominally valued over polygamy. Some men abandoned all but one of their wives to join the church, and younger converts married only one wife. Missionary churches and the colonial state promoted monogamy exclusively but ignored the underlying taboos that made more than one wife "necessary" in the male mindset. This gave rise to the hidden polygamy that is practiced in modern Africa today.

As a result, it could be argued that modern-day women, like multiple wives, are still valued by men for different reasons. The mindset that allowed polygamy to exist is still present in monogamous marriages. If some form of equality is not present, the monogamous wife, like the first wife in a polygamous marriage, is valued only for her procreation and is known as mother. While a monogamous man might not take a second wife, he is still prone to take a lover, who, like a second wife, meets the needs of sexual fulfillment when taboo or man's disinterest keep the monogamous wife from fulfilling that role. If the lover becomes pregnant, the child is often "adopted" by the monogamous wife, who, like the polygamous first wife, is considered the mother of all the husband's children. When patriarchy and the polygamous mindset are both present in a monogamous marriage, without some form of equality, wives are valued for procreation and girlfriends are valued for sexuality.

Mahari *and Relationality*

A second issue at play beyond the tradition of polygamy is the practice of giving and receiving *mahari* (also known as bridewealth or dowry).
In much of sub-Saharan Africa, and especially in patrilineal cultures,
when a woman is married her family is given a substantial gift by the
family of the groom (or by the groom himself). The two families consider
the woman's education level, her supposed fertility, her virginity, and
multiple other factors as they sit down to determine *mahari*. The idea is
that the *mahari* is a thank you gift to the parents and helps them cope in
the absence of their daughter. It also is thought to help repay the investment they have made in their daughter, since they will no longer benefit
from this investment as the girl moves to her husband's family's home. In
addition, *mahari* is thought to bond the two families together, since if the
couple were to separate, the *mahari* would have to be returned.

Collaborators were conflicted as to whether or not the practice of giving and receiving *mahari* should be continued in Tanzania. Only four of
the twelve PAR collaborators thought it should be completely abolished.
Others suggested that it should be reformed. Veronica, for example,
thought that maybe three cows would be less cumbersome than twenty.
Christine suggested that Christians should follow the Islamic tradition of
mahari (as practiced in Tanzania) where a girl named the price and received the gift herself. Some suggested that *mahari* is good if it is seen as a
"thank-you gift" to the parents but is problematic when it is excessive.
Domina, whose husband had not paid *mahari*, believed it should continue. She thought it was a sign of thanksgiving to the parents in appreciation for their raising the daughter.

Grace said that it should be abolished completely. She thought it allowed men to see women as property and therefore hurt women. Joyce
thought it should continue, but it must be changed. She said that in
Sukumaland, where she is from, *mahari* is sealing and even if there are
troubles in the marriage the family will not let the woman return home
after *mahari* is paid. Joyce gave an example of a friend who was forced to
return to a troubled marriage and instead killed herself on the way home.

Mama Gasabile, who is Yao, a matrilineal ethnic group who do not
receive *mahari*, wondered if the name of the practice should be changed
completely. She agreed with Domina that it was a gift, and said that if
that was the case, then we should not call it *mahari* but *zawadi* (which
means gift in Kiswahili). Grace agreed with Mama Gasabile's suggestion.
She said:

> It is a gift. Even when the elders set it up it was not a price to purchase
> a woman, but nowadays people have abused it and made it be like
> buying a person and therefore the man feels he has the right to mistreat
> the woman because, after all, he feels he has bought her.

But the more we talked about it, Grace became more adamant that *mahari* should not only be abolished but should not even be considered as a gift—at least not anymore. She told the group:

> When we talk about *mahari*, *mahari* as *mahari* is an agreement between the parents and maybe the groom or the parents of the groom. They agree we want that many cows, you see? Ok, we pay an advance of that many, etc. It is like you are being priced and that is what brings problems in many marriages because the man says, "I paid a lot of my money, I married you for a lot of money." Therefore he looks upon you like he bought you for a lot of money. And if we talk about thank you, the parents can be thanked even if no *mahari* is paid. If they live in love, they love each other they will come visit frequently. Even you, your heart will be happy the son-in-law has remembered you. He may say, "Come on let us send this money to mother, to father, like this." He remembers because you live in peace, but *mahari* as *mahari*, it has caused us be like slaves! We can't free ourselves because in our culture if you divorce, someone claims *mahari*. Hasn't he bought you? That is why he claims what is his. Even if she gave birth they don't have anything like that, that you have borne children. He gave ten cows. Now he claims his ten cows and they are really taken to him. The parent as parent, if he is fed up he says come and take your cows, let my child be free. Eh, now isn't it like he has bought you!

Later in the conversation Grace summed up her points by saying, "faithfulness and trust are better than *mahari*." Scholastica agreed with Grace and said that in her own marriage, *mahari* had not been paid. She said:

> I think there should not be any *mahari*, because as for me, I got married without *mahari* and I lived with my husband, we lived well. And my parents were just happy. They would pass for a casual visit, if you have a gift, you give it to them and they are very happy. Therefore there should not be any *mahari*. If it is a thank you, when the parent visits you give him his thank you and that is all!

The women pointed out the ways in which *mahari* could cause parents or relatives to make a decision about their daughter's life that was not necessarily good for their daughter. Joyce and Grace talked about the ways in which *mahari* could force a woman to stay in a bad marriage. Veronica shared her own story where she was forced to marry at thirteen because her brothers wanted to take the *mahari* that was offered.

For some women in the study, marriage was forced because of *mahari*. This was the case for Maria. At fourteen, no one ever asked if she wanted to be married. In fact, no one consulted her at all. As we were talking about *mahari*, Maria said, "It is true, some are just ordered, like me, I just found the *mahari* had been brought." She paused to laugh as if she was still overwhelmed by it all. "I was engaged and I refused. I went to my paternal aunt but when I came back I found the cows were there." Because the cows had been brought—the *mahari* had been paid—Maria had little choice but to consent to the marriage. She had no advocate to help her make a new way for herself.

While the women saw the ways in which *mahari* impacted their marriages, they still argued that it was not part of the marriage but was preparation for marriage. During one meeting when we were talking about *mahari*, we also talked about the characteristics for a good relationship, which the women named as understanding between partners, love, transparency, peace, honesty, and trust. Later, when I asked the women why *mahari* had not made the list of requirements for a good relationship, I was told, "*Mahari* did not make the list because it is not in marriage but on the side of the parents." While the women believed that *mahari* was not a key component to the marriage but something that happens outside, they did believe that *mahari* could affect the marriage—especially if the payments were too high.

Christine said that she believed that *mahari* could cause unfaithfulness on the part of the husband. She said, "It makes him be impossible so that as a woman there is nothing you can tell him because, after all, he has paid *mahari* for you." Grace agreed with Christine's argument and chimed in saying, "If, for instance, he gave several million shillings for *mahari*, he tells you I paid so many millions for you so there is nothing you can tell me!"

Yet even with these objections, at the end of the conversations, many women still weren't ready to abandon *mahari*. As a researcher, I wondered if *mahari* was valued by some of the women because it is one of the few spaces where the community shows a form of appreciation for women's work. The *mahari* is given to the family of the young woman to compensate the family for their "loss." The idea is that the girl will no longer be there to help out—to care for the house or younger siblings, or to contribute to the daily life of her family. In an environment where women's work is so rarely appreciated, this is the one remaining space where women are praised for their abilities and virtues. Women who are well educated, smart, or beautiful may bring in a higher *mahari* and, as a result, make their families proud. Though terribly flawed, *mahari* does still provide a space to appreciate women. The problem comes into play when we consider what *mahari* means within the marriage. For all the good *mahari* may bring, in our capitalistic world, it does cause men to see women as purchased property. In this way, the benefits do not outweigh the risks.

As I was finishing my fieldwork in the summer of 2010, legislators in Kenya began to talk about the issue of marital rape. Legislation was being drafted to not only finally recognize but to criminalize non-consensual sex within marriage. The issue was controversial. A June 2010 news article in *The Globe and Mail* began with a quotation from a man in Kenya who responded to the proposed legislation by saying, "I own her. The dowry I paid for her means she's my property." The forty-year-old Linus

Kariuki went on to say, "If my wife refuses to have sex with me, I will rape her. And then I'll beat her because she didn't obey me."[11] For Linus Kariuki and for many of the husbands of the women in this study, paying *mahari* meant that marriage would not be relational, equal, or just.

SELF-SACRIFICE, SEXUALITY, AND CHRISTIAN CHURCHES IN AFRICA

In responding to these issues, we must ask if Christian churches are part of the problem. In Tanzania, in most churches (both Catholic and Protestant) before a marriage takes place, *mahari* must be paid. While some pastors will speak out against abuses of *mahari*, African Christianity on the whole rarely problematizes the practice. In the same way, many Christian churches relegate women to the role of procreation by praising their role of mother and ignoring their capacity to lead in the church or in their communities. By highly valuing procreation within marriage, and by not valuing women's leadership in the church, both Catholic and Protestant churches have created a situation where women's primary means of fulfillment only comes through the traditional roles of wife and mother.

Within both African traditional religions and newer African independent churches, women have been able to participate in leadership positions unavailable in Christianity missionary churches. Women in African traditional religions were responsible for creating rituals of reconciliation and served as women priests or prophets within these traditions. In a similar way, women in African independent churches are known as healers, church founders, and pastors. When women are not included in church leadership, their participation is relegated to the realm of service. They become the caretakers who care for their churches and its children but are not invited to participate creatively in sacraments, ritual, or word.

Beyond excluding women from leadership roles in the church, we must also ask if the African Christian views on marriage are detrimental to women. Within this study, the women cited numerous examples of pastors and priests who encouraged them to return to their unfaithful or abusive spouses and try to work things out. The women also raised the issue of churches who would marry individuals without first checking to be sure that the husband was not already married. Veronica reminded us of her own story as well, where the priest forged a birth certificate to allow her to be married at thirteen years old. Furthermore, the women said their churches encouraged them to sacrifice themselves and obey their husbands. While the women saw the failure in this system on the part of the husbands (who did not love their wives as Christ loved the church), they did recognize that their churches were not doing all they could to empower women.

When I was in Ethiopia in 2007, a doctor working at an HIV/AIDS clinic told me the story of a woman who went to her Pentecostal pastor for help when she discovered her husband was unfaithful. The pastor told her to return to her husband because divorce was not acceptable within their Christian tradition. The woman continued to plead her case to her pastor and said that she was worried her husband might be HIV-positive. The pastor told her that she was required to obey her husband and that if she did, God would protect her. He said that every time she had sex, she should pray in the name of Jesus, and when she claimed the name of Jesus, she would be protected from HIV. This woman is now buried in a grave outside of Addis. She died from AIDS. Her marriage put her at risk, and her faith system did not help her mitigate these risks.

Unfaithful Men, Blamed Women

When it comes to self-sacrifice and love, the biggest issues for African women come in the form of responsibility and blame. As previously mentioned, faith-based HIV prevention programs are more likely to focus on young girls who shoulder both the burden and the blame if they contract the disease.[12] Within many of these programs, marriage is seen as the final destination where they will be safe from disease.

Yet in sub-Saharan Africa, marriage (whether Christian or not) does not make women safe but vulnerable. When patriarchy is not interrogated, women have little control over their bodies, especially within marriage. A 2003 study in Zambia showed only 25 percent of women believed a married woman could refuse sex, and only 11 percent thought a woman could ask her husband to use a condom.[13] In another study of young mothers in Cape Town, South Africa, 72 percent reported having sex against their will, and 11 percent said they had been forcibly raped.[14] All of the women in this study reported having sex with their husband against their will. They also said that if a woman were to ask her husband to use a condom, she could be beaten or thought to be sleeping around.

In response to these statistics and experiences, it can be argued that when Christian churches promote fidelity without an interrogation of patriarchy, they create risk factors for women. Just as a move from polygamy to monogamy cannot happen without a new understanding of the worth of women apart from procreation, a move from unfaithfulness to faithfulness will also not transpire until women are valued apart from men's sexual satisfaction. This is something that should be challenged and interrogated by Christian churches.

As previously mentioned, in much of sub-Saharan Africa, men are thought to control women's sexuality. Yet, the way women are blamed and stigmatized within their communities suggests incorrectly that when it comes to sex, women, not men, are the ones who are out of control. Constance Shishanya says that women are even blamed for their husbands' infidelity.[15] From an ethnographic study of women in the Democratic Republic of the Congo, Bernadette Mbuy Beya created a list of factors that women found to be favorable to fidelity. Those listed that were likely to keep a husband faithful involved factors such as the wife being a "good housekeeper, pleasant . . . calm, watchful of her figure, careful about spacing her pregnancies . . . careful of her hygiene," and so on. It is interesting that none of the factors for fidelity to the marriage had anything to do with the moral formation or character of the husband.[16]

Within this study, the women noted another level of responsibility that makes women susceptible to HIV and noted that this was another space where Christian churches were silent. Both Grace and Christine spoke about ways women's economic vulnerabilities within marriages place them at a disadvantage, particularly if their husband dies or abandons them. When Christine was married, she agreed with her husband that even after she was married, she would continue going to school. She was enrolled in a local college and wanted to continue her education, but soon after she was married she found out she was pregnant and then gave birth to twins. She had to stop going to school. There was no one to keep the twins and there was too much work to do.

A year later she was pregnant again and realized that education was becoming a distant dream. She spoke about her responsibilities to the children and her family and said these responsibilities made her vulnerable. Christine was never able to finish school, and soon her husband died. In the years after his death, she had many offers to remarry. She said that for many women in her situation, these offers are tempting. Christine described these women this way:

> Sometimes, you find a woman who is completely used to having everything brought to her. Therefore when her husband dies she is left behind. She thinks she is not worth anything so she ends up getting infected. Because if that man comes—and he has maybe twenty cars—and he tells her I shall take care of you, she will quickly agree so the children can go to school. Therefore she will be infected with the virus, but why is all this happening? My children should go to school, my children should eat. Therefore, I agree completely that these responsibilities that we have are the reason we are easily infected with HIV.

Grace, like Christine, saw women's responsibility as a space of vulnerability. Grace, as you might remember, contracted HIV from her boss who pressured her to have sex in exchange for his paying her son's school fees. Following up on Christine's comment, Grace said: "Maybe I should also add here these responsibilities really contribute to women becoming infected because we women feel deeply for our families, we feel deeply for the children." Grace continued by giving the example of her son, and said:

> Let me give an example—even me, my son who is in the university, truly had it not been for me he wouldn't be where he is now. Even he himself says: "Mama you brought me from far." This is due to this deep commitment of a mother. His father can't care so deeply especially considering that he has two other women. . . . But me? Won't I look after the ones that came from my own womb?

For Grace, the decision to give into her boss's sexual advances was directly linked to protecting and providing for her son. She told the group over and over about that time when her son was crying, fearing he would be stuck without ever finishing secondary school. She thought she could do this thing for just this one child. She said, "I wished for my child—at least this one only—even if I cannot manage to help the others, but at least this one should be the redeemer of his family."

Grace said that she continued in this relationship with her boss until her son finished school two years later. In this way, she was able to make sure his school fees were paid. Grace reflected on this relationship by saying, "Therefore I can say the responsibilities of the mother, and that deep commitment the mother has to her children, can cause someone to get involved in such things." Grace said she always felt guilty about the relationship. Her boss was married, and she worked in the house and knew the wife well. She always worried the wife would find out but she told the other women in the group that she couldn't give up the relationship until her son had finished his studies!

Grace said, "My son has reached where he is now, but he doesn't know what I went through so he could study. This is my secret here. Maybe on the day that I shall go to my grave I shall tell him—my son, I taught you, but by going through so much. God forgive me." Grace reflected on her actions by calling it a sacrifice. She knew her sacrifice "had negative effects"—it was the reason she ended up contracting HIV. But even still, she did not regret her sacrifice. She saw her son's accomplishments as repayment for the risks. She said:

> In the end, he reached where he is through this. So that means he will save the whole community and the whole family. Especially if you consider that his father did not study, neither did I myself, as you know, so I trust that my sacrifice has at least it has brought a certain light to the family.

For Grace, the benefits of her sacrifice well outweighed the risks, and the eventual consequences of these risks.

Risk, Sacrifice, and Survival

While many women who are living with HIV and AIDS in sub-Saharan Africa have contracted HIV through their partner, some women are at-risk through the daily decisions they make for survival. Since women cannot inherit property in much of the region, and since economic opportunities are unavailable to most women, transactional sex sometimes becomes a viable option for survival. The reality of transactional sex reminds us that women's bodies are often their only commodity. While there are exceptions, in an era of AIDS, transactional sex and sex work in Africa should be primarily understood in terms of self-sacrifice, which is motivated by the need to survive, rather than as a risk that some women choose. [17]

A deeper understanding of risk, sacrifice, and survival can be gained by understanding the prevalence of transactional sex within sub-Saharan Africa, even before the HIV pandemic. Some sociologists and anthropologists working in the region argue that transactional sex has always been present both inside and outside of marriages. Liv Harem, in her study of the Meru people of Tanzania says: "It is normative for women in this cultural setting to receive gifts and favors from their lovers, but, according to most, there is a limit . . . these tokens of affection should not be excessive, and a woman should share them, lest she be called a greedy person (*mchoyo*)." [18] Harem goes on to argue that even within marriages, a woman's primary objection to her husband taking a lover is not because of their husband's unfaithfulness, or even the possibility of their contracting HIV from this unfaithfulness, but from the money spent on the mistress outside the marriage.

Harem gives an example of a Meru girl named Upendo who was the mistress of a married man. When the wife found out about the affair, she objected on the basis that her husband should not buy a plot of land for the girl. [19] Harem says:

> Sexuality—the management of sexual relationships, including procreation—has become increasingly troubled and difficult. For most people, sex deals with matters that go far beyond a concern with health, illness, and the risk of dying: it involves love and affection, desire, money, self-identity, and a way to express maturity, adulthood, and social and economic responsibility. It can become a practical matter: to find a partner and a life companion, to settle, and to have children. [20]

Harem rightly argues that in Tanzania, sex is not just one thing. It is not only about love or children but is never only about the benefits either. Sex in Tanzania—like most everywhere else in the world—is always fairly complicated.

In Mwanza, a study among the Sukuma people showed that greater levels of sexual activity among men did not hurt, but, rather, enhanced their reputations. While women were allowed to have sex before marriage, if they agreed too quickly, had too many partners, wore immodest clothing, or had a child outside of marriage, their reputation could be spoiled. The same was simply not true for men. In Sukumaland, the main taboo on sex before marriage was that school age children should abstain because it would interfere with their studies.[21] Girls were not expected to remain virgins until marriage but were made fun of when they did not receive gifts or money for sex or were paid too little.[22] The researchers described it this way:

> The illegitimacy of sex before some form of marriage, illustrated in the euphemism "an act of marriage" for vaginal intercourse, seems to stem from the lack of payment to the woman's family for access to sex. Transactional sex can, therefore, be seen as a modification of conventional norms: the contentious issue is not the material exchange but that the woman's family does not benefit.[23]

Similar to the issues presented with *mahari*, we learn from this argument that a young girl or woman's sexuality is not always considered her own. Sexuality can be for *mahari*, for the husband, for procreation, or for the benefit of the family or the community. In these ways, a woman's sexuality is being sacrificed. Therefore, it should come as no surprise that women are willing or forced to sacrifice their own sexuality through transactional sex to care for their children, their families, and themselves.

This argument brings us to ask the question of whether at-risk behavior, be it transactional sex or sex with an unfaithful husband, is linked to either self-love or love of neighbor. When self-sacrifice is motivated by survival, then some form of self-love must be present. This self-love, of course, cannot be considered "just" love, to use Margaret Farley's framework,[24] but it is a form of self-love all the same. It is also linked to love of neighbor as African women almost always act not only on their own behalf, but also on behalf of their families. In light of this, it is possible to argue that just as there is no separation between the private and public spheres of life, for African women there may be no separation between self-love and love of neighbor. For in a community motivated by immortality, loving one's child is one way of loving one's self into life beyond death.

In a similar way, Joyce believed that sacrifice was not always completely altruistic but could become a way to avoid problems. She didn't think women sacrificed without reason but were very rational in their choices. She gave an example from her childhood and said that her own mother was chased away from their home. Because the children had seen their father beat their mother repeatedly, they were worried, so her younger siblings ran away with their mother as well. Joyce stayed behind and was forced to prepare meals when her father brought his girlfriends home.[25] She said that as a child, in this home, she learned to be angry and she learned to hate. Joyce seemed to suggest that when her mother fled, this was a sacrifice. She was leaving behind security, but she was also running away from the hate and anger Joyce was internalizing. Joyce summed up the story about her mother by saying, "Therefore, if a woman sacrifices herself she has a reason. . . . That is how it is." As she looked back, Joyce saw her mother's departure not as abandonment, but as a rational choice to protect herself and her young children.

SELF-SACRIFICE AND CHRISTIAN CHURCHES: RETHINKING SEXUAL ETHICS

With the advent of HIV and AIDS, neither African traditional religions nor African Christianity was prepared for the inequalities this disease would expose. The divide between Christianity and traditional religions has been too great to create a strong enough ethics to stand up to HIV and AIDS. As the quick move from polygamy to monogamy has shown us, Christian sexual ethics in Africa has not given voice to African tradition. To see this we need only to compare HIV transmission rates in Christian areas to those in Islamic areas. [26] Where Islam integrated more closely with African tradition, for example, by allowing polygamy, Christianity exported their ethics from the West, and the narrative behind the ethics did not fit the African story.

Within African tradition, the taboo that governed cultural behavior was always motivated by an underlying cause.[27] Sometimes "superstitious," sometimes practical, each taboo was, at least originally, connected in some way to life. Encouraging fidelity or abstinence in sexual ethics without a connection to community is like a taboo that has lost its narrative. A prescriptive ethics exists without a story to give it meaning.[28]

In light of the experiences of sacrifice of women in sub-Saharan Africa, we realize that a simplistic sexual ethics will do little to solve the HIV pandemic. Instead, an approach is needed that draws on intercultural dialogue and sets solidarity as a goal. What Christian churches are doing is not enough. It is not enough for the *True Love Waits* campaign to go to Uganda[29] or for churches to care for the dying. The long-standing suspicion or prohibition of condoms by both Catholic and some Protestant churches can only be seen as the opposite of a concern for life.[30] Even the secular sexual ethics of UN programs are also insufficient; the ABCs provide little safety for women who are unable to negotiate their own sexuality. Marriage is a risk factor for women, which means that Christian churches have much to do.

Though I am arguing that for African women there may be little separation between love of self and love of neighbor, I am not suggesting that this represents a healthy balance. In the era of postcolonialism, the private and the public spheres have become separate, as the family, the clan, and the community are spread between big cities and rural villages. The close-knit communities who were present to make sure women were treated fairly have also dispersed, and sometimes all that remains are the taboos, divorced from their original contexts. A form of separation of love may now be what is required in order for African women to pursue an integrated life. Love of self is deeply and urgently to protect women in the midst of this pandemic.

In rethinking our approach to the African HIV pandemic, an understanding of women's sacrifice can be formative in showing the gaps in our approach to prevention and care. The women in this fieldwork repeatedly asked me to tell their stories so that more help would come. These women recognized the need for global solidarity in response to their suffering. Hopefully, their stories will help us create a new framework for approaching the pandemic in a way that empowers women to make a difference.

In outlining the contours of this approach, we can say that first, the women who are most affected must be "consulted by the theologians."[31] As those who seek out an integrated life, the voices of women will have much to offer. To enable their voices, churches across Africa and around the world must empower women as more than just servants but as full participants in the life of Christ.

Second, an appropriate Christian sexual ethics for Africa must draw primarily from African culture. African Christianity needs a sexual ethics that is more than a list of virtues and vices; it must also have narratives appropriate to the African context that can carry the story and lead to moral formation. Appropriate taboos that protected women can be reintroduced and become part of the practice of Christian churches. In the same way, harmful taboos and cultural practices that put women at risk must be questioned. Even more importantly, sexual ethics needs be part of a wider focus on social ethics. This is important because the problems that fuel the HIV pandemic are primarily social issues that manifest in intimate relationships.

Third, love must take on a new context of mutuality, drawing from the mutuality that has been prized in African culture in the past. Mutuality in Africa could draw on community as a model for right relation, where everyone sacrifices for the common good and no one person bears the burden for the entire community. Oduyoye argues rightly that women's sacrifice can become a model for the church,[32] for if Christian churches were to sacrifice in the way women do, the burdens of survival would be more equally distributed.

Finally, a new sexual ethics must not neglect human sexuality. Oduyoye argues that sexuality has always had a religious function in Africa and that it must be celebrated and not relegated only to the realm of morality within the church.[33] By placing sexuality at the center of the dialogue, a new narrative can be created that replaces the taboo of silence that leads to women's self-sacrifice. As previously mentioned, when a safe space was created in the fieldwork for women to talk openly about sex and sexuality, they embraced the opportunity to speak up and offer constructive advice as they analyzed their own lived experiences. In this way, the simple act of opening up a space for speech proved to be a wonderful place to begin. To move the conversation further, if sexuality is not only placed in the realm of safe speech but also celebrated, then women will be empowered as agents. When women's sexual pleasure is no longer considered taboo, then women will be able to negotiate safe sex. But even more importantly, in this sacred space, women will be able to construct new justice-based sexual ethics for their communities.

In conclusion, while self-sacrifice for women is found in both Africa and in the West, it shares common and differing origins. The commonality comes from colonial missionary movements that relegated women to the home and introduced a Christian love based on sacrifice. The difference comes from the way each group sees community and agency. While gender roles might be more formative for the way Western women are socialized to sacrifice, taboo, and survival are more formative for African women. In the midst of these differences, we share the struggles of patriarchy, as each group of women is too often asked to shoulder more than their load.

Drawing attention to the lack of choices women are given does not mean we believe it will always be this way. We can choose to hope for change. But for change to happen there must be recognition of the ways we have failed each other. As we seek to create change, both inside and outside of the continent, we must learn from our past so we do not create inadequate solutions.

In light of the African HIV pandemic, the sexual ethics of most Western and African churches are inadequate. In response, we are called to an urgent solidarity and a creative re-imagining. As the Akan proverb says, "Wisdom is like a baobab tree; no one individual can embrace it."[34] Together, through a dialogue of difference, we can make space for change. With hands that are joined across cultures, we can stand at the base of the baobab and embrace women's wisdom together. For women's self-sacrifice across the world will only end when women are given space to create new choices.

NOTES

1. Oduyoye, "Church-Women and the Church's Mission in Contemporary Times," 261–62.

2. As previously mentioned, among some African ethnic groups (such as among the Maasai of East Africa) women build their own house before marriage. According to the Food and Agricultural Organization of the UN (FAO), women are responsible for 60 to 80 percent of food production, yet control almost none of the means of production African countries. For more, see FAO, "Women and Food Security," 2011, http://www.fao.org/FOCUS/E/Women/Sustin-e.htm (accessed February 21, 2011).

3. In her work on Christology, Anne Nasimiyu-Wasike notes a fatalistic interpretation by African women of their suffering. See Nasimiyu-Wasike, "Christology and an African Woman's Experience."

4. Haddad, "Living it Out: Faith Resources and Sites as Critical to Participatory Learning with Rural South African Women," 135–54.

5. Sobonfu Somé, *The Spirit of Intimacy*, (New York: Harper Collins, 1997).

6. Daniel Jordan Smith, "Romance, Parenthood, and Gender in Modern African Society," *Ethnology*, 40:2, (Spring 2001), 130.

7. Ibid., 134.

8. Schipper, 58.

9. Mbiti, *Love and Marriage in Africa*, 104.

10. Ibid., 189–93.

11. Sally Armstrong, "Marital Rape in Africa: The right to say no," *The Globe and Mail*, June 11, 2010.

12. Kaplan, 237.

13. UNIFEM, UNIFEM Fact Sheet on Gender and HIV/AIDS, (New York: UNIFEM, 2003).

14. UNPF, *The State of the World Population 2003*, United Nations Population Fund, 2003.

15. Constance Shishanya, "The Impact of HIV/AIDS on Women in Kenya," in Mary Getui and Matthew Theuri, ed. *Quests for Abundant Life in Africa*, (Nairobi: Acton Publishers, 2002), 58.

16. Beya, 160–61.

17. In fieldwork with sex workers in Lubumbashi, DRC, Bernadette Mbuy Beya found that out of twenty women interviewed (which constituted approximately 20 percent of the sex workers in the city), only two cited "adventure" as a reason for their involvement. The rest cited either need or abuse as the reason for turning to sex work. Beya also said many of the women cried and expressed shame when speaking of their work. See, Beya, "Human Sexuality, Marriage, and Prostitution."

18. Liv Haram, "Eyes Have No Curtains": The Moral Economy of Secrecy in Managing Love Affairs among Adolescents in Northern Tanzania in the Time of AIDS," *Africa Today*, Vol. 51, No. 4, (57–73), Summer 2005, 67.

19. Ibid., 67.

20. Ibid., 69.

21. Daniel Wight, *et al.*, "Contradictory sexual norms and expectations for young people in rural Northern Tanzania" *Social Science & Medicine* 62, 2006, 987–97, 990–91.

22. Ibid., 991.

23. Ibid., 995.

24. Farley argues that even when love is not just, love may still be present. See Farley, *Just Love*, 196–97.

25. It should be noted that under Tanzanian law, children are almost always considered the property of the father, not the mother. In this case, Joyce's mother would be allowed to leave with the young children, but the father could demand the children back after they reached the age of seven. Joyce, who was older than seven at the time, was most likely left behind because she was considered her father's property.

26. Laurenti Magesa points out that HIV/AIDS rates are lower in West African countries where Islam is more predominant than Christianity and that these rates are almost negligible in the Arab/Islamic states of Somalia, Egypt, and Sudan. See Laurenti Magesa, "AIDS and Survival in Africa: A Tentative Reflection," in *Moral and Ethical Issues in African Christianity*, J.N.K. Mugambi and Anne Nasimiyu-Wasike, ed. (Nairobi: Acton Publishers, 1999), 200–201.

27. One example could be seen in female circumcision. According to Turtoe-Sanders, female circumcision was begun during a time when newborn infants were dying. When the ancestors were consulted, the people were told it was because the clitoris touched the infant during birth. As a result, it became taboo for women not to be circumcised. (See Turtoe-Sanders, 89). Similar narratives probably existed behind female circumcision across the continent, yet today, most communities who circumcise women have lost the narrative for why circumcision is performed, making it difficult to correct the narrative and make lasting change in the practice. For more see, Ephigenia W. Gachiri, IBVM, *Female Circumcision*, (Nairobi: Paulines Publications Africa, 2000).

28. Here, I am making an intercultural comparison between taboo and virtue ethics. While the comparison is not exact, it can be argued that like virtues, taboos function as shortened discourses to shape moral formation. Robin Lovin sees virtues as compressed stories and says that if the stories (or the context) are lost then the virtues are no longer applicable. (See Robin W. Lovin, *Christian Ethics: An Essential Guide,* Nashville: Abington Press, 2000.) I am arguing that the same can be said for taboo in the African context; and when the narratives are lost, harmful taboos cannot easily be corrected.

29. True Love Waits, a US-based abstinence-only education campaign, has taken credit for the success rate in curbing HIV/AIDS in the country, ignoring that condom distribution and wide-scale advertising campaigns are normally credited for the success. See Don Beehler, "True Love Waits to expand anti-AIDS initiative in Africa," *Baptist Press*, April 12, 2007.

30. Until 2010, official Catholic teaching did not allow for condom use even for serodiscordant married couples (where one partner is HIV-positive and the other partner is negative.) This position on condoms changed in November of 2010 when Pope Benedict XVI was interviewed by Peter Seewald. In this interview, the Pope said that while condoms are not a "real or moral solution" that it could be a step "in the direction of moralization" in that the person is taking responsibility and seeking not to spread the virus or risk infection. See: Benedict XVI and Peter Seewald, *Light of the World: The Pope, The Church and the Signs of the Times,* (Ignatius Press, 2010), 118–19. Before Pope Benedict XVI's statement, many Catholic theologians in sub-Saharan Africa argued that condoms should not be seen as an evil, but as life-giving. For example, Laurenti Magesa argued that being against condom usage was the very opposite of being "open to procreation," especially since condoms are not even permitted for married couples who risk passing the viral load back and forth. See Magesa, 197–216.

31. Edet and Ekeya, 4.

32. Oduyoye, "Church-Women and the Church's Mission in Contemporary Times," 261, 265–72.

33. Oduyoye, *Beads and Strands*, (Maryknoll, New York: Orbis, 2004), 86–88.

34. The baobab is the largest tree in Africa with a base that can span 16–25 feet.

SIX

HIV and AIDS as Communal Dis-Ease

Cultural and Religious Interpretations of Stigma

When Jesca found out that she and her child were living with HIV, she was relieved. She said, "After I tested for HIV, I was happy when I got the answer because I had already had so much trouble, and I didn't know what was torturing me, what was torturing my children, you see." Jesca had already buried one child and another was violently ill. But Jesca's relief in finally knowing what was wrong was short-lived. When she went home, she told her husband the news so they could think together about how to help their child. But her husband called her a liar. "He refused completely," Jesca said. "He told me, 'you are liars, do people with HIV look like this? And first of all they lie to you there at the hospital.'" Jesca said that later that afternoon, her husband stood in the doorway of their house, shouting her status to the whole neighborhood. He yelled to the neighbors, "My wife says she has HIV, but really she is a liar and a witch. She went to witchdoctors to bring this sickness to my house." Then he packed his things and moved out. Jesca said she remembered looking at their sick child after her husband left and wondering what she could do now that she was alone.

In the body of literature on AIDS in Africa, much has been written on the effects of stigma and even on its theological implications. Very little of what has been written has questioned how interactions between Africa and the West have shaped the ways in which stigma functions in postcolonial communities. In this chapter and the chapter that follows, I focus on stigma in intimate relationships and argue that colonialism, neocolonialism, and globalization have weakened African community structures, which traditionally promoted health. As a result, a space has been created for stigma to spread alongside the HIV and AIDS. An intercultural

99

interpretation of stigma is needed in order to point out the places where worldviews collide, because it is in these places where stigma strangles life.

Throughout this and the following chapter, I draw heavily on my fieldwork with Tanzanian women but also supplement this with data from two mixed-gender town-hall style meetings I conducted in Mwanza on AIDS-related stigma.[1] This chapter begins by showing how stigma is tied to the history of colonization through examining intercultural interpretations of stigma, HIV and AIDS, and social systems. I look particularly at the ways in which information about HIV was disseminated by outsiders in an environment that was already weakened by the distrust of imperialism. The chapter ends by examining the ways in which fear, silence, and secret-keeping and taboo and sin function in relation to stigma.

DEFINING STIGMA IN THE CONTEXT OF COMMUNITY

Sociologist Erving Goffman defines stigma as "an attribute that is deeply discrediting," but argues that a "language of relationships, not attributes, is really needed."[2] In saying this, Goffman points to the social nature of stigmatization, arguing that stigma is created in relationships as individuals are included or excluded based on real or perceived traits. Goffman notes that the word "stigma" was first used by the Greeks to refer to bodily representations that were given in the form of cuts or branding in order to signify the moral failure of a person, such as the bodily marks given to slaves or criminals. Goffman goes on to say the word took on a different meaning in Christian history as "stigmata" came to represent a bodily sign or mark of grace.[3] Today, stigma has moved away from bodily representations and has settled on a notion of "disgrace," which can be visible or concealed.[4]

Interestingly enough, Christian churches still play a role in defining who will be stigmatized and who will not. The research collaborators in this research told story after story of how clergy at their churches had called them out from the pulpit or had made statements staying that people living with HIV and AIDS deserved their fate. In these churches, there was no "stigmata" of grace to accompany the stigma of suffering. Because stigma in the context of HIV and AIDS is a social stigma, communities and the churches within them determine who carries stigma's burdens.

By its very nature, stigma could not exist without some form of community consensus as to what defines a tainted identity. Stigma draws its power from the masses—the more people who subscribe to certain definitions of stigma, the more powerful that stigma becomes. In this sense, stigma is perpetuated by those whom Goffman calls the "normals,"[5] as well as by those who are stigmatized. Stigma could not function without the equally problematic category of what is considered to be "normal."

In order to fit in with what is considered normative, individuals in the stigmatized group will often hold the same damaging stereotypes about themselves as those in the dominant group. This was true in my field-work where collaborators said that they had stigmatized themselves or others who were living with HIV and AIDS even while knowing their status. Likewise, some of the worst instances of stigmatization reported by collaborators came from individuals who were living with HIV and AIDS or who had someone in their family who was. According to Goffman, this process of self-stereotyping involves an internalization of stigma in an effort to get along with others and thus achieve a level of social interaction.[6]

When we talk about stigma, we are talking about communities, about who is allowed to belong, and who is pushed to the fringes. Communities can be both life-giving and life-destroying. Social groups that are either overly individualistic or overly communitarian can limit agency and marginalize their members. In order to further analyze stigma and the way it impacts communities, families, and intimate relationships, it is helpful to begin with an intercultural look at the nature of communities and how stigma functions within them.

As we begin to think about communities, it is important for us to first identify different forms of communal association. White American Jesuit theologian Edward Vacek names three types of communal groups: the prepersonal, the associational, and the corporate. In the first group, Vacek defines "prepersonal belonging" as mass or crowd behavior. In this model, everyone is engaged, but no one is individually responsible. Here, Vacek argues that individuals lose their independence. The second type of group participation, which Vacek names "association," can be described as voluntary association, where individuals act at will as individuals within the group. The third group Vacek calls the "corporate person." While the corporate person still consists of individuals, it also possesses an identity of its own. Examples include nations, families, or friendships.[7] Vacek argues that membership in this group may require a form of self-sacrifice but that the group cannot exploit the individuals within it. Also tied into this is the requirement of collective responsibility. Membership in the group means that individuals are responsible for the actions of the whole as well as for their own actions.[8]

Vacek's three models describe well the range of personal belonging for those of us in the West, but because all three models begin with the individual in relation to the group, another model is needed to understand African communities. Within African philosophy and theology, communities that begin with "we" rather than "I" do not fit into Vacek's models because the social construction of these communities does not begin with the individual-in-relation but with the community-in-relation.

Yet at the same time, these communities are not at the other end of Vacek's spectrum and cannot be called totalitarian or prepersonal. They are close to Vacek's notion of the corporate personality, yet they are not one identity constructed by many individuals but one identity, which constructs the individuals with it. The distinction seems slight but is quite significant because without it an intercultural understanding of African ontology cannot be established.

As previously mentioned, the African philosophical maxim that defines communal structures is, *"I am because we are, and since we are, I am."* A possible response to the Cartesian maxim, *"I think, therefore I am,"* this statement places individual ontology as originating from within the community. Congolese theologian Bénézet Bujo argues that, "according to the African people's belief, not only human beings influence each other, but all forces possess a causal and ontological interdependence."[9] The community, in African thought, is part of this "ontological interdependence" that Bujo names. Bujo faults Christianity for starting with the individual and for not recognizing the individual's connection to a concrete community.[10]

Yet, while Bujo recognizes that African conceptions of community may have much to teach the West, he also warns against the dangers of romanticizing the idea of community. When Vacek's understanding of a community as a "corporate person" and Bujo's understanding of all forces possessing a "causal and ontological interdependence" are placed in conversation, a space can be created where we see that communities, like people, possess a form of morality in their relationality. If this is the case, then what does stigma tells us about a community's morality? Or perhaps a better question would be: What does stigma tell us about our global morality?

A POSTCOLONIAL FEMINIST INTERPRETATION OF STIGMA

During one of the sessions on stigma, Joyce told a story of being stigmatized by her neighbor. She said one day she was coughing and a neighbor turned to someone else and said, "Eh, that one, [meaning Joyce] will tomorrow come? She will die." Joyce ignored it but was hurt by the comment. She said that she was on medication so she began to gain weight slowly. Joyce said around the same time, the son of this same neighbor became sick, and Joyce could tell he was also living with HIV. Joyce continued to be kind to this neighbor and tried to ignore her comments. One day, when she greeted her neighbor with the respectful greeting reserved for elders (*Shikamoo*), the woman greeted her back saying, "Are you the one who has passed away?" In making this comment, the neighbor deeply insulted Joyce by linking her with stigma of death.

Within a few months, this neighbor experienced her own tragedy. Her son, who was also HIV-positive, committed suicide. Joyce felt bad for her neighbor and her neighbor's son, but also realized that even though she had been called "the one who passed away," she was the one who was still living. For Joyce, her very life was a symbol of her decision to reject this woman's stigma and the way that stigma pushed her to the fringes of her community. This was something her neighbor's son was not able to do.

In this story, we see an example of community that is broken rather than life-giving. It is far from the model of African community that created *"I am because we are . . . ."* Nigerian feminist theologian Teresa Okure suggests that Africa is a "martyred continent" and argues that during colonialism, the prosperity of whites depended on the martyrdom of black African communities. Okure affirms the sense that, *"I am because we are . . . "* but as she does she also laments that, "The economies of selfishness took over this community-oriented economy," and says, "Martyred Africa has yet to recover from this onslaught." Okure rightly notes that the brokenness that exists in African communities is tied to the alienation created by colonialism.[11] Throughout the world, colonialism was only able to flourish by replacing local forms of community and governance within an imperialistic hierarchy, where diverse groups of people were subject to authoritarian rule.

Colonialism deeply changed familial and societal structures through the introduction of new laws, new systems of governance, and new economies. As a result, today many Africans still live between the old and the new, tied in some ways to African traditions and other ways to the West and the modernization it brought. Perhaps the most important change colonialism introduced was the shift from a community-oriented society to an individualistic way of being in the world. This is why Okure laments the loss of a "community-oriented economy." Yet even in this lament, there is little time for looking back. While colonialism shoulders some blame for the brokenness of society in that it was a violent and oppressive system of rule, we must not buy into the myth that there is or was ever a pristine "Africa" that can be recovered. Even the idea of "Africa" and the states within it were colonial inventions. However, we can make progress by acknowledging that Africa and the West are tied as former colonized and former colonizers, and that colonialism deeply changed the fabric of social life in colonized countries. Therefore, this history must not be ignored when seeking to identify the underlying cause of social illnesses such as stigma.

Musa Dube echoes Okure's concern as she speaks of African communities as being "stigma positive." Without romanticizing community, Dube speaks of what was and what is as she holds the overlapping realms of tradition, colonization, and post-modernity in tension. Dube argues that the extended family has lost some of the "botho/ubuntu, the traditional 'human norms' that made extended family members responsible for the siblings of the deceased." She goes on to say that, "The community spirit, therefore, can no longer be taken for granted, but neither should it be dismissed as non-existent; rather we should acknowledge an ongoing cultural conflict."[12] Writing in 2002, Dube noted that in her home country of Botswana, 270,000 people were living with HIV and AIDS, but only eleven people had come forward to disclose their HIV status publicly. Dube argues that this stigma makes life "socially unlivable" for those with HIV or AIDS.[13]

In speaking of African communities, Bujo talks of the "African spirit of solidarity, which shows itself most clearly during the hour of death of a member."[14] But with HIV and AIDS, this solidarity is strangely absent. Collaborators in my fieldwork talked about the deep secrecy surrounding the deaths of those who were living with HIV and AIDS. Even today, throughout sub-Saharan Africa, people rarely say that a person has died of AIDS, but instead another cause (such as TB) is listed. The stigma of dying from AIDS is still too strong.

To be stigmatized is to be radically individualized, to be denied relationality with the community. It is a social death, which is more than just symbolic in places where community identity trumps the identity of individuals. Stigma is the opposite of *"I am because we are."* Stigma tells the stigmatized, "we are, but you are not." Because stigma denies community, in Africa this means stigma also denies ontology. Just as the virus destroys a physical being, stigma destroys social being, which in many cultures is more important.

One man in the group said that he first found out his status in 1989. At this time period, very few people understood the nature of the disease or how it was contracted. Stigma was understandably at an all-time high. He was engaged to a girl who died from AIDS, and when the community found out how she had died, he was immediately stigmatized. The people in his village tried to force him to leave. They even called in the *sungusungu*, a local police/court system that enforces traditional law. At first, this man refused to leave but then in the middle of the night his neighbors started banging on his doors. He said this was a terrible experience. "My soul was in pain," he said. "I was like a dog in the eyes of the villagers. They even called a meeting about me and the whole village came. . . . I remember everything clearly. It was like I was a stranger." He finally gave in and sold his family's land and moved to Mwanza. He didn't return for ten years, but when he did return, he found that many of the people who forced him to leave had also died of AIDS. While the community was pushing him to the fringes, they were imploding from within.

Stigma not only happens in communities, but it impacts the very fabric of communities as well. It is important to note that stigma is not only a cause of discrimination but is also a cause of the pandemic's spread.

Studies have shown that the regions where stigma is high are the same regions where HIV has moved away from individual and network levels toward pandemic levels.[15] The relationship between stigma and pandemic levels could either result from stigma contributing to the spread of the disease, or from an increase in stigma due to high prevalence. Both are valid reasons, and I suggest both are at play. By examining four key aspects of stigma—fear; silence and secret keeping; sin and taboo; and in the following chapter, sacrifice—we can see how stigma functions in local and global communities and can seek out ways to dismantle stigma and contain the spread of the HIV pandemic.

FEAR: STIGMA'S MOTIVATION

A primary force that fuels stigma is fear. This fear expresses itself in a fear of the disease, a fear of contagion, a fear of being stigmatized, and a fear of death. The fear of the disease is based in a fear of the unknown. Feminist theologian Musa Dube argues that because HIV and AIDS have not been given African names, their natures have not been fully known, and Africans have remained suspicious in light of the history of colonialism.[16] Conspiracy theories abound that claim HIV does not lead to AIDS, that AIDS is really a manifestation of extreme poverty, or that the disease was created by the West to wipe out Africans or bring profit to pharmaceutical companies.[17]

Joyce said that she remembered when she first heard of AIDS in 1986. At the time, a woman in her community returned from Nairobi and was very sick with AIDS. Everyone in the community said that she got the disease from sleeping with white people because it was known as a "white man's disease." One early acronym for AIDS was "American Invention to Discourage Sex." These conspiracy theories and re-namings are evidence of the mistrust between the former colonizers and the former colonized. HIV and AIDS must be known in the African context, but exporting Western scientific names and understandings may create more suspicion than knowledge.

Musa Dube argues that because HIV and AIDS have not been given African names in most countries, their natures have not been fully known and Africans have remained suspicious in light of the baggage of western colonialism.[18] In Tanzania, HIV/AIDS is known as *VUU/Ukimwi*. *VUU*, the abbreviation that is the Kiswahili equivalent for HIV, stands for the Kiswahili name for the virus, *"Virusi Vinavyosababisha Ukimwi"* which means, "virus that causes AIDS." The Kiswahili word for AIDS, *Ukimwi*, is a shortened form of the phrase, *"Ukosefu wa Kinga Mwilini"* which translates as "Acquired Immunodeficiency Syndrome," or more literally reads, "not to have immunity in the body." By using the Kiswahili names rather than the English, people are more able to understand the disease and the way it functions. Tanzania has widespread campaigns to publish literature on HIV and AIDS in Kiswahili. When the collaborators were asked about this, they said that while *"Ukimwi"* still carries stigma, it is better than talking about "AIDS" because at least it is not a foreign concept.

All of the collaborators were optimistic that education could make a difference by reducing stigma. They were especially worried about the rural areas because of the lack of information, clinics and AIDS drugs. They believed that because education and resources were lacking in these areas, stigma tended to take over and prevent a positive discourse about prevention or treatment. Collaborators said that stigma caused people to be isolated, especially in rural areas where even sharing a bowl or spoon with a person who was living with HIV and AIDS is still considered taboo. One woman in a stigma group meeting said, "I want to talk about the village. It is there that if you are sick and it is known that you are a sick person, you will be segregated into your own room. Also the food and the dishes will be segregated. They won't even touch you in there; they'll just push the food towards you."

When HIV and AIDS are not named and understood, their natures are also not integrated into African worldviews. Yet, African worldviews are still used to interpret the sickness and death they bring. One example is that many people in sub-Saharan Africa believe witchcraft[19] causes HIV. When Agnes found out she was HIV-positive, her husband told her someone must have bewitched her. Agnes went to a diviner who agreed with her husband. The diviner told her it was her mother's youngest sister who bewitched her. Agnes said she was so angry that she even considered burning down this woman's house. At the time, Agnes was pregnant, but the child did not live long after it was born. Her husband, who had left Agnes while she was pregnant, blamed the death of his child on witchcraft. He said Agnes was the one who bewitched the child. This was a turning point for Agnes, because her ex-husband had also been with another woman who had lost a child. She knew then that the problems in her life were not related to witchcraft. She countered her ex-husband's accusation by reminding him of "this problem" that they both shared—a positive HIV diagnosis.

Joyce said that one of the reasons that witchcraft was so widely believed to be a cause of HIV transmission is that the wife and the husband often exhibited symptoms at different times because one partner usually contracted the virus earlier than the other. She believed that if both partners would show symptoms at the same time, then the tendency to blame witchcraft would decrease. She gave an example from her own life. When her husband died, Joyce said she was still visibly symptom free. Her husband's clan thought someone in Mwanza had bewitched Joyce's husband and they wanted Joyce to marry someone else in their clan in her dead husband's name. Joyce and her family refused. Joyce said, "If my brain had been small, I would have been married again in the same clan. I would have already killed the clan, you see. Those relatives of his believed completely that their relative was bewitched, that there was no AIDS."

Blaming witchcraft could be a way of saving face and even eliciting sympathy while distancing one's self from stigma and from the disease. Witchcraft also provides an excuse to "property grab," as wives are often accused of causing their husband's illness and are kicked out of their homes by the family after the husband dies. The fear of non-sexual transmission, either through cursing or casual contact, leads to stigmatization, especially in rural areas. As previously mentioned, stigmatized individuals are often made to eat alone as bodily contact or sharing utensils, clothing, or bedding becomes taboo. This fear is also a means of saving face. If transmission can happen by accident or by innocent contact, the individual can create distance from the stigma of sexual deviance.[20]

Beyond the fear of disease and fear of contagion, there is also a great fear of being stigmatized. This fear can lead individuals to delay or completely avoid testing. It also means that when a person does test positive, stigma can lead them not to disclose their status, putting their partners at risk. The greatest danger stigma poses is that it limits information and therefore causes those with HIV to knowingly or unknowingly spread the disease. Thus, the fear of stigmatization affects not only the individual but others the individual interacts with as well.

This was especially true for the women who participated in this study. They said that when their husbands got sick, the men either did not test out of fear or tested and kept their status a secret from their wives. None of the women in this study found out their status because their husband disclosed it to them. Almost all of the women were positive their husbands had contracted the virus first and either ignored the symptoms or kept their status a secret. Most women found out their status either because they were pregnant or because their husband was dying from AIDS.

Some women told stories of husbands testing positive and even starting medication without ever telling their wives. Grace told a story of a friend whose husband had been on medication for three years without ever telling his wife. Eventually, the man's wife found the medicine hidden in his clothes and then knew she should also be tested. Domina told a story of a colleague who had been hiding his status from his wife for three years as well. Domina was sure, though, that this man was "being beaten by God with a stick" for his actions, because every time he went to the doctor his CD4 count was very low. Veronica's husband didn't disclose his status either. He was taking medicine, but when she asked him what it was for, he said it was to clear up his cough. He was sick for seven years—and having unprotected sex with her the whole time—before she finally figured out he was HIV-positive.

Maria found out her status as the result of intervention from her in-laws. Her husband's younger brother and his wife were concerned about her. They had seen Maria's husband with a woman who the community believed was HIV-positive, so without saying why, they encouraged Maria to be tested. It took them three tries to convince her to go in for the test. When she was tested she found out she was HIV-positive. She told the women in the group:

> I was told I was infected and I asked myself where did I get this? When I was pregnant I got tested and I didn't have anything. Today, where did I get it? Now we came to my husband's brother and he sat me down and he told me, "When this man (your husband) comes, don't agree to share with him, because he brought this woman here and I know her health quite well. I sat him down and I confronted him about the woman who he married to kill your family, but he kept quiet. That is why we came for you."

Maria's story was an unusual one in that her in-laws intervened to protect her from further harm.

Social psychologist Diane Quinn notes that the way stigma affects an individual is directly related to the visibility of the stigma and to whether or not it can be concealed.[21] Stigma presents dangers beyond discrimination as people go to great lengths to conceal their status, such as skipping medication or medical appointments.[22] In the African context, this also means that many mothers living with HIV and AIDS will sometimes choose to breastfeed and risk passing the virus through their breast milk, because in communities with HIV and AIDS, those who do not breastfeed are stigmatized as being HIV-positive.[23] It also means that a positive test result will not be disclosed to current or future sexual partners, even if that puts others at risk.

TABOO AND SIN: STIGMA'S RATIONALE

Conceptions of taboo and sin provide a rationale for HIV and AIDS and the stigma that accompanies it by equating the disease with deviance or a trespass. While stigma can exist without taboo and sin, such as when the stigmatized person is considered unlucky or an innocent victim, the presence of sin or taboo strengthens stigma by sanctifying or moralizing it. While taboo is a category within indigenous African religions, and sin a category within Christianity, the two often overlap. Taboos can become sin, and sin can turn into a taboo. South African anthropologist Isak Niehaus reminds us that taboo is not only a part of the past but is present in contemporary Africa as well.[24] The two exist concurrently, sharing both meaning and function. As cited in chapter 3, common African taboos center around blood, bodily fluids, death, and sex. The very nature of the HIV and AIDS virus evokes numerous taboos and therefore the disease is easily interpreted as the result of a transgression.

It is understood in many African cultures that breaking a taboo can lead to illness or death.[25] Unlike moral rules, taboos are thought to directly avenge themselves, exemplifying a cause-and-effect-type relationship for those who transgress.[26] Zimbabwean theologian Ezra Chitando suggests that modern understandings of disease are rooted in indigenous notions that see illness as a curse from the ancestors.[27] Where illness equals curse and transgresses multiple taboos, stigma will abound. For the purpose of this discussion, I will limit my focus to the two categories of taboo that have the greatest effect on HIV and AIDS stigma: death and sex.

While HIV is becoming a chronically manageable disease in the West, it most often equals death in sub-Saharan Africa. As of 2010, only 37 percent of those who needed antiretroviral treatments in this region were able to access these life-saving drugs.[28] In countries where drugs to treat HIV are still not universally available, death is still the primary interpretation of the virus. The images of death which surround the pandemic have come both from contact with the dying and from prevention campaigns.

Isak Niehaus argues that a culture of denial surrounding the disease has created a form of social death for those who have HIV or AIDS. According to Niehaus, African communities see those who are infected as zombies, people who are living but are socially dead because they are carrying a terminal disease. Niehaus calls those with stigma the "living dead,"[29] a term particularly poignant because in African cultures the ancestors who are thought to still live on after their death are also known as the living dead. Yet, those who die of AIDS might not be considered ancestors within some communities, because a requirement for becoming an ancestor includes living a long life and not dying a violent death.[30]

During the sessions on stigma, I asked collaborators what they thought of Niehaus' argument. The collaborators agreed that this resonated with their experience of living with HIV and AIDS. A recurring theme in my fieldwork centered on early death vs. longevity. Many of the collaborators reported that others had said they were "close to death" or "almost dead" or had simply treated them as if they were dead or dying. Yet as the collaborators would tell stories about those who had stigmatized them in this way, they would often end the story by saying that the person who stigmatized them is now dead but they are still living.

Maria's story of a time when she was admitted to the hospital is a good example. When Maria got sick, one of the village leaders took her to the hospital and dropped her off. On the second day she was in the hospital, her children arrived, crying. They were accompanied by a large group of people from her community, who were peeking in at her through the hospital doorway. Maria was confused and asked her children, "Why are you crying? Have you been beaten?" The children replied that they were crying because the elder who brought her to the hospital had told them she was dead. When Maria walked out of the room, she said her whole community was amazed to see that she was alive. She concluded the story by saying, "Surprisingly, it was him, the one who told them this, who got sick from shingles, and now he is already dead."

Another man at the stigma meeting said that after he found out he was HIV-positive, he decided to stay in Mwanza rather than return home to Shinyanga. He was trained as a counselor and worked with a local HIV support group. Four years later he returned home to find out that everyone thought he was already dead. Five men who knew his status told the whole community he had died. The story ended on the same theme of death vs. longevity as the man told the group "All those five who announced this about me are now the ones who are underground."

Collaborators were also called names that linked them with death. Agnes and Maria were called "the deceased-to-be." Maria was called a "carcass" and said to have "rotted already." Esther and Joyce were called "the one with electricity" meaning they had been electrocuted and died. One man was said to have "gone bankrupt."

Based on Niehaus' argument and on my fieldwork, I argue that a close connection can be made between stigma and taboos surrounding death. If a person is seen as a zombie, or as nearly dead, the same taboos that apply to contact with a dead corpse can be transferred to the living. African taboos regarding death include restrictions on touching or interacting with the dead to avoid ritual impurities.[31] In many ways, these taboos also shape stigma for those living with a terminal disease as they see themselves as untouchable or as a source of pollution (or perhaps as a burden) to their families.

A second level of taboo comes into play because HIV is transmitted sexually. From the beginning, HIV and AIDS have been equated with sexual promiscuity in Christian churches and in society in general. Maria, who attends an Anglican church, shared her story of being in church services where the pastor said that those who have HIV are "hopeless adulteresses." She said that in one church service the pastor said that if a person died of HIV, they shouldn't call a pastor to conduct the funeral because "we pastors have been purified."

As Maria illustrates, many Christian churches in sub-Saharan Africa have proclaimed that death from AIDS is God's punishment for sin. Here, I would argue that there is a connection between Africa and the West. In the early days of HIV and AIDS in the United States, Christian churches preached that HIV was a punishment for homosexuality, which they called sin. This stigma made its way to Africa through missionary movements and connections between Christian churches in Africa and the West. Unfortunately, I know this personally. In the fundamentalist Baptist church that I grew up in, I remember hearing multiple sermons asserting that AIDS was God's way of cleansing the world from homo-sexuality. And when I went to Kenya for the first time in 1998, I talked to Kenyan Baptists who learned this same rhetoric in seminary classes or from visiting evangelists or mission groups. Even today, not much has changed. The 2011 murder of gay activist David Kato in Uganda can be directly linked to propaganda from US evangelical pastors who preached in Uganda calling homosexuality a sin and AIDS God's punishment.[32]

This same association of HIV with sexual promiscuity and "sin" showed up not only in churches but also in public awareness campaigns. In the early days of the disease, the ads that didn't show images of death portrayed women in mini-skirts standing by men in bars. With this asso-ciation between promiscuous sexuality and HIV, when a person in the community is infected, they are thought to be at fault for their contracting the disease. The association of HIV and promiscuous sexual behavior is especially true for women, even if they have had no other sexual partners other than their husbands. As previously mentioned, African feminist theologian Constance Shishanya reminds us that women are even blamed for their husband's infidelity.[33]

White, feminist Catholic theologian Rosemary Radford Ruether argues that taboos surrounding menstruation and childbirth have caused women's bodies to be seen as polluted while men's bodies embodied sacrality. Ruether suggests that the separation of women during their menstrual cycle may have originally been a sacred gathering of women and not a separation due to pollution. [34] While Ruether uses this to en-courage women to redeem a sacred embodiment in liturgy, the same could be suggested as a form of advocacy against HIV and AIDS and stigma. Women must find a way to reclaim the sacredness of their bodies. This is not only a task for African women but must become a goal of our global moral response to the African HIV pandemic. As long as preven-tion is reduced to the "do's and don'ts" of sex without a focus on under-standing sexuality as part of our embodiment, women will be stigma-tized and blamed for the spread of HIV. When HIV prevention cam-paigns tell women what to do with their bodies, an important opportu-nity is missed for women to cultivate a body-knowledge that shapes their way of being in the world.

A focus on women's bodies without attention to embodiment spreads fear rather than hope. Within this fear of HIV and AIDS, sex, and child-birth—activities that are normally seen as life-giving—become seen as vehicles for death. Stigma, though reprehensible, can be thought of as a grab in the dark for life. It is possible that the severe stigma attached to women with HIV comes from the potential disruption in their assigned role as child-bearers. The identity of women, their life, and their immor-tality is wrapped up in their children. Parents cannot become ancestors when children are not left to remember them. As previously argued, in the African context, children insure immortality. In interpreting the "fall" in Christian tradition, the North African church father, Augustine, argued that the loss of immortality was Eve's punishment for her sin.[35] Perhaps the same line of reasoning is being applied today in the sub-Saharan African context as the loss of immortality (defined as being forgotten) is equated with committing a sin or breaking a taboo.

Within the African context, dying young or dying a violent death—both of which are characteristics of dying from AIDS—are often thought to prohibit someone from attaining immortality by becoming an ancestor. This is because in these circumstances death is considered to have a cause. This reason for one's death could be that the person has violated a taboo, or that someone has harmed them through witchcraft. John Mbiti notes that punishment (such as sickness or death) is sometimes seen as a sign that something is evil rather than retribution for evil. Mbiti gives the Nuer people as an example and says that for them, "Something is evil because it is punished: it is not punished because it is evil." In this way, it could be argued that when Christian and African beliefs on evil and sin were combined, a person's health and well-being became indicators of their morality. This is certainly evidenced in the appearance of prosperity gospel theologies within both African Independent Churches and Pentecostal churches across sub-Saharan Africa.

In the postcolonial African context, understandings of taboo and sin tend to collapse into one another, creating teachings in Christian churches that fuel stigma. Ezra Chitando argues that sexuality as a taboo subject in African cultures has been intensified by the negative connotations given to sexuality within Christian history.[36] Similar to understandings of taboo, sex in the Christian tradition also carries with it interpretations of purity and pollution that are wrapped up definitions of sin and salvation. Among some Christian communities both inside and outside of Africa, it is even debated whether people living with HIV and AIDS can even be saved.

Mama Gasabile, who works with pastors throughout the Anglican Diocese of Victoria Nyanza, agreed that this was a problem in Tanzania as well. She said that in 2002, a consultant from Dodoma came to hold a seminar for pastors and their wives about HIV and AIDS. The consultant began the seminar by asking the pastors what they thought communities should do for those who are living with HIV and AIDS. One pastor raised his and said, "I think that if someone is heard to have AIDS he should be given an injection so that he dies." All the other pastors laughed and the consultant responded by saying "Is that so?" Once the laughing died down the consultant said that maybe this pastor had a wise idea, and she thought she would follow it. She went on to say that she had everything with her, and she could begin testing immediately with the pastors and their wives who are present, because after all, pastors should be role models and practice what they preach. She continued the drama by asking two of the youth who were helping to close and lock the back doors while she set up a testing station. The pastors attempted to excuse themselves, saying they must run to the toilet or had to take a phone call. Some were afraid this consultant might just follow through with her plan. Mama Gasabile ended the story about the consultant's clever illustration by saying, "It is true that many pastors have no education, and it is true that the pastors must be educated."

Domina followed Mama Gasabile's story with a similar story. She worked with a small self-help group for women living with HIV and AIDS that met on property owned by the Diocese of Victoria Nyanza. The Anglican diocese had allowed the women to use an old shipping container and the area surrounding it as an office and workspace. They cooked lunch each day for nearby workers and had a garment-making business where women living with HIV and AIDS learned how to sew to supplement their income. When they initially approached the then Anglican bishop about getting an office, he said, "You are infected. Why do you need an office? A person who is already dead doesn't need an office at all." Domina and her group were eventually given an office on the church compound after much persuasion from the bishop's son, but the bishop still never supported their work. As Domina told the story she said it was ironic, since the bishop was now the one who was dead. She said, "He died and he left us, and still now, we don't die. Not today or tomorrow — we are still around." All the women laughed at her story.

Margaret Farley argues that our perceptions of sexuality "remain immersed in the economy of defilement."[37] Drawing on the work of Paul Ricoeur, Farley points out that taboos associated with sexuality do not allow for reflective rationales. When they are broken, purification is the only means of restoration. Sin, on the other hand, for both Ricoeur and Farley, is a rupture of a relationship. Building on these definitions, it must be asked whether or not "sin" can be used as a category for a sexual morality that is tied to expectations of purity and fear of defilement. Farley argues that the belief in the defilement of sexuality is pre-ethical in that it pre-dates Christian morality and has little to do with the definition of sin that Ricoeur proposes.[38] If Farley argues correctly, then "sexual sin" in the context of stigma functions more like taboo. In this sense, both represent a pre-ethical attempt at containing pollution rather than a reflective ethic that seeks to restore relationships. With this in mind, stigma can best be understood as an inadequate and life-destroying attempt to keep broken taboos from affecting communities.

Religious abstinence-based campaigns that have branched out into HIV prevention have reinforced this stigma by naming purity as necessary requirement for the Christian life. Yet the short-sightedness of abstinence-only programming is its assumption of full agency and unlimited choice, which, as I argue throughout this book, is simply not a reality for many African women.

SECRET-KEEPING AND SILENCE: STIGMA'S CONTINUATION

Silence and secret-keeping create an atmosphere where stigma can thrive because stigma's greatest enemies, speech and truth-telling, are closeted with those who are afraid to disclose their status. Collaborators in this research saw status disclosure as a sacrifice they made for the good of others. For most, it took years for them to speak publicly about their status, if they had at all. Of the twenty-two people present at the first meeting on stigma, only sixteen had publicly disclosed their status. Of these people, only five disclosed their status within the first year. Another nine people disclosed their status in the second year, and the rest waited longer or still had not publically disclosed their status.

Chitando reminds us that taboo also functions on a level of speech, as even the words needed to talk about sex are taboo.[39] The same verbal taboos that surround sex now also surround HIV and AIDS. Though communities know HIV is present, the silence that surrounds it provides a perception of distance and creates a false consciousness where it is thought that not everyone is affected.

Secret-keeping and silence makes HIV and AIDS someone else's disease and isolates those who are living with HIV and AIDS. Through a process of "othering," silence creates a false confidence that diminishes the felt need for regular HIV testing, and secret-keeping discourages status disclosure. Secret-keeping hides the spread of the disease and dangerously distances individuals from the real risks it presents.

Grace talked about the process of othering as she reflected on stigma. She said:

> I also want to contribute here about those who think they are ok and we who are seen to have the virus. It is like there is a wall between us that separates us. I can only talk about my example—it felt as if I were completely alone. You see, it felt like I didn't have peace, because haven't they said they are all clean? Now I, because I have the virus, I feel like I am in a world all to myself. . . . Therefore, there are issues that hurt people who are infected, and truly we are hurt tremendously to a great extent. There is a wall that separates us. They are in their world as they see themselves and we are in another world.

As Grace talked about the wall that separated the infected and unaffected, others chimed in to tell similar stories from their lives where they were stigmatized by family, health care workers, neighbors, or even their children. Collaborators said that stigma is what encourages silence over status disclosure. It causes people to not talk openly about HIV, yet at the same time creates space for gossip about those who are presumed to be living with HIV and AIDS.[40] Silence and secret-keeping perpetuate the scandalous nature of the disease as it is assumed that people would not hide a disease that comes innocently. In this way, the perception that those who have HIV and AIDS are sinful, deviant, or have violated a taboo is reinforced.

Musa Dube's writing is pivotal in linking this silence to the experience of globalization. Dube argues that practices of confidentiality when testing for HIV isolates individuals, because in Africa, the sickness of one is to be shouldered by the community. According to Dube, the practice of doctor-patient confidentiality, which has been exported from the West, deepens stigma and leaves no room for a communal response.[41] In addressing confidentiality, Dube proposes an African response, suggesting that HIV should be challenged through communal divination where a traditional healer gathers the community to explore where broken relationships exist and how they can be healed. Dube believes this would bring to light issues such as patriarchy, poverty, and other forms of marginalization that make people vulnerable.[42]

In her volume on AIDS in Africa, Stephanie Nolen tells the story of Prisca, a woman who experienced extreme discrimination when she found out she was HIV-positive. Prisca experienced discrimination from doctors and clinicians and was forbidden by her husband from telling anyone her status. Now an AIDS activist, Prisca reflected on the practice of doctor-patient confidentiality and said, "This confidentiality is killing a lot of people."[43]

Collaborators in this research also believed that doctor-patient confidentiality did more harm than good. Joyce said that when her husband was sick and in the hospital, no one told her about her husband's condition because her husband didn't choose to disclose his status. Joyce's husband was in an overcrowded hospital in Mwanza, where family members care for patients—they feed them, bathe them, change their soiled clothes, and even tend to their sickness. During this time, Joyce was at risk because she was caring for a person living with HIV and AIDS, yet this risk was never disclosed. Joyce's husband died while he was in the hospital, and she buried him, never knowing the truth about his illness. Because Joyce was poor, and had few options after her husband died, she found boyfriends who helped provide for her. Joyce had no idea she was HIV-positive or that her husband died of AIDS. She reflected on this saying, "After my husband died, it is not as if I did not get other men. I was going out with them and later I found out I infected some of them because of this 'confidentiality' of the doctors. If only the doctors had called me and given me advice, I would have protected these other people. As for me, this confidentiality has hurt me deeply."

The concept of confidentiality and whether or not confidentiality about one's status should be kept is certainly a complex issue. On one hand, confidentiality is essential because stigma is rampant. In sub-Saharan Africa, there are few enforceable laws to keep a person from losing their job, their land, or children if their status is disclosed. And as we have seen, status disclosure tends to strain or disrupt familial and marital relationships. So in one sense, confidentiality is of upmost importance. Yet, on the other hand, because of this same stigma, individuals are not likely to voluntarily disclose their status—even to their sexual partners or caregivers. In this way, confidentiality puts others at risk.

This issue is even more complex when you consider that some men in sub-Saharan Africa do not see their female sexual partners or caregivers as equals but as property. This was a concept that arose in the conversations on *mahari* (or bridewealth), as many of the women in the study said their partners saw them as property rather than as equals. To use Kantian terminology, we could say that within these patriarchal power structures, men are tempted to treat the women in their lives as a means to an end rather than as ends in themselves. When this mindset is present, women become the means for procreation and the means of providing for the family or the community. When men are sick, women become the means whereby men recover as women nurse them back to health. When this mindset is present—when women are not seen as ends in themselves—a moral obligation to disclose one's status and protect another may not be sufficiently compelling since the other is not considered an equal. Simply put, until all women around the world are seen as ends in themselves rather than a means to a patriarchal end, they will continue to bear the burdens of sickness, poverty and violence. When women are not seen as equals, keeping men's confidentiality could be putting women at risk.

In thinking through stigma, we must also acknowledge that another major source of stigma is that HIV and AIDS has been seen for too long as a death sentence. We cannot expect stigma to diminish or individuals to voluntarily disclose their status if they and those around them do not have access to life-sustaining drugs. As long as only 37 percent of those who need medicine are getting it, then a positive HIV status still means death for far too many. Those of us in the developed (or overdeveloped) global north have a responsibility to our sisters and brothers in the global south. As part of this global community, we are morally obligated to help provide life-saving drugs to developing countries. This moral obligation stems from a basic demand for distributive justice and a recognition of structural violence. We are also morally obligated to provide access to drugs because much of our current knowledge on HIV and AIDS comes from research centers in developing countries. In order for the benefits of their participation to outweigh the risks, we must do more to provide access to drugs for individuals within these communities.

One way to accomplish this within the sub-Saharan African context is to consider the communal aspect of health and seek to bring families and communities into the testing process together. Perhaps stigma could be diminished if clinicians and public health practitioners took a more familial or communal approach to HIV testing and status disclosure. If we encouraged entire families and communities to test together, then a space for equality and compassion could be created. In testing together, even those who tested negative could experience compassion for those who tested positive as the experience of testing together could create solidarity.[44] Testing at a community level also creates opportunities for education about prevention. Familial or communal testing could also create a space of accountability within intimate relationships that could protect women, as it could prevent a woman from being blamed for bringing HIV into the marriage. Currently, women are usually the first tested for HIV because they are tested when they become pregnant. If partners were routinely tested together—and fortunately this practice is on the rise—then women would not have to face their husbands alone with the news and might be less likely to be blamed for bringing the disease.

According to the collaborators in this study, even when they were tested for HIV with their partners, the clinician always asked them if they wanted to receive their results separately. While this practice honors confidentiality and a Western understanding of autonomy, it can put a partner who is negative at risk if the other partner is positive and chooses not to disclose their status. As Agnes' story of testing with her partner showed, a doctor's breaking the news about a partner's status can provide a way of saving face for the HIV-positive partner who may not know how to break the news.

Keeping confidentiality is not the only way to prevent stigma. We need more creative solutions that honor the traditions of communities who shoulder sickness together. Perhaps in thinking through best practices for testing and prevention, we need to employ Dube's idea of "communal divination." This practice, while rooted in African traditional religions, still offers an important solution for Christian churches that are seeking ways to listen to each other and to their communities. By employing this practice, space could be created to abolish stigma through encouraging a moral obligation to listen, which is also a Christian practice.

If silence and secret-keeping ensure stigma's continuation, then speech and truth-telling will bring about its end. But in order for speech and truth-telling to flourish, safe spaces must be created where marginalized voices can find life. Only in speaking against silence and secret-keeping is it possible for us to being "hearing each other to speech."[45] Even those who may not be ready to talk (or to disclose their status) can be heard when we learn to embrace an ethic of listening. In this pursuit, a global/communal divination can be engaged where truth-telling and speech are given new space to flourish.

NOTES

1. These meetings came out of the participatory action portion of the research as we decided that stigma was a topic that would be good to discuss at a wider level with more collaborators. Each of the two meetings had around twenty-five people in atten-

dance, including almost all of the twelve women from the PAR portion of this research. In the first meeting, collaborators decided to go around the room and each tell a story of being stigmatized. In the second meeting, we focused on some of the themes that emerged in their stories such a doctor-patient confidentiality, secret-keeping, and stigma within intimate relationships.

2. Erving Goffman, *Stigma: Notes on a Spoiled Identity*, (New York: Simon & Schuster, 1963), 3.

3. Ibid., 1.

4. Ibid., 1–2.

5. Ibid., 5.

6. Stacey Sinclair and Jeff Huntsinger, "The Interpersonal Basis of Self-Stereotyping," 235-59, In *Stigma and Group Inequality: Social Psychological Perspectives,* ed. Shana Levin and Colette van Laar, (New Jersey: Lawrence Erlbaum Associates, 2006), 235.

7. Ibid., 82–84.

8. Ibid.

9. Bénézet Bujo, The Ethical Dimension of Community: The African Model and the Dialogue Between North and South, (Nairobi: Paulines Press Africa, 1998), 16.

10. Ibid.,18.

11. Teresa Okure, "Africa, A Martyred Continent: Seed of a New Humanity," *Concilium,* 2003, 39-46.

12. Dube, "Fighting with God: Children and HIV/AIDS in Botswana" *Journal of Theology for Southern Africa,* 114, Nov 2002, 31–42, pg. 36.

13. Ibid., 39.

14. Bujo, 21.

15. Chris Beyrer, "HIV Epidemiology Update and Transmission Factors: Risks and Risk Contexts—16th International AIDS Conference. Epidemiology Plenary," *Clinical Infectious Diseases,* 44 (2007), 981–87.

16. Dube, "Adinkra! Four Hearts Joined Together," 131-51. For an alternative view, see Jenny Trinitapoli and Alexander Weinreb, *Religion and AIDS in Africa* (New York: Oxford University Press, 2012). Trinitapoli and Weinreb argue that based on the "contact hypothesis", generalized epidemics cannot sustain stigma precisely because everyone knows people who they love who have died of AIDS-related complications.

17. Ibid.

18. Dube, "Adinkra! Four Hearts Joined Together," 131–51.

19. A belief in witchcraft is present in most of sub-Saharan Africa, both rural and urban. In my own study, many of the women said they believed in witchcraft, or that they went to a traditional healer when they thought they had been bewitched. In a study by the Maryknoll Institute of African Studies in Nairobi, Kenya, witchcraft was defined as "doing willful harm to a fellow human being. It is an evil act practiced by witches and wizards through the manipulation of vital forces of nature for malevolent reasons. It is the evil thought sand deeds that lie within the human heart and actions...The effects of witchcraft are evident through accidents, sickness, injuries and whatever causes harm to people." For more see, "Witchcraft/Uchawi" African Cultural Theme No. 11, Maryknoll Institute of African Studies, Nairobi, Kenya, August 2003.

20. Virginia Bond, et al., Kanayaka "The light is on," Understanding HIV and AIDS related stigma in urban and rural Zambia, (Zambia: The Zambart Project, 2003), 29–33.

21. Diane M. Quinn, "Concealable Verses Conspicuous Stigmatized Identities," 83-103, In *Stigma and Group Inequality: Social Psychological Perspectives,* ed. Shana Levin and Colette van Laar, (New Jersey: Lawrence Erlbaum Associates, 2006).

22. Margaret A. Chesney and Ashley W. Smith, "Critical Delays in HIV Testing and Care: The Potential Role of Stigma," *American Behavioral Scientist,* Vol. 42, No. 7, (1999), 1162–74.

23. Bond, *et al.*, 34.

24. Isak Niehaus, "Bodies, Heat and Taboos: Conceptualizing Modern Personhood in the South African Lowveld," *Ethnology*, vol. 41, no. 3 (Summer 2002): 189–207, 205–6.

25. J.D. Kriel and Molebatsi M. Mapogole, "To be clogged up by an impure woman: A male malady among the North Sotho," *South African Journal of Ethnology*, Vol. 21, Issue 4, (December 1998): 181–84.

26. Niehaus, 192.

27. Ezra Chitando and M.R. Gunda, "HIV and AIDS, Stigma and Liberation in the Old Testament," *Exchange* 36 (2007) 184–297.

28. See Avert.org, ""Universal access to AIDS treatment: targets and challenges" http://www.avert.org/universal-access.htm (accessed November 28, 2010).

29. Gerrie ter Haar, "Religion and Development in Africa: Focus on HIV/AIDS," unpublished paper given at the African Association for the Study of Religion Conference, Gaborone, Botswana, (July 11, 2007).

30. Bujo, 16.

31. Niehaus, 192–93.

32. For more on this connection see, Candace Chellew-Hodge, "Ugandan Gay Rights Activist Murdered, US Evangelicals Must Take Responsibility," *Religion Dispatches*, January 27, 2011; Sarah Posner, "Recounting (Again) The Role of American Religious Activists in Uganda Anti-Gay Violence," *Religion Dispatches*, January 27, 2011; Candace Chellew-Hodge "Gay Rights Activists Condemn 'Spiritual War' in Uganda," *Religion Dispatches*, February 10, 2011; Jeffrey Gettleman, "Ugandan Who Spoke Up for Gays is Beaten to Death," *The New York Times*, January 27, 2011.

33. Shishanya, "The Impact of HIV/AIDS on Women in Kenya," 58.

34. Rosemary Radford Ruether, "Women's Body and Blood: The Sacred and the Impure," *Through the Devil ' s Gateway: Women Ritual and Taboo*, ed. Alison Joseph, (London: SPCK, 1990), 7.

35. Elizabeth A. Clarke, ed. *St. Augustine on Marriage and Sexuality*, (Washington DC: Catholic University of America, 1996), 40.

36. Chitando and Gunda, 187–88.

37. Farley, 177.

38. Ibid., 174–78.

39. Chitando and Gunda, 187.

40. Bond, *et al.*, 44–45.

41. Dube, "Adinkra! Four Hearts Joined Together", 131–51.

42. Ibid.

43. Stephanie Nolen, *28: Stories of AIDS in Africa*, (New York: Walker, 2007), 65.

44. An example of this type of approach can be found in The Rwanda-Zambia HIV Research Group (RZHRG), which is connected with the Rollins School of Public Health at Emory University. RZHRG encourages couples to test together and receive their results together. In doing so, they have created a model that is closer to the African understanding where the community shoulders the burden for sickness. For more, see their website at: http://www.rzhrg.org

45. Nelle Morton, "The Rising of Women's Consciousness in a Male Language Structure," *Andover Newton Quarterly* 12, no. 4 (March 1972), 177–90.

SEVEN

Learning from Stigma

Living as an Outcast in Intimate Relationships

During the fieldwork, talking about stigma brought us back to the issue of sacrifice. Many women in the PAR group saw disclosing their status and risking stigma as a place where they sacrificed themselves. Domina gave an example of going on a local radio talk show where she not only used her real name but also told everyone where she lived and worked. At the time, Domina worked as a *"Mama Lishe,"* meaning she sold snacks on the side of the road. She said that when people heard the radio show, many stopped buying from her. She described the consequences by saying, "Oh boy, this radio, people listened to it! They went to tell each other, 'Listen to *Mama Lishe*! Come listen—even her Kiswahili is that of the Haya people. . . . So, she lives with HIV, eh! We eat her doughnuts! By God we are gone!' You know, this news spread throughout."

In the PAR sessions, the women talked frequently about why they disclosed their status and would often begin their statement by saying, "I sacrificed myself because. . . ." They said informing and protecting others was one of the main reasons they sacrificed themselves by disclosing their status. As a result of their disclosures, most faced a great deal of stigma and were affected personally, relationally, and economically. For many of these women, this was not their first major act of sacrifice as many had contracted HIV as a result of sacrificing themselves within an unequal intimate relationship.

The women's articulation of status disclosure as self-sacrifice can bring us back to Mercy Oduyoye's claim that women are not only sacrificing themselves but being sacrificed by their communities. Building on this, I suggest that one specific way stigma functions is as a form of communal sacrifice. In articulating this claim, the work of René Girard in

121

his text *Violence and the Sacred* is illuminating.[1] Girard argues that the concept of sacrifice (especially human and animal sacrifice) originated as a way to curb "mimetic rivalry" where violence always begat violence. In order to end or appease perpetual violence, a sacrifice involving a "surrogate victim" was required. This "sacred violence" then appeased the community's need for retribution, and thus, ushered in a time of peace.[2]

Using Girardian theory, I suggest that communities stigmatize certain individuals as a form of sacrifice, hoping to keep clear the line between pollution and purity. Girard argues, "As long as purity and impurity remain distinct, even the worst pollution can be washed away; but once they are allowed to mingle, purification is no longer possible."[3] By pushing people to the outskirts of the community, by separating those presumed to be infected from those presumed to be uninfected, the community could be seen as seeking to purify itself in order to salvage what life is left in the face of certain death. Because stigma is best understood as social death, this marginalization is a symbolic killing as individuals are sacrificed for the sake of the community.

Mary Douglas also takes on this topic in her book *Purity and Danger.* Here, Douglas argues that while beliefs about pollution and moral norms in a community are not congruent, they do often overlap.[4] Douglas sees the body as "model which can stand for any bounded system" and argues that its boundaries can represent "any boundaries that are threatened or precarious."[5] Drawing on Douglas' work, we can see how HIV introduced a new dynamic where threatened boundaries—such as sickness and health—were both manifested and carried by human bodies. Yet as a means of scapegoating, some bodies are more greatly burdened (or sacrificed) than others.

The parallel between stigma and sacrifice can be seen most clearly through an exploration of who is most often stigmatized. Here, we can learn a lot from looking at intimate relationships. As women are blamed for their husband's infidelity, or as they internalize the blame for their family's misfortune, their bodies become the symbolic space where boundaries are transgressed. To use Girard's term, they become the "surrogate victims" who bear the violence of HIV and AIDS. Girard's understanding of the surrogate victim as one who is not to blame for the violence can also apply to HIV and AIDS. Since HIV is primarily a sexually transmitted disease, some responsibility must rest on individuals who knowingly or unknowingly spread the disease. Yet the primary stigma is built around the person's HIV status, not whether or not they infected others. This is seen most clearly when women are stigmatized more visibly than men, even though studies have shown that 60 to 80 percent of women living with HIV and AIDS have only had one sexual partner.[6]

Douglas also theorizes that in places where male domination is secure and accepted, rules regarding sexual pollution are less likely to be present. Yet when male domination is threatened by women's indepen-

dence, rules regarding sexual pollution are developed to keep this independence in check.[7] As rules on pollution are developed, the threat of
danger replaces the actual human punishment, such as those punish-
ments that come from strictly controlled patriarchies.[8] Here, we see another parallel, as both male domination and rules concerning pollution
are present in the sub-Saharan African context. Perhaps both are being
asserted as a broken attempt to keep the contagion of HIV at bay.

Turning back to theology, we can put the work of Mercy Oduyoye in
conversation with Girard and Douglas. As previously mentioned, Oduyoye argues that in Africa, women's self-sacrifice should be separated
from their being sacrificed. She points out that different forms of sacrifice[9] have always been a part of indigenous African religions, but in the
past it was not relegated only to women but was shouldered by the
community.[10] In other words, sacrifice did not always scapegoat women.
Building on Oduyoye's critique, a postcolonial reflection would point out
that in light of colonialism and globalization, stigma might represent a
confused attempt in both assigning blame and in choosing surrogate victims. The burdens carried by women's bodies—and the sacrificing of
women's bodies—could represent the fear of threatened boundaries as
Douglas suggests.

The process of stigmatization functions by blaming the victim. It involves a process of distancing and othering as the "dominant group"
separates itself from the "out-group." Yet the distance created is a false
distance. One study of HIV and AIDS stigma in Zambia pointed out that
the dominant group holds greater responsibility for the actual spread of
the disease because the distance created allows the risk to be projected
onto the "out-group" and therefore not taken seriously.[11] In the scenario
of the African HIV pandemic, men lead the dominant group. They are
less vulnerable biologically, they are more likely to have multiple partners, and they are the least likely to volunteer for HIV testing or to disclose their status. They also experience less stigmatization and carry less
blame for the disease than women.

In reflecting on the role of men and women in myth, Girard argues
that it is adult males who, because of their responsibility in the sacrificial
crisis, are those who have the "greatest need to forget."[12] If Girard is
correct, then Oduyoye's argument that women are being sacrificed by
men carries new meaning, for it is the men who carry a greater responsibility for what has gone wrong and therefore are the ones who are
looking for a surrogate victim to symbolically (or even literally) sacrifice.

In a group meeting on stigma, one research collaborator told a story of
how he heard that another man was telling everyone that he was HIV-
positive. One night, when he was having a drink with a girl, the date
ended quickly when this same man told the girl he was with about his
positive status. The collaborator said that he was so angry that he made
up his mind to get revenge. He told the group:

> The Almighty God will forgive me, but I knew this man had a woman.
> So I made every effort to seduce this woman. Yes, what I did—may the
> Almighty God forgive me, I did not buy sex, but I had to deal with this
> man's wife. I went with her—God forgive me, God forgive me—I went
> with her because he announced me like that.[13]

By having sex with this man's wife, the collaborator intentionally attempted to spread the virus in order to get revenge on the man who wronged him. In this way, this woman literally became a surrogate victim for a dispute between two men. Her body was used as a site of violence to connect the "unaffected" man with the "affected" man whose status was disclosed.

Within the parallel between stigma and sacrifice, stigma must be understood as a failed or misguided sacrifice because its practice only incites more violence.[14] According to Girard, in order for the surrogate victimization to cease, in order for the violence of stigma to end, the true sacrificial crisis of the HIV pandemic must be identified.

I have suggested that stigma functions as sacrifice locally as individuals are pushed to the fringes of their communities through stigmatization. Yet there is also a global dimension. Africa itself, as a colonial invention, as a continent of many peoples, is stigmatized as well. Globalization has placed us in a new scenario where borders can be built or broken at the whim of political ideologies and power. Between sunrises, a free trade agreement can expire, causing multinationals to move a production facility from Lesotho to China. Globalization, like its predecessor colonialism, is dependent on sacrifice to keep the violence at home at bay. As a system of movement, it hides the means of production—the violence of blood diamonds or the labor of sweatshops. In the process, people are literally sacrificed to growing markets, which are given more "agency" than the people trapped within them.[15] The honest question must be asked: When individuals are blamed for their positive status, are those with HIV and AIDS in the Global South being sacrificed and stigmatized by the global community?

This question takes on new relevance in looking at the focus of US aid organizations and churches on behavior change as the primary form of prevention. For example, the "ABC" (abstinence, be faithful, condoms) strategy promoted by PEPFAR (The President's Emergency Plan for AIDS Response) in its inception focused prevention on sex, barely acknowledging how factors such as poverty, gender inequality, or poor health are also responsible, if not more responsible, for this pandemic. Is this a way of deflecting the blame? If the individual is solely responsible for contracting the disease, then globalization cannot be blamed for creating scenarios of poverty or limiting agency, which have opened up spaces for HIV to spread like wildfire.

In his work on public health responses to HIV and AIDS, Paul Farmer argues that we must pay attention to systems of structural violence that affect the health of the poor. Pulling from liberation theology, Farmer argues that we must have a preferential option for the poor, because "diseases themselves make a preferential option for the poor." [16] Through his organization, Partners in Health (PIH), Farmer attempts to put this preferential option into action through practicing "pragmatic solidarity." Farmer defines this concept by saying:

> Pragmatic solidarity is different from but nourished by solidarity per se, the desire to make common cause with those in need. Solidarity is a precious thing: people enduring great hardship often remark that they are grateful for the prayers and good wishes of fellow human beings. But when sentiment is accompanied by the goods and services that might diminish unjust hardship, surely it is enriched. To those in great need, solidarity without the pragmatic component can seem like so much abstract piety. [17]

An example of how pragmatic solidarity works can be seen in Farmer's experiences treating those with tuberculosis in Haiti. Within public health programs, individuals who are not able to take their medications as scheduled or return to the clinic for follow-up visits are often labeled as "noncompliant." In listening to the experiences of patients, Farmer realized that the reasons for "noncompliance" were rooted in economic hardships. When PIH began to give stipends for food and transportation through what they called an "enhanced package," the cure rate for the sample study rose to 100 percent. For those who did not get this additional support, the cure rate was barely half of the cure rate for those who did. [18]

I have detailed Farmer's methodology here to make the point that there is a place for global solidarity, but for this solidarity to work, a long listening is required. We must understand the risks and experiences of living in resource-poor settings as well as we understand the diseases that are prone to spread in these environments. We cannot talk about prevention or "risky behavior" until we understand the context in which people take risks and the factors, such as extreme poverty, that make life itself risky.

Farmer argues that in order to get to this place of pragmatic solidarity where the poor are actually helped, an analysis that is "historically deep" and "geographically broad" is required. In Haiti, Farmer reminds us that a historically deep analysis remembers that "modern-day Haitians are the descendants of a people enslaved in order to provide our ancestors with cheap sugar, coffee and cotton." A geographically broad analysis reminds us that we are all still interconnected. Farmer puts it this way, "In our increasingly interconnected world ('the world that is satisfying to us is the same world that is utterly devastating to them'), we must under-

stand that what happens to poor people is never divorced from the actions of the powerful."[19] In this way, for us to truly embrace a global
solidarity that works to end both HIV and stigma, we must recognize
both our connections and their histories if we seek to respond in a way
that is effective and just.

STIGMA AND INTIMATE RELATIONSHIPS

The issue of stigma is of particular importance to this book on HIV and
AIDS and marriage because stigma disrupts intimate relationships. Stigma not only makes status disclosure difficult and puts partners at risk,
but it also shifts the blame to women. Stigma names women as surrogate
victims as they not only bear the burdens of the HIV pandemic but also
unjustly shoulder the blame for the pandemic's spread.

The women in my fieldwork told story after story of men who did not
disclose their status. Even in the HIV support groups in Mwanza, the
women drastically outnumber the men. It is the women who test first.
The men, even if they suspect something is wrong, are less likely to test
and even less likely to disclose their status if they do test.

Joyce gave her opinion as to why men do not come forward about
their status, saying it is because they have multiple partners. She said,
"One reason why men do not come forward like women is this. That one
man has a wife inside, the house girl is also his, and his sister-in-law also
belongs to him. Outside there he has five or six cooking stones.[20] So he
thinks if he comes forward maybe those ones will be afraid of him." Joyce
went on to say that men also refuse to disclose their status or even be
tested because of all they stand to lose. She described men's behavior by
saying:

> He gets money and then he spreads that money about. Therefore that
> man will not disclose—the reason is that he has too many people of
> whom he is ashamed to come forward to. But we women—we don't
> have anyone we fear. It is your husband who died; you remain
> alone. . . . You remain alone, why shouldn't you come forward?

Here, Joyce ties the unequal ways in which men and women disclose
their status to their economic and social power. In this way, the inequalities that are already present in intimate relationships cause additional
violence when a partner chooses to not disclose their status because there
is too much to lose. This speaks volumes about what is valued. For men
who chose to hide their status, the marital relationship is not something
that they fear losing. There are other relationships and relations that are
more important.

To be honest, this is probably a safe bet. Because women often lose
power when they enter the marriage relationship, and would lose even

more power by ending the relationship, men don't have much to fear. In my fieldwork, story after story was told of women who contracted HIV from a partner, were then abandoned by that partner, but still ended up caring for him once he became sick.

For instance, there's the story of Rose, another woman who attended a focus group on stigma. When Rose found out her status in 2004 and told her husband, he became abusive. He blamed her for contracting the disease and said he was not infected. But even in the midst of this abuse, she still stayed with him and cared for him until he died of AIDS a year later. After her husband died, she moved with her children into a new place she rented from a teacher. A few years later, in 2007, she became very sick, and the landlady called her family to come and care for her. Her family came but refused to help. They said, "This one came to experience prostitution here in Mwanza, so we don't know her. She knows where she got this from." As she was abandoned by her family, Rose's landlady felt compassion and was worried about her situation. So she began to care for her. Rose said that even now, her relatives have not come back, but her landlady continues to care for her and even sponsors one of her children by paying their school fees. Rose endured abuse but still did not leave her marriage. Even after her husband died, Rose continued to experience abuse by being abandoned by her family.

The story of Rose and her landlady gives an example of a relationality that sustains health in the face of sickness and stigma. It is unfortunate that this type of relationality within marriage was considered rare and out of reach by many of the collaborators in this project. A turn to relationality is exactly what is needed to dismantle stigma. This is one place where Christian churches could really do some important work. While focusing on prevention is an important effort, Christian churches should spend less time talking about being abstinent until marriage and more time talking about relationality and relational justice within marriage relationships. Because Christian churches sanction and preside over marriage ceremonies, they have some public health work to do. By focusing on justice in all our relations, we could not only see stigma end but could come closer to seeing an end to the HIV pandemic as well.

POSTCOLONIAL THEOLOGY AND AN ETHICAL RESPONSE: AN EXERCISE IN COLLECTIVE RESPONSIBILITY

Beyond a turn toward relationality at the familial/communal level, a global response is also needed in order for stigma to be abolished. I have made the argument in this and the last chapter that stigma in sub-Saharan Africa is tied to the history of the colonized and the colonizer. In order to abolish stigma, nothing short of a paradigm shift is needed where the responsibility for the spread of HIV is carried on the wide shoulders of the global community rather than overwhelming the limited capacities of local communities. Instead of focusing the blame for HIV and AIDS on personal responsibility, we need to turn to collective responsibility and shoulder the blame together.

When HIV begins and ends with "infected" communities and we are not all "affected" by the disease, then the overwhelming stress of dealing with a devastating and life-destroying disease will always lead to stigma and the isolation it brings. A postcolonial critique brings our attention to the ways stigma has been used by the global community to avoid taking responsibility for the HIV pandemic. If HIV can be confined to the realm of individual responsibility, then communities—both global and local— are not forced to face their role in the crisis. To put it simply, prevention programs have focused primarily on individual behavior rather than on broken structural systems that have helped to fortify stigma. Many of these programs have come from developed countries via aid programs and missionary movements. Because of this, we all must carry the burdens and blame of stigma if we truly hope to eradicate it at the source.

A postcolonial theology that recognizes these connections is not a space of blame, but a hopeful, empowered space in which to discover collective responsibility. This is especially important for those in the West who seek to respond to this crisis, because a postcolonial approach can define the lines between the imperialistic "white man's burden" and the Christian love of neighbor. It can function as a communal divination for the global community, pointing out how former colonizers and former colonized play various roles in the African HIV pandemic.

Mujerista theologian Ada María Isasi-Díaz argues that "giving is an ethical behavior today only if it is understood and carried out within the context of solidarity."[21] With this we must ask where our space of solidarity will be. Is there a postcolonial solidarity that can be imagined, and if so, how will we imagine it? As I have suggested, I believe it would first involve an ethic of listening as a way of creating room for self-reflection and transformation. Isasi-Díaz tells us that solidarity begins with the oppressed who become agents of their own liberation. "The first word in this dialogue is uttered by the oppressed. The oppressors who are willing to listen and to be questioned by the oppressed begin to cease being oppressors—they become "friends" of the oppressed. Friendship, according to Isasi-Díaz, is essential to true solidarity.[22]

COLLECTIVE RESPONSIBILITY AS A COMMUNAL RESPONSE TO STIGMA

A normative ethic for addressing stigma must be an ethic of listening, solidarity, and friendship. Yet these connections are not possible without a collective responsibility that commits to shoulder the burdens of the

HIV pandemic together. Collective responsibility is still an underdeveloped category in Western Christian ethics. Most of the work on a Christian ethic of responsibility focuses on the responsibility of the individual agent. When collective responsibility is addressed, it is often within the context of social responsibility or a "community of agents" where groups are held responsible for their actions.[23] In these articulations, conceptions of responsibility have been heavily influenced by the individualism of Western philosophy.

William Schweiker articulates three theories of responsibility within Christian ethics: agential, dialogical, and social. In the agential model, responsibility is placed with the agent, or the self.[24] In both Western philosophy and theology this has been the primary location of responsibility, finding its roots in Aristotle's conceptions of praise and blame. The dialogical model extends the responsibility of the self by focusing on the demands of the other. Schweiker sees both the divine command model attributed to Karl Barth and the I-Thou-It model seen in H. Richard Niebuhr's work as part of this category.[25] In this model the focus is still on the individual agent but in relation to the other. In Barth's ethics the other is God and in Niebuhr's the "fellow-knowers." The third model identified by Schweiker is that of social responsibility, which he defines as focused on roles and identities of persons, or the responsibility of organizations.[26] This model is appropriated in Christian ethics primarily in terms of blaming corporations or groups for their irresponsibility.

Schweiker's own proposal of an "integrated Christian ethics of responsibility" adds to the conversation by taking power seriously and arguing for a Kantian understanding of individuals as ends in themselves. While Schweiker rightly argues for increased responsibility in the face of increased power, (a concept he builds from Hans Jonas' argument), he never answers the practical question of how. How can we live responsibly? How can we, to use Schweiker's argument, fulfill the imperative of responsibility and "in all actions and relations . . . respect and enhance the integrity of life before God?"[27] Perhaps Schweiker's own conceptualization of action within a "community of agents" is not enough.[28]

While the concept of the acting agent is an appropriate model for individual responsibility to those we can tangibly touch, it may not provide a strong enough connection to compel us do something about the global HIV pandemic and the stigma that accompanies it. H. Richard Niebuhr's dialogical model can provide an illustration toward this end. Niebuhr argues that the idea of responsibility is bound up in our "response." He articulates this by saying, "Responsibility affirms: 'God is acting in all actions upon you. So respond to all actions upon you as you respond to his action."[29] This standard can speak formatively in teaching us how to react to those we meet, but what about those we have never met?

These models fall short because they do not allow for responsibility when there is not a direct causal link to the individual or to the group. This leads us to ask if we have created room within a Christian ethic of responsibility for the global community to feel responsible for a history of colonization, to which we may not be directly linked, or the current state of globalization, which we may feel powerless to change. A postcolonial theology can make space for a needed collective responsibility through an analysis of how our history as colonized and colonizers shape our current discourse and interactions.

Moving beyond Christian ethics, the concept of collective responsibility has been used to attribute both blame and praise without a direct causal link. It recognizes the way ideologies and histories can create unstable environments that become a factor in both collective and individual actions. Philosopher Larry May uses this theory to establish a link between racist attitudes and hate crimes,[30] and Hannah Arendt used collective responsibility to identify the "co-responsibles" in the Holocaust as those who were sympathetic to Hitler's regime.[31] Hans Jonas makes an important contribution to an ethic of responsibility by arguing that responsibility is increased with power.[32] When the idea of collective responsibility without a direct causal link is added to a postcolonial Christian ethic, new space is created for us to be "co-responsibles" in the African HIV pandemic. And in becoming a "co-responsible," we can find a place for hope and change. As we take responsibility for the sins of our governments and churches, the burden of blame will be shifted resulting in a new awareness of co-factors in the spread of the HIV pandemic.

The possibility of collective responsibility offers the greatest hope of change for issues like HIV and AIDS, which affect us at a macro-level. For it is in the process of shouldering responsibility together, in recreating communities who claim *"I am because we are,"* that we will find the greatest hope for ending stigma, and even ending HIV and AIDS. Collective responsibility teaches us to ask: Who benefits from stigma, and who is saved by its sacrifice? It then teaches us how to end the sacrifice of the few by distributing the burdens among the many.

From the perspective of the Christian tradition, it has always been the responsibility of everyone to protect the most vulnerable. In the Hebrew Scriptures, commandments and covenants were given to the community who either kept them or broke them together. The prophets were called to remind the people that defending the poor, the stranger, and the orphan was the only way to participate in the life of God. And in the Christian New Testament, Jesus announced his own mission by saying he had come to "proclaim release to the captive" and "let the oppressed go free."[33] When the vulnerable were not defended, when their cries were ignored, the entire community came under judgment. In Matthew 28 the gospel writer tells a story of "all the nations" being gathered. They are judged based on how they reacted to the hungry, the stranger, the sick, the captive, those who were without. In the story, the "Son of Man" sees the rejection of these people as a rejection of himself.[34]

Yet somewhere in Western Christian traditions, conceptions of individual sin and salvation have replaced the idea of collective responsibility and judgment. Responsibility has been relegated primarily to known relationships of the agent and any action that crosses these boundaries is done not out of responsibility, but charity. Perhaps this is why Reinhold Neibhur believed that even when assuming responsibility beyond our borders, our action would be confined to the realm of "generosity," not justice.[35] The language of foreign policy speaks the same message as we choose where to give "aid" and how international aid can be used. This aid is not seen as a responsibility, but as a gift. Liberation theologies have reminded both church and state that charity fixes few problems. Instead, a recognition of structural sin and a "preferential option for the poor" is necessary to readjust what has gone wrong in the world.[36]

Far away from the burdens of the African AIDS pandemic, how can the unaffected use responsibility as a basis for their response? Most Americans, busy with grocery lists and soccer practice and teaching Sunday school will never see the stories of women in Tanzania as a call to action on their lives. Because of this, they may not feel a responsibility to respond. Reaching beyond our borders may require a new appropriation of collective responsibility that emphasizes the deep interconnectedness of our actions and responses in relation to the world.

CONCLUSION

In articulating a postcolonial feminist interpretation of stigma, I have argued that colonialism, neocolonialism, and globalization have weakened African community structures which promoted health and in doing so have created space for stigma to spread alongside HIV and AIDS. I have attempted to paint some broad postcolonial feminist strokes around four key aspects of stigmatization by articulating the ways in which stigma functions on global and local levels through fear; silence and secretkeeping; taboo and sin; and sacrifice. I have also given examples from my fieldwork that show how stigma impacts intimate relationships and have argued that Christian churches should focus on just relations in intimate relationships as means of promoting prevention. I have also argued that a postcolonial feminist interpretation of stigma demands a normative Christian ethic that turns to collective responsibility as a way of addressing the issues HIV and AIDS in our world.

The idea of collective responsibility opens space for the burdens carried by individuals to be shouldered by the entire community. It holds the promise of ending stigma's violence as the community absorbs the violence of HIV and AIDS rather than scapegoating its victims. It also holds the greatest potential for solidarity as it asks us to own up to our part in both the history of oppression and the current state of globalization. Postcolonial theology asks us to speak the truth about the complexity of our history. If global and local communities are not silent about the forces that have created stigma, then the collaborators in this study and all who follow might find a safe space imagined by solidarity. And in this space, they might just find the freedom to speak their own truth and end stigma.

NOTES

1. It is important, especially in the context of using Girard's work to interpret stigma in African communities, to reject his underlying myth of progress. Girard contrasts "primitive" religions and "primordial" religions with Judaism and Christianity, suggesting that the latter were more advanced than the primordial religions from which they originated, yet this premise is imperialistic at its root. To put Girard's work in dialogue with African philosophy and religion, this premise must be rejected in order not to diminish the credibility of African indigenous religions. While Girard's work is helpful in articulating the way sacrifice (and I suggest stigma) functions, I would argue that the distinctions made between so-called "primitive" and modern religions may not be as clear as Girard might like to believe. I would also argue that any understanding of African indigenous religions as "primitive" or "primordial" is imperialistic and unfounded.

2. Rene Girard, *Violence and the Sacred,* (Baltimore: Johns Hopkins University Press, 1979), 30–33.

3. Ibid., 38.

4. Mary Douglas, Purity and Danger: An Analysis of Concepts of Pollution and Taboo, (New York: Routledge, 2003), 153–65.

5. Ibid., 135.

6. Aylward Shorter and Edwin Onyancha, *The Church and AIDS in Africa — A Case Study: Nairobi City,* (Nairobi: Paulines Publications Africa, 1998), 116.

7. Douglas., 168–69.

8. Ibid., 159.

9. In this article, Oduyoye is not referring to human or animal sacrifice, (to distinguish her usage from Girard's usage) but sacrifice defined as giving up something for the greater good of the community.

10. Oduyoye, "Church-Women and the Church's Mission in Contemporary Times," 259–72.

11. Bond, *et al.,* 4.

12. Girard, 139.

13. The Kiswahili phrase that here translates "went with her" (*" Nimetembea naye"*) is a euphemism for having sex with someone.

14. One reading of Girard is that sacrifice as he describes it is also ultimately a failure. While the surrogate victim could bring temporary peace through ritual violence, Girard does not suggest that these sacrificial acts brought any lasting peace. He ultimately sees this as the importance of Christianity, that it provides a final sacrifice, (in the form of Jesus' death), which could end ritual violence. For an extensive theological analysis of Girard's claims, see S. Mark Heim, *Saved from Sacrifice: A Theology of the Cross,* (Grand Rapids: William B. Eerdmans Pub. Co., 2006).

15. For more on this line of thought see, Patrick Bond, *Looting Africa: The Economics of Exploitation,* (London: ZED Books, 2006).

16. Paul Farmer, *Pathologies of Power: Health, Human Rights and the New War on the Poor,* (Los Angeles, CA: University of California Press, 2003), 140.

17. Ibid., 146.

18. Ibid., 150–51.

19. Ibid., 158.

20. In some ethnic groups in Tanzania, girls are told that you need three stones to build a place for cooking so they should keep three men to provide for them. Joyce hints that men keep double the amount of women as women keep men.

21. Isasi-Díaz, 32.

22. Ibid.

23. One example is found in the work of William Schweiker who uses the phrase "community of agents." Schweiker envisions a collective responsibility, but because it is causally linked to the individual agent, it might not be broad enough to encompass a person's responsibility toward people they have never met. See William Schweiker, *Responsibility and Christian Ethics*, (New York: Cambridge University Press, 1995). Another view can be found in H.R. Neibuhr who speaks of responsibility by saying, "'God is acting in all actions upon you," but his conception does not necessarily embrace the idea of collective responsibility but rests only with the acting agent. See H. Richard Niebuhr, *The Responsible Self*, (Louisville: Westminster John Knox Press, 1963), 126.

24. William Schweiker, *Responsibility and Christian Ethics*, (New York: Cambridge University Press, 1995), 78.

25. Ibid, 94–105.

26. Ibid,93.

27. Ibid, 125.

28. Schweiker sees responsibility as focused on the agent but does identify with a view close to H. Richard Niebuhr's by speaking of a "community of agents" (See Schweiker, 151). Here, he also reflects the Kantian notion of a "kingdom of ends" (See Schweiker, 80).

29. H. Richard Niebuhr, *The Responsible Self*, (Louisville: Westminster John Knox Press, 1963), 126

30. Larry May, *Sharing Responsibility*, (Chicago: University of Chicago Press, 1992).

31. Hannah Arendt, "Organized Guilt and Universal Responsibility," in *Collective Responsibility*, ed. Larry May and Stacey Hoffman, (Savage, Maryland: Rowman & Littlefield, 1991), 273–83.

32. Hans Jonas, *The Imperative of Responsibility*, (Chicago: University of Chicago Press, 1984).

33. Luke 4:18, NRSV.

34. Matthew 25:31–46.

35. Reinhold Niebuhr, An Interpretation of Christian Ethics, 105.

36. See Gustavo Guttierrez, *A Theology of Liberation*, (Maryknoll: Orbis Books, 1973).

EIGHT

Reimagining Christian Marriage in the Midst of a Pandemic

Marriage has always been risky. When two people enter into an exclusive partnership, there is always the possibility that one (or both) of the people involved won't live up to their end of the deal, putting the relationship and those in it at risk. When vows are exchanged, there is always the potential that they will be broken. These risks are inherent in any intimate partnership. Yet, in places where marriage partners play by rules based on gender and structural inequalities, marriage is even riskier.

In East Africa, marriage is not only simply risky; sometimes it is outright dangerous. For the twelve women that participated in the PAR study, nine contracted HIV within their marriages despite their being faithful to their partners. Two other women contracted HIV through transactional sex after their marriages ended. The final collaborator (who was single) contracted HIV when her boyfriend was unfaithful.

On the basis of this small study and on other literature from the region, it is reasonable to hypothesize that the primary reason marriage in East Africa is dangerous for women is that men are unfaithful.[1] UNDP and UNAIDS confirmed this in a 2001 study which indicated that 80 percent of all infected married women contracted the virus from their partners.[2]

Moreover, marriage is not only life-threatening for women because of unfaithfulness, but when the marriage ends, whether through death, separation, or in civil divorce, women are often left with few options or resources for survival. There is rarely an equal (or even unequal) division of the marital assets. And if the woman is the one who leaves the marriage, her family is responsible for repaying the *mahari* (or bridewealth) to the husband.

While marriage in East Africa (and much of sub-Saharan Africa) has become increasingly dangerous, the faith-based prevention messages remain the same. Many Christian churches tell women to be abstinent until marriage and faithful within marriage.[3] This message creates the illusion that marriage will be a safe space, when nothing could be further from the truth. In this way, Christian marriage as it is practiced creates an even riskier scenario as the real dangers of infidelity within marriage are obscured, rather than addressed. Additionally, pronouncements and conceptualizations of Christian marriage in East Africa tend to reinforce strict gender roles while counseling women to obey their husbands.[4] This patriarchal practice limits women's agency, especially regarding sexual activity and the use of prophylactic measures against STDs within these patriarchal forms of marriage.

Yet despite these shortcomings, the women in this study saw Christian marriage as a potentially liberative practice. Only three of the women in the study had been married in a church. The rest had been married traditionally or informally. However, even the women who were not married in a church still attended church on a regular basis before and after their marriage. In this way, they said the teachings of their churches influenced their conceptions of marriage. This illustrates the complexity of modern day Africa where many people live between multiple co-existing worldviews as they are influenced by tradition, multiple religious traditions including Christianity, and modernity.

While all of the women in the study identified as Christian and almost all attended church regularly, not all were able to have a "Christian wedding." Joyce and Scholastica reported that they were unable to be married in a Catholic church because their husbands were not Catholic.[5] Maria said if her marriage had been a Christian marriage, it would have been better. Christine, who was a Roman Catholic when she married but later joined a Pentecostal church, also thought her marriage would have been better if she had been married in church. She said,

> I would have liked it if my marriage had been a church marriage. It would have been a peaceful marriage of two people who know God . . .
> I was saved after my husband died while I was sick, during a time of many tribulations. That is when I decided to get saved. Maybe if we had been in a Christian marriage, we would not have had these problems.

The women saw Christian marriage as a more liberative practice than traditional marriage because Christian marriage encouraged men to be faithful and to love their wives. In this way, Christian marriage offered something that according to the women traditional marriage did not.

Despite their bad experiences of marriage, almost all of the collaborators in the PAR study believed women should obey their husbands. They equated this with Christian teaching but simultaneously gave examples from tradition about why it was important to obey one's husband. When asked, ten of the twelve women said it was important for wives to obey their husbands. Four of these women qualified their statement by saying that while obedience was important, it must be matched with respect and love from the husband. When pressed, they made exceptions, saying that women who were being abused should not have to obey but should appeal to the elders or to someone outside the marriage for help. The women believed Christian marriage could be seen as a liberative practice because the command to obey was met with a second command for husbands to love their wives "as Christ loved the Church."[6] While none of the women believed that a Christian marriage would have solved all their problems, they did see Christianity as having tremendous potential for reforming marriage practices and making marriage a safer space for women.

SPEAKING NORMATIVELY: WHAT SHOULD MARRIAGE BE?

Speaking normatively is a complicated but necessary endeavor. Yet, in light of my experiences learning from these women, I am profoundly aware that when women are risking their lives for the sake of their relationships, there is no longer any morally neutral space in which the descriptive onlooker can stand. Even so, when one speaks normatively one always risks being wrong. While as a researcher I am critical of missionary movements that imposed Western interpretations of Christian marriage on African societies without carefully considering the cultural ramifications, I realize that the same possibility for overstepping is potentially present in my own work. For even when one attempts to speak in solidarity with others, there is always the possibility of misunderstanding and misinterpretation.

As I attempt to move forward by speaking normatively, I will do so carefully, seeking to first listen to the women who are the heart of this study. As I have throughout this book, I will attempt to let these women speak through their own words as often as possible. Further, I will differentiate between their direct recommendations and what I believe I can recommend after listening to and analyzing the field research and triangulating it with other relevant data and theological literature. Finally, I admit that I will not always agree with the women in this study as to their recommendations or opinions about Christian marriage. We come from varying social locations and have spent differing amounts of time thinking philosophically and theologically about marriage. Our lived experiences are different. For this reason, when I speak normatively in ways that diverge from the opinions of the women in this study, I will note these differences, and when possible, seek to explain them.

While speaking normatively is not an easy endeavor, it is an important one, especially in a postcolonial Christian context. As a theologian who identifies as Christian, I admit that the faith that nurtured me is also part of the problem. Current Christian practices surrounding marriage in East Africa have failed to make marriage safer for women. In fact, the normative speech of the past has even created problems for the present.[7] For this reason, to borrow a phrase from postcolonial theory, I believe it is important for African women *to speak back* normatively from their lived experiences. I hope this *speaking back* will be accomplished in some degree in retelling their stories and in citing their normative claims. Yet, because the focus of this book is listening to the lived experiences of women in Tanzania, it must be noted that this particular project is not universally normative but contextually normative. While there will be pieces of this work that apply to multiple cultural contexts, the primary audience for this work is Christian churches and congregants in East Africa and those who attempt to work interculturally in the East African context.

Why Marriage?

Before we begin to talk about *what marriage should be*, I believe it is necessary to first ask *whether or not marriage should be*. As John Mbiti argues, in African contexts, marriage is an expectation for everyone.[8] While in the West some individuals might choose not to marry,[9] traditionally this choice has been rare in sub-Saharan Africa. However, in light of the HIV pandemic, more women are choosing to remain single. This is a trend that is becoming prevalent in places such as South Africa. Here, women still want to have children but are choosing to do so while remaining unmarried because of the risks associated with marriage.[10] One example of this is seen in migrant-based industries such as mining, which have created a culture where men spend long periods away from their families. When the men do return home, they often do so having contracted HIV in the mining camps.[11] South African theologian Philippe Denis reflected on the effects of migrant-based industries such as this saying, "For large numbers of people, the institution of marriage is not threatened: it has simply ceased to exist."[12]

Similarly, many of the women in this study were adamant about not wanting to remarry. Agnes and Esther, the youngest members in the group, said they still hoped to remarry one day, but most of the women did not share their sentiment. Joan, who chose not to marry the father of her children, said that not being married gave her freedom. Reflecting on the fact that many women in South Africa are choosing not to marry, she said,

> I can believe this because maybe someone hears the history of a certain person who married a husband, but he troubles her, he doesn't love her. It means he is not faithful; he has affairs. Now you find this thing enters someone's mind very much and she thinks, if I get married, this person is going to trouble me. So I shall give birth only so that I can also be seen as someone who has a child, but I should not marry. [13]

Joan valued her freedom and decided not to lose this freedom for the sake of marriage. In this and similar situations, the decision not to marry (or not to remarry) is an example of women exerting agency over a culture with double standards regarding sexual fidelity in marriage and that expects wifely submission.

From their example, we must ask whether or not marriage as it is practiced should be considered a moral good at all. If traditional marriage with its double standard regarding sexual fidelity has put wives at risk, can it be redeemed? And can Christian churches participate in this redemption even if they have turned a blind eye to patriarchy for so long? Or instead, if traditional or Christian marriage limits women's ability to protect herself from STDs then we should ask, should marriage be abandoned?

As we seek to answer these questions, a lesson can be learned by momentarily turning away from the heteronormative context of East Africa. [14] Some theologians in the West writing on same-sex marriage have questioned whether the institution of marriage itself is worth defending. Mary E. Hunt argues that because marriage is a hegemonic institution, it will not necessarily lead us toward the common good or greater relational justice. [15] Marvin Ellison continues Hunt's argument by saying that marriage is problematic because it has always been about the regulation of sex as well as a "means of male control over women's lives." [16] Emilie Townes raises the issue of commitment in marriage, arguing that the institution of marriage enforces structures that keep a marriage going long after it should have ended. [17] Townes calls this "bad sequencing" and says, "If we can talk about, think through, and live through relationality and commitment, then marriage might flow more naturally than it does." [18]

All of these theologians challenge the elevation of marriage as the primary form of commitment for relationships. Hunt argues that we might be better off eliminating the language of marriage altogether and proposes the terms "relationship-based contracts" and "religiously connected commitment ceremonies" as alternatives. [19] Interestingly enough, the women in this study, as I will later show, also resonated with the language of contracts when rethinking marriage.

Returning to the African context, Signe Arnfred argues that Christian marriage is problematic because it undergirds both heteronormativity and entrenched gender roles. She says:

The importance of marriage, in Christian as well as in Muslim contexts, points to the shared axioms of heteronormativity, and also of male/ female double standards, pillars of patriarchy. . . . Acknowledgement of same-sex relations . . . pulls the carpet from under such axioms, implicitly endangering patriarchal power.

Arnfred goes on to argue that same-sex practices have always existed in Africa though they have not always existed as "identities."[20] In other words, while traditionally (and even today) people do not often identify as gay or lesbian, same-sex orientation and sexual activity has always been present in African cultures. Yet, because procreation is the goal of marriage and of heterosexual relationships, homosexuality exists concurrently with heterosexual relationships. Here, Arnfred makes the distinction between sex for pleasure and sex for procreation.[21]

As we consider the question of "why marriage?" a rethinking of the original purpose of marriage is in order. In both African and Western contexts, marriage was originally instituted for the community. In reflecting on this within the context of Western history, Margaret Farley argues that, "In the beginning of Western civilization and for a long part of its history, marriage was undertaken primarily to meet the needs of families and kinship groups—economic, political, and social needs."[22] The same argument is made from an African perspective by Laurenti Magesa who says, "The survival of kinship in the social structure of Africa depends on marriage. . . . In the long run, marriage always establishes very strong bonds between the individuals belonging to different families and clans, particularly when children are born."[23] In thinking through the idea of marriage originating for the community, we can ask the question of whether or not marriage still protects and contributes to the community.

Because marriage has become a risk factor for HIV, it now threatens the community rather than contributing to its survival. Yet, even so, marriage itself is not blame but the lack of communal protection for marriage. If marriage was taken more seriously, if the original intentions were guarded more closely, then perhaps marriage could again become an institution that provides for communal flourishing.

This in itself poses a compelling reason for faithfulness in that the original intention of marriage cannot be fulfilled when marriage becomes a space of risk. A refocusing on marriage for the sake of community can also challenge patriarchal allowances for men having multiple partners as this threatens not only women but the entire family and clan. In this way, incorporating an African worldview on marriage within the African context might provide the most compelling reason for protecting marriage by encouraging faithfulness. With this context in mind, marriage should not only be seen as a space of danger but a space of hope. In returning to the original intention of marriage as a way to ensure "survival of kinship"[24] we quickly realize that in not protecting marriage, we are participating in communal suicide.

The Purpose of Marriage in the East African Context

With this in mind, we can begin to look deeper into the purpose of marriage in the East African context. When the women in this study were asked the reason for marriage, their first response was "children." In sub-Saharan Africa, marriage is for community, and the expected outcome of marriage is children. Other reasons for marriage included love and companionship, but these were not identified among the primary reasons for marrying.

When asked if sexual pleasure was a factor in marriage, the women responded that for many women, sex within marriage is not pleasurable. Obed Kealotswe, a pastor and theologian from Botswana confirms the women's reflections by saying, "The general nature and belief is that women are made for men, and they have to satisfy the sexual desires of men."[25] In this way, it can be argued that sex within marriage is considered to be for procreation and men's pleasure while women's pleasure is not a consideration.

Some of the women in the study identified the unitive dimension of marriage but placed it as secondary in importance to the procreative dimension. This could be because in East Africa, if the procreative dimension is not present, the unitive dimension never has a chance to form as the marriage is quickly ended. In her article, "A Coming Home to Myself," Mercy Oduyoye talks about her own experience of not being able to bear children. She talks about the stigma she experienced as a result of being childless and how her other contributions—such as her education and work for the church, or her caring for other children in her family—were diminished in light of her childlessness. Oduyoye, a Methodist, faults Christian churches for being silent, for not speaking out on behalf of those who experience infertility.[26] Oduyoye says:

> On marriage and childbearing the Christian church is often as unswerving as the Hebrew and African religions and cultures. . . . There is no empowering word and no ceremony to strengthen what may, for many reasons, turn out to be a childless marriage. On this the church is at best simply silent. . . . The general taunting of the community is reflected in sermons from our pulpits. Whether intentionally or not, the church participates in blaming (the woman) and casting stones. . . .[27]

Oduyoye reminds us that when Christian churches are silent, they are complicit in the suffering of women. Extending Oduyoye's argument, we can ask whether an expansion of the purpose of marriage would be one way of making marriage a safer space for women.

In light of the primary focus on procreation and male pleasure within marital sex, we can begin to understand why marriage has become an unsafe space for women. While a high valuing of procreation originally protected the community by ensuring life would continue, today it can endanger life as some women risk their lives to have children at any cost. In the same way, a focus on male pleasure without equal consideration of female pleasure limits women's ability to negotiate sex. Ugandan Catholic theologian Therese Tinkasiimire reminds us that women are often unable to negotiate sex because of cultural practices such as *mahari* (or bridewealth).[28] Tinkasiimire says:

> Symbolically, this payment deprives the woman of the ownership of her sexuality; the man owns her sexuality and has unlimited access to her for sexual relations. She cannot deny him anything. She is expected, per the payment, to make herself available on his demand. She is culturally powerless to defend or protect herself, and any request on her part for a condom creates the suspicion that she has been unfaithful. She fears to raise the request, since it can easily end in divorce or violence.[29]

In light of this, a refocusing of marriage is needed. The original intent of procreation as a way to guard life can be expanded as we consider not only future children but also the parents who will raise them. In the midst of this pandemic, protecting life must become more than just having children but protecting the entire community. A focus on procreation could be expanded to include encouraging male fidelity and eliminating traditional practices that endanger women.

Though most of the women in the study were Roman Catholic, very few knew about the Catholic Church's articulation of the dual purpose of marriage—that it should be both unitive and procreative. An expansion of the unitive purpose of marriage could be a helpful starting place in a rearticulation of a theology of marriage in East Africa. In many ways, this focus within Catholic theology fits well with the African conception that marriage is for community.

Unfortunately, within the African context, the primary understanding of the unitive dimension of marriage is expressed in the concept of male-female complementarity. Conceptions of complementarity have been well inculturated into African Catholic theology, and it even appears in Protestant conceptions of marriage.[30] For example, the women in this study—who were primarily Catholic and Anglican—frequently talked about men and women as having separate but complementary roles within marriage. It is possible that this particular theology is well accepted in the African context because it fits with traditional understandings of gender roles within marriage. Examples of this include the idea that women are responsible for working inside the home, whereas men are responsible for work outside,[31] or that women are responsible for procreation to the extent that they are even blamed for men's impotence when children are not born.[32] As these examples show, if the unitive purpose of marriage is only expressed in terms of male-female complementarity, then the Church will only be trading one oppressive patriarchy for another.

CHRISTIAN MARRIAGE IN AFRICA IN POSTCOLONIAL PERSPECTIVE

In order to think about how to make marriage a safer space for women, it is important to think first about marriage as it is and as it was. Marriage in sub-Saharan Africa exists in postcolonial space. It is a mix of tradition and modernity, yet it is still deeply formed by the period of colonial rule. Christian marriage was introduced in sub-Saharan Africa as part of the colonial project. Among other things, it was a way of regulating behavior and subduing subjects. For this reason, it is important that we begin by looking back in order to allow us to listen more fully to lived experience as we look forward.

Looking Back: Traditional Marriage and Early Missionary Movements

When we look back on the ways in which marriage functioned (and to some extent still functions) in sub-Saharan Africa, we must begin with a recognition that marriage was (and still is) for the community. While love and compatibility have often been desirable traits to be shared among marriage partners, marriage has always been about something more. In the African context, the purpose of marriage almost always revolves around the community and the desire to enrich the community through procreation.[33]

To further explore the argument that marriage for is the sake of community, we only need to look at the types of marriages present in sub-Saharan Africa and the ways in which marriages are initiated within these communities. The first thing we can say about marriage in sub-Saharan Africa is that everyone is expected to marry. John Mbiti describes marriage as "a normal rhythm of life through which everyone must go."[34] Those who do not marry, or at least those who do not have children, are seen as existing outside of the community and are often stigmatized.[35]

Second, for many ethnic groups in sub-Saharan Africa, strict rules have been created to prohibit incest, exogamy (marrying outside of one's ethnic group), or pregnancy outside of marriage. The goal of these rules, which vary by clan, is to ensure that marriages fulfill the aim of enriching the community.[36] Mbiti describes marriage by saying:

Marriage is not just an affair of two individuals alone: it brings together
families, relatives and friends from each side of the partnership. This is
the case both in our traditional life and in the changing type of life. You
do not just marry one man or one woman: you marry the relations of
your partner. . . . The radius of kinship extends very wide, and on
getting married you bring together the many hundreds of other people
who fall within your radii of existence. . . . Ultimately, society makes
your marriage a marriage or otherwise, and you cannot get away from
that.[37]

The social dimension of marriage is so important that poor family relations are often reason enough not to marry. Joan, who was the only PAR
collaborator who never married, decided not to marry the father of her
children in a formal ceremony because his family spoke ill of her. After
the birth of her first child, her fiancé's sister came to visit but always
returned home with bad things to say about Joan. While the sister had
been perfectly kind while she was visiting, the things she said later made
Joan distrust the family. Though she was planning to marry, because of
this she instead entered into an informal marriage. She called her partner
"husband" because he was the father of her three children, but *mahari*
was never given and a formal marriage never took place. This resulted in
the marriage not being recognized by either family.

We can further see the communal purpose of marriage when we look
at the different types of marriage. Polygamous marriages are one example. In these marriages, the goal is to enrich the community through
procreation and to create wealth through an abundance of offspring. Similarly, widow inheritance, ghost marriages, wife-sharing, and woman-to-
woman marriages are all arrangements made for the sake of procreation.
Even monogamous marriages can be easily dissolved if no children are
born of the union.[38]

In one sense, marriage for the sake of the community could be seen as
a praiseworthy goal. Yet in communities that are patriarchal, marriage
rarely honors women as ends in themselves. To be more precise, it could
be said that marriage in sub-Saharan Africa as it is currently practiced in
both patriarchal Christian and patriarchal traditional forms is not primarily for the sake of the whole community, but rather it is primarily for the
benefit of men in the community. The women in this study named multiple ways men benefited from marriage including having women cook for
them and work in the farm, proving masculinity via their prodigy, exerting control over women's sexuality (and therefore ensuring male pleasure), and enjoying unchallenged power within the relationship. If marriage is to truly live up to the African ideal of being for the community,
then it must be for the entire community as it seeks the flourishing of
women as well as men.

When marriage serves patriarchal aims, it severely limits women's
agency. This is seen not only through limitations on women's abilities to

negotiate sexual agency, but it extends to other matters as well. Wives have less spending power than their husbands because of limited economic opportunities and even less free time because of their responsibilities at home. As previously mentioned, women have more to lose if the marriage fails and therefore are not in a position to challenge their husband's decisions. These factors limit the decisions women can make regarding their own well-being and the well-being of their children.

Women are also asked to put the needs of the community always first in their decision-making, even if it means neglecting their own needs and desires. An example of this can be seen again through procreation, where women are expected to have children even if it endangers their lives through complications. Women are also asked to begin a marriage or remain in bad marriages so the family can benefit from *mahari* payments.

With the advent of colonialism and early missionary movements, marriage began to change but not necessarily for the better. Early Christian marriage in sub-Saharan Africa also had community as a goal but served the aims of creating a new Christian community rather than benefiting the family or clan.[39] While the goal of creating Christian community was certainly well-intentioned, it disrupted existing family systems as individual converts were forced to chose between their church family and the clan. Bujo argues that the arrival of Western Christianity changed marriage from a communal relationship to a private relationship between two individuals.[40] Perhaps the biggest problem in the change in marriage from traditional to Christian systems was that the early missionaries did not seek to inculturate the Christian message in the African context but instead worked to replace one patriarchal system with another. In this way, valuable insights from African culture that could have complemented Christian theology were neglected.

Early missionaries to Africa saw regulating marriage and sexuality as key to keeping new converts converted.[41] Toward this end, they introduced (or redefined) concepts such as fidelity and sought to change marriage by outlawing polygamous unions.[42] Missionaries reshaped marriage by shifting an oral tradition to written records, whereby missionaries asked parishioners to live up to their recorded commitments to be faithful or to marry only one wife.[43]

Marriage was also changed as missionaries encouraged converts to not only marry other converts but to live and work at the mission station.[44] This shift pushed marriage out of communal structures rather than seeking to reform troubling marriage practices within the context of the community.[45] In this way, missionaries limited the influence family members (especially fathers and brothers) could exercise over the new couple. In his work on the history of marriage in Tanzania, Derek Peterson describes early Christian marriage practices in East Africa by saying:

Missionaries believed that the bond between husband and wife took precedence over all other relationships. They ruled that no polygamist could be admitted to the catechumenate unless he separated from all of his wives except the one he had married first. Many people found this paring down of their human relationships to be dangerously antisocial.[46]

Of course, this version of Christian marriage was an inherently Western interpretation of Christian practice. By setting up Christian marriage as an individual commitment, rather than a commitment grounded within existing communal structures, early missionaries missed an important opportunity to transform marriage in Africa into a life-giving institution. Instead, they offered one form of patriarchal marriage to replace another. While Christianity made important contributions in challenging the double standard of sexual fidelity, it ultimately failed to truly transform marriage because it, like many African traditional forms of marriage, did not challenge patriarchy.

Looking Forward: Listening to Lived Experience

The women in this study tended to approach the idea of Christian marriage in a more holistic way. They believed that because Christianity pushed one to be a better person, Christian marriages would naturally be better because the marriage partners would attempt to live out Christian virtues. As a Western researcher who came to my own convictions about marriage reading feminist theologies, I found it interesting that some aspects of Christian teaching that I rejected—such as its call to mutual obedience in marriage, or the significance of Eve being formed from Adam's side—were seen as liberative by the women in this study.

Joyce, who married a Muslim and was unable to marry in the church, believed that a Christian marriage would have saved her heartache. She said:

> In my opinion, Christian marriages have made a difference and have done so to a great extent. It is clear that a person who has a Christian wedding is educated, a person who knows God. One who is still involved in traditional customs is the complete opposite of the Christian. You will find that traditional marriages and Christian marriages are different as the Christian marriage is more peaceful. The husband knows that the woman is his rib, a part of his life, but in a traditional marriage he sees the woman as a servant, a person to just give birth to children, to just work for him in the farm. He takes the woman as a slave as opposed to the Christian who takes the wife as a part of him. Therefore there is a very big difference.

Others said that Christian marriages were more respected than traditional marriages and they provided more rights to the woman as it prevented some of the problems with *mahari* (or bridewealth). Esther said:

Christian marriages can protect the woman and provides her rights as a woman. Also in the case of a Christian marriage, my parents cannot take back *mahari* in order to dissolve the marriage. If it was the customary marriage then they would easily do that and it brings the marriage to an end.

Grace echoed Joyce and Esther's comments by telling her own story. She said:

I could give an example of my own case. My marriage was the customary one, not the Christian one. Therefore in my case when my husband looks at me he does not see anything that binds him to me. I also do not see anything that is binding me to him. On the other hand if it is a Christian marriage, the wedding is done in the presence of many people in church and these people and God are your witnesses. You also vow in the presence of these people and God. Therefore it becomes very difficult to walk away from such a marriage and before you do it you must give it a second thought wondering is it right for me to do this? But if it is the customary marriage, if things become very tough for you, you can just walk away or he can walk away leaving you, as there is nothing binding you.

Here, Grace was arguing that making a vow to God was a vow that should be taken seriously. While it is *mahari* that binds a couple in a traditional marriage, she believed it was the vows taken before God that seals a Christian marriage.

Jesca, the only woman in the group who was still married, didn't think Christian marriage made much of a difference. Jesca was married in a church, and her marriage was not the idealistic scenario that the other women were describing. When I asked if Christian marriages could help make marriage a safer space for women, she said:

As far as I can see the church will do very little because it will give you the ethics you should follow, and make sure you both unite, but after staying together we shall change. We shall go to test for HIV before marrying, because for us Catholics that is compulsory,[47] for you to go and to test and to bring the results. And yes, indeed, you will be married, but even then, we have already accomplished it. We have already stayed together.

For Jesca, while the church gave "ethics," it didn't prevent people from co-habiting before marriage nor did provide a compelling enough argument to keep people faithful within marriage. In other words, Jesca did not see the church as making a real difference in a person's moral formation. Jesca's marriage was an informal marriage for two years before she and her husband made it official through a church ceremony. But this decision to have a church wedding did not keep her safe. Her husband still went outside the marriage, and she contracted HIV as a result. For Jesca and other women in the study, a primary frustration with their churches was that they preached fidelity without actually confronting men about their infidelities. While they understood that a Christian marriage could not guarantee fidelity, they still thought the churches could do more, especially in regard to holding men accountable.

Christine, who attended a Pentecostal church, thought that Christian marriage did make a difference:

> In my view, I look at it this way. I think the church is a safe place for marriage because we get good ethical codes of conduct. Therefore if we follow the behavior of Christ, it will be safe because no one will go outside (the marriage). (If someone does go outside the marriage) it means we haven't followed what the Bible says.

Grace disagreed with Christine. While Grace believed that her marriage would have been better and more binding if it had been a Christian marriage, she did not believe a Christian marriage would make marriage safer, because the church itself was not a safe place. She said:

> Regarding the question of whether the church a safe place for women in regard to marriage—I can say it is not. Because if we look at it, even the church has nowadays been infiltrated by strange, strange things . . . Priests rape—I don't know, they do shocking things . . . if you investigate the church you find that a pastor is moving around with a certain lady. Therefore you find it right in here. In here, the pastor has the virus; the Bishop also dies of AIDS. Therefore, where to do we turn? So I see that the church is also not a safe place to stay. It is not a safe place but it should be a safe place for us to turn. Yet, if we look at the church, we still don't know where to turn.

Grace believed that the biggest problem with marriage in the church was that people did not take the vows they made seriously. She said:

> As for now things have changed. We get married when people have already moved around with each other.[48] You are already tired of each other. Now it means you swear in front of the Almighty God, but there is nothing you are swearing because you are already used to one another. Some get married while they are pregnant. The pregnancy is there but they exchange the veil. Therefore, I think the church should find another way to change the law. This oath should be changed. Because if we look at it, a great percentage of people do not fulfill their promises. They don't fulfill them at all. Maybe 25 percent, but as for 75 percent really there is nothing there at all.

Others believed it was not the church that needed to change marriage, but that people simply weren't living up to the church's vision of marriage. Mama Gasabile put it this way: "Marriage was taken from the Bible. Since ancient times marriage was there. Therefore I don't think the solution is for the church to change the system of marriage. There is a problem somewhere, but it is not in the church." Joyce echoed Mama Gasabile's comments. She said:

> When the church conducts your marriage, you two have agreed saying,
> "We love each other, let us go to get married." Therefore the church
> only implements your ideas, they complete your ideas. If, in the future
> things go wrong, that is not the fault of the church. It is the fault of the
> two of you who have cheated God. You have said, "We love each other
> today, but tomorrow I am going to refuse." Yet, you went to the church
> and took an oath that you love each other. Now what do you expect the
> church to do? You went to tell them that you love each other and that is
> why they married you. And as for the marriage in the Roman Catholic
> Church it is a long process so that when you hear a girl got married you
> know she really wanted it. . . . In the Catholic marriage you accept your
> husband in bad times and good times. . . . And for the man it is the
> same: Do you accept her in bad times and in good times and he agrees:
> Yes I accept her. But after how many days, the agreement is no longer
> there. Now what is the priest supposed to do? It is your fault. It is you
> who lied to God; it is not the fault of the church.

In this statement, Joyce expresses the sacramental nature of Catholic marriage where the church witnesses a couple conferring a sacrament on one
another. For many of the women, this space of witness and sacrament
was a key liberative aspect in Christian marriage.

Joan also agreed that the failure of marriage was the fault of individuals and not the church. She said that these days, people married too
quickly, often before even getting to know each other. She said if you
marry someone without knowing their character, you can't blame the
church if the marriage fails. Most of the women believed that the teachings of Christian churches weren't to blame for the failure of marriages;
the blame was rather with individuals who did not live up to the teachings of their church or made poor decisions when it came to marriage.

The disconnect came when we began to talk about who made up the
church. The women agreed that the church should be defined as the
people of God who gather in a place. The church, for them, was not the
hierarchy or the buildings but the people. And when we begin to talk
about the people, they quickly acknowledged that it was the men who
led the people in the church, but the majority of the people were wom-
en.[49] Jane said, "When I look at the churches, the ones who appear the
most are women. Those that make up the church are women." I asked the
question of whether or not anyone had been to a church in Tanzania that
had more men than women and everyone in the room began to laugh.
Agnes said, "No, there is not one. It is not there." When asked why, she
went on to say:

> In the church we women arrive early; the men are late. If they ask
> maybe why is your wife on time while you are late? Meaning the
> woman has come early the man is the one who is late. He tells you I
> have many responsibilities. They claim they have more responsibilities
> than us while we have more responsibilities than them.

In Tanzania, it is the women who are expected to be late due to their household responsibilities. Yet when it comes to church, not only do the women show up more often than the men, but they show up early. All of the women agreed that part of the problem was that churches educate women about marriage but pay little attention to men. This is simply because the men are absent. They do not attend church regularly the way that the women do. Therefore, when there are sermons on faithfulness within marriage, the pastor is preaching faithfulness to the faithful.

Grace expounded on Agnes' comment by saying that women were more active in Christian churches because of the role they played in caring for the family. She said:

> Maybe yet another reason is that the woman feels the pain for the family. . . . Therefore you find the woman has things she is touched by, issues that continue to affect her family, more than a man. Therefore, the woman cries to her God. The man will not remember but the woman will, due to her commitment to her family and her children and her husband. That is why the women are the majority.

In saying this, Grace was arguing that women are at church each week because they believe that going to church will help their families. Here, she indicates that if men were more involved in their families, they might also be more involved in their churches as well.

Veronica compared women's disproportional church attendance to their disproportional attendance at HIV support group meetings. She said, "We have the courage to come forward." Jane said women make up the majority membership at churches because, "Women are people who were created with a merciful heart." She went on to trace this to the origins of Christianity, saying, "That is why even at the time when Jesus died, the first ones to reach the grave were women. So we follow the tradition of that generation. That is why in the church, women are many."

Mama Gasabile noted that it was not only at the church where women outnumber men but other events important to the community as well. She said that women are always ready to volunteer. She gave funerals and tending to the sick as other examples where women outnumbered men. She said that the only place in Tanzania where men outnumbered women was at the bar!

While women make up the vast majority of the members in Christian congregations across sub-Saharan Africa, Christian churches are still not places where women can fully exercise leadership.[50] This may be the primary reason that these churches are not yet making marriage a safer space for women. If women were more able to participate in leadership roles including preaching and worship, issues that intimately affect women might more easily become important issues in their churches. Instead, many churches in Tanzania tend to overlook the experience of women and encourage not mutual submission but the unilateral obedience of wives to husbands without a critique of patriarchy. Change is needed, and if churches really want to help in the work to end HIV and AIDS, marriage is the most appropriate place to begin.

MARRIAGE AS SOCIAL ETHICS

An expansion of the meaning and purpose of marriage is precisely what is needed if marriage is to become a safer space for women. I have argued in this chapter that in much of sub-Saharan Africa, Christian marriage is still articulated primarily in terms of a procreation telos, and teaching on marriage is confined to discussions on sexual ethics and gender complementarity. What has been lost in the Christian articulation of marriage on the continent is what was present before the missionaries arrived—the understanding of marriage as a social institution that enriches the community.

What would a theology of marriage look like if we began not with sexual ethics but with social ethics? During one PAR session on sex and fidelity, our group began to talk about the reasons fidelity was important. In our conversation, I encouraged the women to think together about a metaphor that could symbolize fidelity. The metaphor we agreed on was that of a fence, such as those that surround traditional homesteads throughout East Africa. The fence around the homestead marks off the boundaries of the home. It is not built to keep neighbors out but to keep those within safe. The farm animals are protected from predators, and small children have a space to play without wandering off. Sometimes, extended family members will build homes together on a plot of land and build the fence around the houses. In this way, the land in which the fence marks off is a gathering space. Meals are often cooked outside in the open air, and young children sit around the fire to listen to their mother's stories. The women agreed that fidelity was like a fence; it kept the family safe and allowed the marriage and the family to grow.

Perhaps, in light of this articulation, we could argue that it is not helpful to articulate concepts such as fidelity in terms of sin and salvation. When churches focus exclusively on "abstinence until marriage" and "faithfulness within marriage," they tend to do so without evoking a positive rationale for why fidelity is important. If we expand our focus and begin teaching about marriage in terms of broader social values (like its potential service to public health) as well as the interpersonal value of sexual exclusivity, space could be opened to honor some African understandings of marriage and interrogate others with the goal of making marriage a safer space for women.

In the PAR project, we attempted to do just that. During our fourth week of meeting together the women were asked to complete a Rawlsian exercise where they imagined a village that would be fair to all who lived within it. I began the exercise by explaining who John Rawls was and his understanding of justice.[51] I told them that Rawls imagined justice by creating a scenario he called the "original position." He believed that taking a group of knowledgeable people and putting them behind a "veil of ignorance" would be a way to discern justice. Behind this veil, they would be asked to imagine a just society, but they would not know what position they would be in once the veil was lifted.[52] In Rawls' "original position," the person would be unable to know whether she or he would be rich or poor, well or sick, HIV-positive or HIV-negative. I told them that according to Rawls' theory, this uncertainty would cause those in the original position to choose the maximum advantage for the greatest number of the world's people.[53]

I then asked the women to imagine that they were in Rawls "original position." Their task was to imagine the world as a blank slate and beginning there, they should imagine a village that was fair and just. They were told that in this village they would not know whether they would be male or female, rich or poor, married or single, HIV-positive or HIV-negative.

The activity took us two weeks to complete. When the idea was first introduced, the women had a hard time thinking about society and culture as a blank slate. Instead, they described things as they were with slight improvements (i.e., men should be faithful). As a result, the activity shifted to a "homework" assignment. The women were asked to spend the week imagining what life would be like if they were in charge of a village. They were asked to imagine a situation where women where village leaders rather than men.

The following week, the women came to the meeting with new ideas. They began by saying that family should be the starting point for the village. Marriage would be the way to begin families, and traditional and Christian marriages would be allowed, but there could be no polygamy. Christine said that if we took to heart the concerns of the women we simply couldn't allow polygamy.

Eliminating polygamy was the most important concern the women expressed when articulating their idea of what the village should be. At one point, Christine turned to Grace and asked her to share her story about her own marriage turning polygamous in order to remind the group about the dangers of polygamy. Grace gave her story and ended it by saying, "Therefore, as for marriage, I request that in our village that we want to create there should not be a situation of a person having more than one wife." The women agreed and then went on to talk about what should happen in the village if a person took more than one wife. Jane suggested they be reprimanded. Joyce said they should be isolated and not even allowed to draw water from the well or use the same market as everyone in the village. Jesca went even further and said they should be expelled from the village altogether.

Interestingly enough, eliminating polygamy was a key goal in early Christian missionary articulations of marriage. Yet, based on the presence of continued male infidelity—even among Christians—and the presence of "hidden polygamy" it could be argued that this reform simply did not work. Perhaps the reform failed because it came from outside the community rather than inside. If this is the case, then we have reason to be optimistic that if women are given space and voice to think about these issues, then marriage can still be transformed into a space of exclusivity when changes come from the inside out.

Contracts and Covenants

As we continued to talk about marriage in our village, Grace proposed an entirely new idea to the group, saying that marriage should be based on a contract. She said, "If I were to create my own world, marriage would be by contract, and that is that. Marriage should be a contract. That way if you see the marriage is good, you renew it. If it is too much for you, after the contract it ends—*shhhhhhh.*" Grace made a motion with her hand to signal a swift separation, and then she went on. "There should be no certificate nor ring that commits you—no! Only a contract!" When asked to describe the idea of a contract marriage, she said it would be like a trial marriage. It could be set up to last for three years or five years, but at the end of that time, the contract, which would take the form of a civil binding document, could either be renewed or dissolved. The commitment to the marriage would be based on the actual commitment present within the marriage, rather than a commitment to an abstract ideal.

In many ways, what the Grace was proposing was similar to the idea of trial marriage, which is already present in African tradition. Yet, in traditional trial marriages, the process of marriage was spread out in multiple steps that took years to complete in order to ensure fecundity in the marital union.[54] Interestingly enough, Grace's suggestion turned this traditional idea upside down, suggesting that a new type of "fruitfulness" be honored. Rather than a trial marriage to prove that the union would give life to children, Grace was proposing a trial marriage to ensure the union protected the life of the woman.[55]

After Grace mentioned the idea of a contract marriage, it quickly became a popular topic in the group. The women continued to bring up the idea in the weeks that followed. The elevation of this idea signaled that the women did not trust marriage as a long-term commitment. While they valued marriage as a means to have children, they did not trust their husbands to remain faithful through the entire course of the marriage.

The idea of contract marriage is in some ways already present in the culture in the form of a come-we-stay (or informal) marriage. Christine described these relationships this way:

> Come-we-stay relationships are now on the rise as people do not trust one another. What many are doing nowadays is staying together for some time then if they feel they are compatible then they legalize the marriage customarily through payment of *mahari*. Also in my culture, if a man does not pay *mahari* and the woman dies, he must pay all the *mahari* on that day so this scares so many people.

By not legalizing a marriage initially, women could be given more power in that they are free to leave the marriage with fewer repercussions if their partner is unfaithful. Yet in these relationships, women have few protections. If the husband decides to leave the marriage before they do, they are often left without property or resources when the husband claims them as his own.

This is exactly what happened to Scholastica who was in an informal marriage for her second marriage. When she found out she was HIV-positive, she told her husband. The following week, while she was away at a funeral, her husband took all her belongings and left her with an empty house with no money to pay the rent. If Scholastica had been able to negotiate some type of contract for her informal marriage (which was in a sense a trial marriage), then she would have been afforded some legal protection when the relationship was dissolved.

Rethinking Mahari

The difference between a formal and an informal marriage largely depends on whether or not *mahari* (or bridewealth) is paid. In fact, the inflation of *mahari* is one reason informal marriages are on the rise. Domina, Scholastica, Agnes, Jesca, and Joan all had informal marriages for some period of time. For most of these women, the cost of *mahari* was the reason they chose to make only informal marriage agreements with their spouses.

Domina's marriage was informal because *mahari* had not been paid. Domina described her relationship by saying, "I was not paid for with *mahari*. My husband was one of those sly fellows who takes off and does not want to pay *mahari*. We stayed together for three years, and he never took any *mahari* to my family, and we separated after that. So in my case the *mahari* went with the wind." Domina told this story with regret. While she had given a great deal to her husband (and had contracted HIV as a result of this relationship), she had nothing to show for her marriage. Her family had not even benefitted from *mahari*, and therefore she lost status with her family.

As articulated in chapter 3, many of the women in this study found *mahari* problematic. While only four believed it should be abolished completely, all of the women believed it should at least be reformed. In reflecting on this, *mahari* is one area of marriage where the church could have a tremendous impact. According to the women in this study, in most Tanzanian churches,[56] two individuals cannot be married until *mahari* is paid. While this is not universally true for all churches on the continent, in cases where this practice is enforced, we can see how African traditional systems have become part of Christian practice.

Realistically, the church might not be very successful in doing away with *mahari*, but it could have a voice in reforming the practice. Setting maximum modest payments on *mahari* would allow couples to more easily marry rather than entering into informal marriages where women are often at risk. The church could also suggest that a certain percentage of *mahari* go directly to the couple rather than the extended family as a way of helping the couple ease into marriage. Further, instruction that *mahari* should not be returned in the case of divorce would allow women more freedom to leave a marriage where they were at risk from their husband's abuse or infidelity.

Reforming *mahari* (or similar cultural practices of exchanging dowry) is an issue in African theology. Bujo advocates for reform on the basis that, "Dowry today has become a commercial matter."[57] In stating this, he notes that when a high price is paid for dowry, women can be abused. Bujo says, "Her husband may do with her what he likes and may reduce her to an object because the dowry has lost its humanizing dimension to mere commerce."[58] Bujo notes that the Archdiocesan Synod of Kinshasa (DRC) took this position in 1988 when they argued against the "exaggerated and unreasonable demands of dowry" and said that, "Christians who practice such abuse are sinning grievously before God and excommunicate themselves from the sacraments."[59]

While the reform Bujo speaks of is a starting place, he still does not problematize the concept of dowry from the perspective of women's experience. He approves of exchanging dowry as a practice because it is part of African tradition, yet he does not interrogate the concept to first discern whether or not the tradition should be maintained. More work is needed from African feminist theologians to discern whether or not the practice was ever good for women.

In thinking through *mahari* and similar exchanges of dowry, Christian churches should first employ a hermeneutic of suspicion. By asking who benefits from and who carries the burdens of *mahari*, it quickly becomes apparent that it is women who carry *mahari*'s burdens. While *mahari* can bring women esteem and status, it can also lock them into a dangerous marriage. Additionally, *mahari* imposes an extensive burden on the newly married couple, especially if the husband is working to pay his own *mahari*. The financial strain on the marriage adds stress to a relationship that is just starting to grow. And if the *mahari* is excessive, the husband will quickly resent the wife, making demands of her and limiting her agency.

Marriage Age

Related to the issue of *mahari*, the problem of marrying too young was of considerable importance to the women in this study. In Tanzania, marriage is legal for girls when they are fifteen years old and boys when they are eighteen years old.[60] Yet even with this legal stipulation, girls are often married much younger. In Tanzania, nationwide, 6 percent of girls are married before they turn fifteen, and in some regions the rate is as high as 14 percent. The rate is even higher when you consider those who are married before eighteen years old, which is 39 percent nationwide and 59 percent in certain regions of Tanzania.[61]

When we were designing our ideal village, Christine suggested that no one should be allowed to marry before the age of twenty-one because before that age, a girl does "not even know how to live with her husband." Mama Gasabile agreed and suggested an imprisonment of thirty years for any man who broke this law! As the women talked about marriage age, they spoke from their own experiences. As previously mentioned in chapter 2, four women in the group were fourteen or younger when they married. Another three women were twenty or younger. The remaining women were in their early twenties.

Almost all of the women in the PAR study said they wished they had been older when they were married. Maria, who was married at fourteen, thought twenty-five would have been a better age. Veronica, who was married at thirteen, thought she should have been at least twenty-four and should never have been allowed to marry to a man seventeen years older than she. Jane, who was married at fourteen, said that all women should wait until they were at least thirty. "Why?" she asked herself, "Because when I got married I was young, and I did not know what marriage was. As a result you get divorced at a young age and you start meandering here and there." Agnes upped Jane's age, and said thirty-five might be better. Grace said if she had it to do over again, she wouldn't marry at all.

Bringing the matter closer to home, I asked the women if they were encouraging their daughters to wait and marry later in life. Veronica said she wanted her daughters to be at least twenty-seven before marrying. Both Scholastica and Jane said they were thankful that they each had a girl who was more interested in books than boys. Joyce said she would have liked to prevent her child from being married completely. When I asked her why, she said it was because of the way her own marriage turned out. She said, "as a result of how I got married, the life I led, I think that maybe all men behave like that."

Veronica told the group that she had already dodged one bullet that would have forced her to marry earlier. In 1984, when Veronica was only seven, her uncles arranged her engagement to a sixty-year-old man. The man had paid *mahari* for her and given her family twenty-five cows. But she refused to be married so she ran away. But because she ran away, and because the man had already paid *mahari*, he was given Veronica's sister instead. As Veronica told her story, she provided details and gestures that made the women laugh about her antics of running away. But Joan spoke up in a serious tone after Veronica's story and said, "This is exploitation." All the women agreed.

Unfortunately marrying young is often connected to economic motives that completely disregard the well-being of girl children. When a young girl is married early, then her family is given *mahari* early. In Kenya, after the 2008 post-election violence, families in the IDP camps began to encourage their daughters to marry early. Because these families had lost nearly everything, they saw their redemption as coming through their daughters' marriages. School-aged girls in the camp were under tremendous pressure to end their schooling and get married in order to rescue their families.[62]

When it comes to marriage age, this is another area where the church could have a tremendous impact. Veronica reminded the group that when she was married, the church should have intervened rather than helping her husband to forge a birth certificate that made her look older. Through education campaigns against child marriage, and through lobbying for better legal protections, Christian churches could play a formative role in protecting girls who are too young to marry.

Preparing for Marriage

The women in the study were also very concerned about educating young women before they married. Mama Gasabile brought up the issue of kitchen parties and asked the group their opinion. In Tanzania, a kitchen party (similar to a bridal shower) is an event for a young woman who is about to be married. In this ceremony, women who are friends and family of the bride are gathered together to teach the young woman about marriage. Guests bring gifts for the bride and also give candid advice about sex and the responsibilities that come with marriage. The kitchen party tradition started in Dar es Salaam and quickly spread to other cities such as Mwanza. When these parties first began, only married women were allowed to attend, but now even young girls are invited. While women in the bride's family organize the event, the women in the groom's family are allowed to come as spectators but do not give advice.[63]

In one way, kitchen parties could be a valuable space for preparing girls for marriage because at these events, taboos around sexuality are lifted and women are able to speak freely about sex. Yet, at the same time, kitchen parties can be dangerous because the primary advice given to women is on how to be a submissive wife and maintain peace in the home, no matter what the cost. Women are instructed on how to keep their husbands happy but not about how to protect themselves. Non-profits in the region have been critical of kitchen parties because there is very little warning about HIV and AIDS at these events. To remedy this, some non-profits are giving out *kangas* (traditional cloths that are worn as clothing) with HIV prevention messages on them to encourage talk about HIV prevention in marriage.[64]

In Tanzanian churches, kitchen parties have become controversial, not because they reinforce gender roles, but because they encourage candid talk about sex. Churches object to these parties primarily because sex talk happens in a non-Christian setting. Other objections include the financial burden on the family and the fact that the groom is not invited (and therefore receives little instruction on marriage).

When talking about kitchen parties, the women in the group were mixed as to their effectiveness. Jesca said they were inappropriate primarily because young girls were allowed to attend. Christine and Agnes thought they were important but said that these parties should instead be an opportunity for the church to teach the youth. Christine said,

> It is true that the churches fight against kitchen parties, but we have reached a point whereby we Christians we are forced to do them, aren't we? We just say, let us invite ladies who know God so we put that girl in line with what is required in the Christian context, how she should live with her husband. But even with this, the young man will not know what we are teaching. . . . For this reason, things should change. . . . The young man should be sat down with the girl they should be taught together . . . teachings should be there for the girl and for the boy. That is how we can get marriages of love and peace.

While Christine makes the important point that both partners should be taught together, I believe this woman-centered space should still be protected. Kitchen parties could become important places to teach women about marriage in order to make marriage a safer space for women. If instruction focused on empowering women within their marriages and instructing women about HIV prevention, these events could be formative to Christian marriages. Similar events could be created for young men who are about to marry in order to give them instruction on the ways in which they could also benefit from equality and respect within the marriage. Because kitchen parties invite women of all ages, including many who are married, they could provide a community forum for advice on strengthening marriage. Those who attend could also be asked to help protect the newly married couple by making sure if abuse or infidelity takes place in the marriage that the couple knows where to turn for help.

In the same way, Christian churches could have a tremendous impact by creating a similar rite of passage for young men who are about to be married. Ghanaian theologian Osei-Wusu Brempong makes the point that men are also vulnerable to HIV because of cultural constraints. Citing a UNAIDS report on this topic, he says, "The conventional teaching that expects men to be more knowledgeable and experienced about sex puts particularly young men at risk of being infected." Brempong believes that the only way for this to change is to create programs that attempt to reshape gender roles and improve communication between men and women.[65] Toward this end, Christian churches could play a formative role. Before men are married, a meaningful ritual could be created where the groom and other men in the community and church are invited to come and listen to teaching about marriage. These events could include using scriptures that point to gender equality within marriage and passages that exemplify the way Jesus treated women. Instruction could also be given on women's legal rights within marriage and on the importance and reasons for fidelity. Because these events would be repeated each time a person in the church is married, the repetition could create a space where men both inside and outside the church receive frequent instruction on marriage and family. Additionally, these events would likely be well attended because individuals in the community would want to show their support for the groom.

Defending Women's Property Rights in Marriage

Another important issue that came up in the research was the role of Christian churches in existing marriages. The women were concerned that although it is the church that sanctions marriages, the church did not help when problems arose in the marriage. Grace gave the example of property grabbing. She said:

> In my experience, the church talks mainly about faithfulness, love, things like that. But one thing I haven't known yet is how the church looks at the way a woman inherits her husband's property if the husband should die. How does the church help her? I haven't heard how the church helps that woman. Because you find many women after the death of their husbands have their property taken away from them. She has to run to other institutions. I don't know, the government or wherever. But the church—I haven't known how it helps this woman even though she got married in the church. When her husband dies she is left to face the problems alone. The problems are between her, her brothers-in-law and the clan. How does the church intervene? The question I remain with is how does the church help the woman regarding inheriting the wealth she created with her husband?

The other women in the group agreed with Grace. They also were unsure as to how the church helped these women. Grace went on as she made her case, saying:

> The woman is deprived of her rights. What wins out is our tradition as Africans. For the woman—she has struggled with her husband all this time—and the brothers-in-law and the in-laws come and chase her out of the house. They tell you the property is not yours, but that of our child. Now the church has married you, how does it defend you here?

Mama Gasabile responded to Grace's question by saying that "the church has no proper answer for matters of inheritance . . . because the church assumes that when the husband dies the wife is the head of the household. . . . The church just assumes that the husband and wife live together always." Mama Gasabile went on to say this is not how it should be. One solution she had been proposing was education seminars to teach married couples how to write a will that would protect the wife in the event of the husband's death. Mama Gasabile had taught several of these seminars and hoped to see the church conduct more in the future. She said, "The church has to stand up and defend those who are left behind."

One reason Christian churches may not be addressing this issue is because many are rooted in the same patriarchal foundation that makes women's property inheritance a low priority in African cultures. For example, when Kenyan theologian Frederick Wangai takes on this issue, he says that, "It is Christian duty for the husband to provide for the family not only during his lifetime but even when he is dead."[66] Yet, Wangai goes on to say blame part of the problem on the women by saying, "Unfortunately the heirs are poorly trained to manage the assets."[67] The advice Wangai ends up giving is that before a man dies, he should both create a will and then train his wife to manage the money after he is gone.[68] Of course, this patriarchal advice points to the problem, in that women are not deemed capable in either African tradition or African Christianity to manage the assets of the home or inherit property without the help of men.

In reflecting on this, Christian churches again must employ a hermeneutic of suspicion to ask who benefits when women do not inherit property. The responsibility to care for widows and orphans is fundamental to Christian practice. Therefore, advocating for women and children in the midst of property grabbing should be an automatic response for Christian churches. Yet here again, patriarchy trumps the basic Christian obligation to care for those who are oppressed. When we employ a hermeneutic of suspicion, we realize it is the men—the fathers and the brothers—who benefit when a property is taken away from their dead son's wife and children. The lens of care for widows and orphans demands that we not only help meet individuals in their time of need, but advocate for better laws that protect women and children from being victims in these situations.

As we reflect on the issues within marriage that make women vulnerable, we quickly see how a social ethics approach can empower communities to make marriages safer. If the church were to begin with important issues such *mahari*, marriage age, preparing men and women for marriage, and defending the rights of widows and orphans, then marriage could be reimagined in a way that enriches the entire community. In this way, women's flourishing can serve as a lens for a justice-based approach that considers first the needs of those who are most vulnerable in intimate relationships. The primary barrier to this approach is that it means that Christian churches would be speaking out against patriarchy, which not only threatens culture but threatens the institutional church as well. Yet, I believe as women are given more of a voice in Christian churches, these issues will take on a more prominent place in the mission of the church.

MARRIAGE AND SEXUAL ETHICS

A primary focus on marriage as social ethics does not mean that a focus on sexual ethics is not needed. Rather, in places where sex is taboo, a paradigm shift could be created by choosing to talk about sexual ethics as a part of social ethics. In doing so, there is a need to recognize that sex is not merely a private act between two people but rather a communal act that can enrich or destroy communities and the families within them.

Rethinking Abstinence

One of the first public health responses to the spread of the HIV pandemic in sub-Saharan Africa was a three-fold approach focusing on abstinence, being faithful, and condoms. Called the ABC method of prevention, this initiative was successful in some ways, primarily because of its widespread public messaging campaigns and promotion of condoms. Yet when most faith-based organizations adopted the model, condoms were dropped in favor of an AB approach focusing only on abstinence and faithfulness. This was particularly problematic for women because, as previously argued, the decision of whether to not to be abstinent or faithful was often out of their control.

When faith-based initiatives began to focus on abstinence and faithfulness, they did so using biblical concepts of purity and sin without adequately addressing the cultural obstacles to abstinence and faithfulness.[69] And since women are often blamed for promiscuity—even their husband's promiscuity[70]—women who contracted HIV tended to be stigmatized rather than empowered through these initiatives. Even the church's focus on virginity was seen by some as confusing. For example, some of the women in this study defined virginity as having an intact hymen. Veronica, for instance, thought that when girls carried water buckets on their heads their hymen could break or that a man with a small penis could leave a girl's virginity intact. Jesca thought that when a girl got her period she was no longer a virgin.

In East Africa, virginity is revered by some ethnic groups and less important to others.[71] Within some groups, sex is seen as a cultural expectation during the engagement period that proves fertility. Bujo notes that for many African cultures, sex should not be considered "premarital" but instead is a stage in the marriage process that happens before the marriage is finalized. He sees this as a space of difference between Christian marriages and traditional marriages and argues that Christian marriages neglect African cultures because they do not recognize the progressive nature of traditional marriage.[72] While I do not necessarily agree with Bujo's argument on this topic, he does make the important point that Christian and traditional marriages understand sex to come at different places in the marriage process. This may be a primary reason that even the language of abstinence-until-marriage has proven to be an ineffective strategy in sub-Saharan Africa.

The women in the study said that in most of their cultures, even if premarital sex were off-limits, "tasting" was generally permitted. Veronica said that her ethnic group had a custom where foreplay was required before marriage to make sure the boy who was to be married was not impotent. He was required before the marriage to lie naked with the girl and count the beads around her waist. If he counted all 200 beads before getting an erection, then he was considered to not be a man and sent home with the wedding called off.

Joyce said that today, in her ethnic group, virginity is no longer prized like it used to be. She said that even young men think virgins are "troublesome." She gave an example of a young man in her family who was married and on his wedding day his older brothers taunted him saying that if his new wife was a virgin they would beat her. Joyce said, "These days, the youth don't like virgins; they want the path to be weeded so they can move as they like."

Agnes said that even an engagement begins with sex. She said, "He will tell you, 'Let us go to have sex, let me taste you. Now you taste me, am I a side dish?' He tells you again, 'I desire to taste you.'" Agnes gave an example from her own life. "Imagine I got a fiancé, and he told me I want to elope with you; let us sleep with each other first, and then tomorrow I come to introduce myself. He puts sex first, which is different from my expectations."

Most of the women in the group agreed that abstinence before marriage was a good thing, but they did not think it was a realistic goal. Between cultural expectations of "tasting," the frequency of rape and forced sex, and the general inability of women and girls to negotiate sex within intimate relationships, they were pessimistic that abstinence could work. Yet even still, some of the women saw abstinence as a space where women could be empowered, especially single women who had more power than married women.

During one exercise, the women were asked what they would do differently if they were young and single again and had not yet been married. Domina answered quickly with a well-formulated plan:

> If there were a chance to get married again I would do it like this: First if the fiancé I got told me, for example, "I love you, I want to marry you," you know there is this habit of getting a taste. I would refuse to taste. I would refuse him. I would not allow him to taste because once he has tasted you get exactly that kind of problem. . . . So once I know he still wants to marry me I would give him conditions. He should send his parents to see my parents. . . . Once they have investigated I would ask my parents, "Are you satisfied?" I would tell them, "Now if you are satisfied, I don't like him for his looks or his income, I like him so I can live with him forever, meaning I will live with him for my whole life." So then I would marry him. I have already seen being impulsive does not bring a good life.

Domina saw an advantage in not giving a "taste," even though this was culturally expected. But Domina came to this perspective as a woman of wisdom, having lived through the experience of two marriages that ended in separations. She was unsure that her own adolescent daughter would be so wise.

This brings up another problem—the pressure to marry. Because in Tanzanian society all young women are expected to marry, young women often feel pressured into sex because it is often seen as a requirement for engagement. This is especially true for poor girls who are uneducated and who will not receive much *mahari*. If we really want girls to be abstinent or to delay sexual debut, basic education may be more important than abstinence education.

Furthermore, abstinence as it is preached and practiced by faith-based organizations is highly problematic because of its focus on purity and virginity and because it sets marriage up as a safe space. Too often, delay of sexual debut is not something a young girl can control. Rape is all too common, and the societal responses to rape are inadequate. According to the World Health Organziation's ten-country study on women's health and domestic violence, 30 percent of women in Tanzania said that their first sexual experience was not consensual.[73]

When the women in this study were asked about their first sexual partner, three of the women mentioned that their first sexual encounter was rape. When they counted their sexual partners, the rapists were among their boyfriends and husbands, because in Tanzania, women are seen as responsible for sex even when it is forced. Beyond rape, when girls are poor, they may turn to transactional sex to pay their school fees or to feed their family. And when a poor girl is looking for a husband, she has little space to negotiate whether or not sex will happen before marriage.

Faith-based abstinence education is also highly problematic because of its focus on abstinence-until-marriage. In this paradigm, marriage is promoted as a safe space where women no longer need to think about protection. Yet there are times within marriage where a woman should be abstinent or use protection, such as when she suspects her husband of being unfaithful. The failures of the ABC method to protect women from HIV remind us that solutions to the African HIV pandemic are more complex than we're often willing to admit.

Reimagining Faithfulness

The women in this study were well aware that they were at risk because their husbands were likely to go outside the marriage for sex. Mama Gasabile used her own marriage and created a possible example of how women can be vulnerable within their marriages. She said:

> I can have my husband, I am married to him but now he comes to say, "You are my wife so we must sleep together, are you not my wife?" I have said that we obey him. So I do the act of marriage. Then, maybe, he comes to you, he does the act of marriage. He says, "This wife of mine I have already left her." But you agree because maybe you want children. Maybe you agree and you get AIDS. Now I've got it, you've got it, and still he goes to yet another one. Because we obey, a man cannot come and say, "Let us go to do the act of marriage," and you reply, "No, I can't." That is where we are trapped. What I want to say is, you are married aren't you? You got married in church. You said, "I will love in hardship, in joy, in sickness, in what." Now your husband comes at night, will you say, "No, my husband, I don't want the act of marriage?" That is where we get infected.

Veronica agreed with Mama Gasabile, saying that even when they knew their husbands were unfaithful, women could not refuse the "act of marriage." She went on to say that women "are also weak." She said, "The man can catch you in adultery, and he divorces you completely. But if you catch him in adultery, he will tell you, 'My wife, I got carried away, it is the devil.' But while he is there, he has gone to get the virus."

The women agreed that while there were times when you might be able to refuse sex—such as when you were menstruating or when you were tired or sick—the ability to refuse sex was no guarantee. Grace said, "If a man feels like it, whether you like it or not, it will come out the way he wants." Veronica agreed, saying, "You will just see, if this man wants you, even if you tell him 'I am tired,' he will just tell you 'keep still and I will do it.'"

Several of the women worried that when their husbands made love to them, they were thinking of other lovers. Agnes said that once when she asked her husband for sex, and he was not in the mood, he asked her to stimulate him so he could imagine his other lovers. Several of the women agreed and said that their husbands would also point out past lovers or even name other lovers while making love or sleeping.

The women collaborators said that in many ways, the men were not ashamed of their other lovers and did not try to hide them from their wives. Jesca said that one day her husband had been away from home for the entire week, and she didn't know where he was sleeping. When he finally returned, he told Jesca to expect a visitor the following day. When the next day came, a woman showed up and she was given Jesca's bed, forcing Jesca to sleep on the couch. Jesca was forced to prepare a bath for her husband and this woman, and after the two had taken a bath, they left again. Jesca was horrified by the incident. She said, "They slept in my room on my bed. I slept on the couch in the living room. He told me, 'you don't know how to prepare for a man, and since you don't know, let me bring someone to teach you.'"

While the women agreed that men were often unfaithful, they said that women rarely went outside of their marriages. Two of the women in this study said that women were generally faithful until men were unfaithful. One woman said that she learned how to be unfaithful in order to get revenge on her husband who was sleeping around. Grace described women's faithfulness this way:

> According to me, women are forced by their husbands to be unfaithful. This is to a very big percentage. If you find a married woman being unfaithful then investigate and you will surely find that the marriage has problems or the man is hardly at home for his wife or that he is the kind that comes back home at one in the morning or something like that.

Several women in the study believed the difference in men and women's faithfulness was linked to income. In this way, they illustrated that the line between sexual ethics and social ethics cannot be so clearly drawn since the two are intertwined. Domina said that money changed everything in regard to fidelity:

> A man can persevere and love you so much when he does not have money, but the moment he gets money things change. He no longer is yours alone. For instance, in my case, when I married my husband he not have much money. In fact, at that point if a woman approached him he would rebuke her and not give in. He even used to travel to meetings and other places and he had no problem with that. . . . But when his economic situation improved and he got money, he treated me like a dog.

Grace agreed with Domina and said that she believed her husband's improved economic status was the reason he took a second and then a third wife.

In reflecting on the experiences of the women in this study, and on the experiences of the men who were also interviewed, I believe that men are not faithful because they lack a compelling reason to remain faithful to their marriages. When some Christian churches preach faithfulness, they tend to preach faithfulness for the sake of salvation or religious devotion. One's relationship with God and the church provides the rationale instead of relationality with one's spouse. In this sense, the church speaks like a dogmatic parent using "God told you so" language as the primary rationale.

A more compelling reason for faithfulness within marriage would be to protect the relationship between two marriage partners. Like the women illustrated with the metaphor of the fence around the homestead, fidelity is important because it can protect the relationship. In this way, fidelity should be seen as a servant virtue.[74] In other words, it is not an end it itself, but it protects other ends within the marriage, such as love, relationality, and care for children. Yet, in a patriarchal culture, relationality with one's spouse has little meaning for men who do not consider their wives to be equals. Therefore we must ask if faithfulness can have any meaning at all without gender equality.

In a relationship where two partners are not equals, male faithfulness can only serve a protectionist agenda where a benevolent patriarch seeks to care for his wife by not going outside of the marriage or perhaps a concern for one's self or public health where men make a choice for faithfulness due to fear of HIV. Yet, as previously argued, in the midst of a fatalistic culture where you can be killed by hunger or road accidents or water-borne illnesses, a fear of HIV is not even compelling enough to ensure fidelity. Some of the women in this study talked about how the men who brought HIV into their homes were good, upstanding men. Some went to church every Sunday and were community leaders.

During one conversation with Jane about her husband, Mama Gasabile stopped the interview to tell me that although Jane contracted HIV from her husband, he was still a truly good man. He never abused her, he went to church every Sunday, and he was well respected in the community. When we're talking about men's infidelity, we're not talking about bad men but men who are the product of a patriarchal culture where male fidelity has traditionally not been a societal expectation. In fact, traditionally, multiple wives and multiple children (inside or outside of marriage) have been not only valued but have been seen as a symbol of male virility and even God's blessing.[75] These examples remind us that a virtue-based approach that encourages fidelity is insufficient in light of systematic violence and gender injustice.

In these patriarchal relationships, it is the women, not the men, who have more to lose and more to fear. As Veronica said, a woman is more likely to take back an unfaithful husband than a man is to take back an unfaithful wife. When women are not considered equals, they are certainly not seen as irreplaceable. Therefore, men can go outside their marriage for sex without being very fearful that they will lose their wives.

If Christian churches really want to promote faithfulness, they have to start with addressing the underlying issues of gender equality. They can do this by emphasizing the ways in which patriarchy (and infidelity) not only hurt women but harms men and children as well.[76] There is also the need to for churches to challenge Christian and traditional notions that family structures are dependent on patriarchy for their survival.[77] Cultures and religions are always deeply intertwined, but as African feminist theologians have argued, both an interrogation and retrieval of culture are needed.[78] If Christian churches seek to create change, they must not seek out spaces of retrieval without first doing the work of interrogation where it is urgently needed.

If Christian churches are not naming equality as a reason for fidelity, then their arguments may simply not be compelling enough for men to follow. Instead, they will only encourage women to be faithful to relationships that are harmful and dangerous. Practically speaking, men need to be convinced that fidelity is good for them as well. While we've been talking about the dangers male infidelity poses to women, we must recognize that it also poses dangers to men. After all, the women in this study were those who were left behind to tell their dead husbands' stories. If the church wants to keep women and men safe, they must begin with a compelling argument for fidelity that does not neglect gender justice.

Re-evaluating Condoms

The issue of condoms has long been controversial in faith-based responses to the HIV pandemic. In 2009-2010, when I was completing this field research, neither Catholic nor Protestant churches in Mwanza were openly endorsing or distributing condoms, although some churches made exceptions for serodiscordant couples (where one partner is HIV-positive and the other partner is HIV-negative).[79] In sub-Saharan Africa, the Catholic Church has long prohibited condoms while Protestant churches have varied on the issue. Protestant mission churches in the West (such as the United Methodist Church or the Evangelical Lutheran Church of America) have made statements supporting condoms as a solution for the African HIV pandemic, yet many local churches in these denominations still have not completely accepted condoms.[80] In my own interviews in Mwanza, I found that Western missionaries (even in typically conservative traditions, such as Southern Baptist) were more willing to acknowledge the necessity for allowing condoms than the clergy they worked with. However, the resistance to condoms for some of these churches and their leadership may be more based on African cultural perceptions of condoms than on Christian sexual ethics. [81]

Shortly after the field research was complete, Pope Benedict XVI made a brief but important statement that opened up new space to talk about condoms in Catholic churches and Catholic development agencies. In the book, *Light of the World,* Benedict XVI begins talks candidly about condoms by leaving some room for condom use in high-risk populations. He says:

> There may be a basis in the case of some individuals, as perhaps when a male prostitute uses a condom, where this can be a first step in the direction of moralization, a first assumption of responsibility, on the way toward recovering an awareness that not everything is allowed and that one cannot do whatever one wants. But it is not really the way to deal with the evil of infection. That can really lie only in a humanization of sexuality. [82]

The reporter writing the book followed up on this comment by asking the Pope if the "Catholic Church is actually not opposed in principle to the use of condoms." Benedict XVI responded by saying:

> She of course does not regard it as a real or moral solution, but, in this or that case, there can be nonetheless, in the intention of reducing the risk of infection, a first step in a movement toward a different way, a more human way, of living sexuality. [83]

While these statements are not extensive, they do open up a significant space for new conversations on prevention within the Catholic Church and even with other churches that have been following the Catholic Church's lead on this subject. Benedict XVI argues rightly that while condoms do not provide a perfect solution they can be a "first step in the direction of moralization." In this way, he designates condoms as a temporary measure that can protect people even though he does not see them as a "moral solution."

However, the weakness of this statement lies in the fact that a male prostitute is used as an example. In this way, Benedict XVI continues the current line thought that sees condoms as needed in casual relationships but not needed within marriage. Marriage is still naively portrayed as a safe space where the "humanization of sexuality" is taken for granted.

To his credit, in this statement, Benedict XVI does accept condom use as a temporary measure that can lead us toward more responsibility for life. Extending this argument, we could ask if condoms could be used within marriage as a temporary measure that would give women more space to negotiate the terms of sex with an HIV-positive husband (or a husband who is thought to be HIV-positive). This could be a great asset when the woman thinks her husband may be cheating and is thus newly infected and highly infectious. Throughout East Africa, men are hesitant to use condoms regardless of their religious convictions, but if more churches encouraged (or at least did not discourage) condom use, then some men might be more open to using this form of protection.

Joyce said that Catholicism was to blame for part of the reason men won't use condom. She said:

> One thing that causes those in marriage not to use condoms or makes it so a woman cannot decide to use condoms is religion. It plays a big part in the fact that people don't use condoms. For example, with the Roman Catholic Church, I am involved in home-based care. When a kit comes to the diocese, the kit comes with boxes of condoms. The church gives us everything else but the condoms are forbidden. They will tell you the Church does not know about condoms. Even if AIDS kills or does whatever, they don't talk about condoms. When a husband and wife are married there is no condom use allowed there. Let them just fool around anyhow. Let them infect each other whichever way, because they have taken an oath. The Church contributes to the spread of infections because they don't want people to use protection. While all this time they know that it is hard for a man to eat from only one pot.

Mama Gasabile followed up and said that it was not only the Roman Catholic Church in Tanzania that was not talking about condoms but Protestant churches as well. She said that the Christian Council of Churches in Tanzania has yet to endorse condoms.[84] She said that the CCCT asked its churches not to talk about condoms in church but only to stress abstinence and faithfulness.

By disallowing condoms for either prevention of STDs and/or family planning, churches reinforce a patriarchy where women's lived experiences are unimportant. Limiting condoms in sub-Saharan Africa results in forced pregnancies and contracting HIV. As previously argued, condoms are already seen as negative within male culture in sub-Saharan Africa, and churches simply moralize this form of patriarchy.

Joyce and Veronica (both of whom were Catholic) talked about how hard it was to get men to use a condom. Joyce told her own story about attempting to use condoms for family planning. She said:

> I think a woman has no voice at all regarding condoms. I am an example. When I had given birth to the first child when it was nine months I got pregnant with the second child. When I was pregnant with the second child the moment I gave birth—eh, again! Now I saw this giving birth round the clock as truly being too hard. So I discussed it with my husband. . . . I pressured him (to use condoms) and he wore one. . . . But when we reached the chorus—to use the expression—suddenly the man throttled me. He tells me a child is more important than me. He removed it and threw it to the side. He throttled me! *iih!* It was now a fight. Therefore regarding condoms, for a woman to tell a man to use a

condom inside the house, if he himself hasn't decided yet, that is a big job.

Joyce's husband told her that "a child is more important" than she was. The possibility of life (or perhaps proof of male virility) became more important than her own life. While Joyce's husband's statement is shocking, this is what the church tells women every day when they speak against condoms. Women's lives are simply not as important as church doctrine.

For some women in the group, their husbands refused to use condoms inside the marriage but used them freely outside. When Agnes and her husband found out they were HIV-positive, the clinic sent them home with a box of condoms. Agnes tried to talk her husband into using them, so they wouldn't pass the viral load back and forth but he refused. A few weeks after coming home from the clinic, Agnes noticed that half of the box of condoms was gone. When she confronted her husband about it, he accused her of selling them, even though he had been using them outside of the marriage. Agnes used this story to say, "As a woman, I had no choice about using condoms in the house." In this way, as a wife, Agnes had less power than her husband's girlfriend(s) who benefited from the use of condoms.

Like many of the women in this study, Musa Dube is critical of the church's support of abstinence and asks who is served when Christian churches continue to cling to their "values" while people are dying. She asks if Christian churches can claim that it is not a party to HIV and AIDS since they encourage poverty by focusing on heaven as the final reward while not speak out against unequal gender relations.[85]

Condoms are not a perfect answer for prevention, but until we have better solutions, Christian churches can simply not exclude any options. An option that leads to prevention should be considered a moral option. In the case of condoms, when they prevent HIV, they are life-giving. Yet, condoms are not a perfect answer because they still do not provide a woman-centered approach to prevention. When a woman has to ask her husband to use a condom, she is not able to prevent, or even reduce the risk of infection by STDs. Her fate lies in the willingness of her husband to agree to condom use, rather than in her own agency. For this reason microbicides along with other woman-controlled prevention methods are desperately needed until a vaccine is found.[86]

MARRIAGE AND SEXUAL VIOLENCE

As we talk about sexual ethics and relationships, there is also a deep need to address issues of sexual violence and domestic violence. As previously mentioned, Tanzania, like many countries in sub-Saharan Africa, has few enforceable laws against marital rape. While domestic violence is finally getting attention, many women in Tanzania, especially those in rural areas, still see physical abuse as normal and are hesitant to report it to the authorities.

The Anglican diocese in Mwanza runs an effective initiative to end violence against women called "The Tamar Campaign." This campaign, which originated with feminist theologians in South Africa, uses the biblical story of Tamar as a way to address abuse against women.[87] Volunteers with the Tamar Campaign conduct public advocacy programs and walk through the legal system with victims of violence. Mama Gasabile, who runs the program in Mwanza, says that she often encounters people who are unaware that they have any recourse after being abused.

Violence against women happens not only within marriage but can actually lead to marriage. In Tanzania, if a woman is raped, she is sometimes given to her rapist in marriage. This happened to Jesca. She was only fifteen when she was raped, and when her family found out, they arranged a marriage between her and the man who raped her. Jesca said that in her tradition, "Once a girl has slept with a man, she is taken there even if the man is old. She has to stay there and be married." Jesca, after losing her virginity to rape, was then given in marriage to this same man who committed violence against her. She said she couldn't bear it, so she appealed to her aunt for help. As she did, she was sure her father would beat her, but he finally allowed her to return home.

Maria was also raped when she was a teenager. A boy in her village grabbed her as she was leaving a store and forced her to have sex with him. Maria was scared and ran home to tell her sister. But her sister's advice was to keep quiet about the matter so their father wouldn't beat Maria. She couldn't keep quiet for long. Soon she found out she was pregnant as a result of the rape, and she had to tell her father. Her father did not beat her, but he forbid her to tell anyone about what happened.

When violence or rape happens within marriage, women are even less likely to report the abuse, and if the abuse is reported, authorities will not always respond.[88] A 2009 study by The Human Rights Committee found that one reason marital rape was not considered a criminal activity was due to religious understandings of marriage. The delegation reported that, "Tanzania had no law against marital rape because it did not exist. Most of the people in Tanzania were Christians. They were married in church where through marriage two bodies became one and one body could not rape itself."[89] Reflecting on this statement, we realize that ending marital rape is also a theological issue and requires a new understanding of bodily integrity within Christian marriage.[90]

When talking about why marriages—both Christian and traditional— were vulnerable, Joyce talked about the behavior of men within marriage, specifically about the frequency of marital rape. She said:

> Very often our African men, in many marriages, they are used to rape.
> There is no love there. He'll come from here, he'll come from there,
> knowing he did not sleep inside for two days. He is with someone but
> when he comes back inside he wants to hide that he has been with that
> person, so he will want to sleep with me by force. He can't ask himself,
> how does my wife look at herself after I stayed two days with this other
> person? So when you try to refuse, he throttles you, he throttles you, he
> beats you. Now are just trying to protect yourself against being
> thrashed.

As Joyce talked she became animated and swung her hands in the air
mimicking the punches. Throughout her story the women agreed with
her by saying things like "continue" or "yes." After her story was finished, the women begin to laugh at Joyce's animated gestures that accompanied her story, saying that her account was very true.

The story Joyce tells is particularly frightening when you consider the
way HIV is most commonly spread. After a person contracts HIV, there is
a period of about two weeks when they are most contagious. If a husband
goes outside of the marriage for sex and contracts HIV and then returns
home to have forced sex with his wife, then she is very likely to contract
the virus. The risk is further heightened when sex is forced since rape and
rough sex often involve vaginal tearing, increasing the likelihood of
contraction.

There is an urgent need for Christian churches to speak out against
marital rape and to advocate for legal measures to protect women against
rape and abuse. The women in the study said that too often, women are
encouraged by their priests, pastors, or families to return to an abusive
situation. In these cases, avoiding marital separation is seen as more important than women's flourishing. The hesitation to recommend separation or divorce is not only based on Christian understandings of marriage, but also on African culture, which sees marriage as indissoluble.[91]
Yet too often, families and churches that send women back to their marriage are sending them to their death.

MARRIAGE AS AN EXPRESSION OF BODILY INTEGRITY AND RELATIONALITY

When we talk about women and HIV and AIDS in sub-Saharan Africa,
we are talking about the ways in which women's bodies bear the burdens
of this pandemic. I have argued from the fieldwork that when women get
married, they no longer have full control over their bodies. Their bodily
rights are very often sacrificed as a result of marriage. This is not a new
problem. Theologians of embodiment have argued that wherever patriarchy exists, women will not have full agency in regard to their bodies.[92]
This is the reason that marriage is not safe. Until women are seen as

embodied agents, and allowed to exercise the rights and responsibilities that embodiment demands, marriage will never be safe.

What is needed urgently is not only a new sexual ethics but, more importantly, a new social ethics that emphasizes the importance of bodily rights in regard to sexuality. If we begin with sexual ethics without first addressing violations of bodily integrity, then we will only create rules without enabling agents. We need to turn to the lived experiences of women in order to make a turn to the body. The goal for our social ethics and sexual ethics must be the goal of just and fair relations, the goal of mutuality and relationality. Toward this end, simply empowering women is not enough. Instead, oppressive masculinities and patriarchies that sanction violence and infidelity must be deconstructed.

As we chart this course, we can turn to women's bodies as a lens for prevention, for caring for the sick, and for articulating right relations between partners. And in the process, Christian churches will be forced to ask themselves hard questions, such as whether or not women's bodies actual matter within their theologies and practices. As we begin to think through bodily integrity, I want to look at the issue of forced sex. In doing so, I will ask what these experiences can teach us about the importance of a turn to the body to seek out solutions for the HIV pandemic.

Marriage and Bodily Integrity

One way of understanding the lack of respect for women's bodily integrity within marriage is to begin with women's bodies and sex. I have argued that within marriage, many choices regarding sex are forced choices. This is not unique to marriage but an issue faced by young girls as well. One week during a session on sexuality, the group was asked whether or not abstinence until marriage campaigns were having any impact in Tanzania. In response, Domina brought up the issue of forced sex. She said:

> You know, some (girls) don't engage in sex because they like it but because they are forced into it. You find someone maybe comes from a low-income home. Now you give her 100 shillings to go return to school, but the bus driver doesn't want her to travel for this 100. He tells her if you have 150 shillings, get in. If you don't have it, we will leave you here. These things overwhelm her, and that bus driver has a moustache in the style of a cock and he tells her, "If you are reasonable, let us go." The first day she might refuse, the second, doesn't she have to agree? And this also contributes to children losing their virginity.

In responding to Domina's statement, the women made a distinction between the girl choosing to have sex and being forced into a choice. Agnes said, "She is forced to chose because in her situation she is hungry. And if she looks at the man, he has money, and he is the one who enables her so she is forced to agree. She gives something and she gets something."

In reflecting on Domina's comments, we not only recognize the problem of forced sex but of male sexual predatory behavior as well. Unfortunately, society tends to turn a blind eye to this problem as even in these situations. If the girl were to become pregnant, she would be blamed rather than the predator who preyed on her vulnerability.

Veronica said this forced choice does not only apply to young girls, but to women as well. "Sometimes, if I have children for example, I might not have any money inside to feed them. So maybe I meet a man who tells me I will give you 5,000 shillings. He eats me and my children eat. I can't let this opportunity pass. This is the harshness of life!"

The collaborators agreed that for many women, their bodies are their only commodities. For a woman who does not have a plot of land to farm or a business that generates income, her body becomes an avenue to feed herself and her children. Grace believed the biggest problem was that women too often are forced fend for themselves. She said:

> I think if you look the women who live alone, their number is higher than those who are married. Now if you investigate how they keep their families, even those who have businesses . . . it is not as if the business would enable her. . . . For a high percentage it is her body, even if she has a business, it is her body. . . . Therefore a great number of women depend on their bodies. I can say that.

As we listen to the lived experiences of the women in this study, we realize that preaching abstinence or faithfulness is useless when women and girls are only left with forced choices. Girls learn from an early age that it is the way they use their bodies in relation to men that enables their survival. From young girls who carry water and dig in the garden on their father's land to adolescent girls who trade sex for money to pay school fees, women and girls are dependent on men and the patriarchal structures that give them power. When we begin to think of their situations, it comes as no surprise that the subjugation of women's bodies continues in marriage. In the marriage event, choice is even further limited as women lose control of their bodily rights.

This leads us to ask—what are the preconditions that are requisite for bodily integrity? If forced sex is a result of poverty and the lack of basic human needs, then we could argue that women are disembodied (or unable to maintain bodily integrity) when they lack resources for survival. If we as a global community want to end the HIV pandemic, then we must not ignore basic needs. Clean water, food, health, and safety were not always available to many of the women in this study. Basic human rights such as safety from violence or the ability to inherit land were also not in place. Many of these women lacked basic resources that would enable them to earn an income or provide for their families in ways that did not force them to use their bodies for survival. Fostering respect for the bodily integrity of all persons requires support for their basic needs.

As we continued to talk about the problem of forced sex, Jane reminded the women in the room that not all women turn to sex to feed their children. She said that after she contracted HIV in her marriage, she made an oath to God that she wouldn't have sex because she didn't want anyone else to contract the disease. She told the group that she didn't give into the problems she faced. She said, "I knew my body could feed my children, but I was worried this would only bring more harm." She said she told God, "God, I got this problem through the act of marriage. It was brought to me. Now I don't want to give it to anyone else so I have handed it to you."

Instead of remarrying or starting a new relationship to provide financial security, Jane used a recommendation letter from the social welfare office to beg for money on the streets. She said some people offered to take care of her children in exchange for sex, but she refused. She said:

> I don't want the devil to bear down on me. Now even us in our lives, those who have husbands and those who don't, we should take care that our bodies are handled according to the ordinance to which we swore that I will die with you alone. If we give into problems, they will take us to a bad place. . . . Truly I ask the women, whatever age we are, those who have husbands and those of us who don't have husbands, let us live by the ethics of marriage to which we have sworn.

Jane saw her vow of celibacy as an extension of her marriage vows. She said when she made this oath to God she prayed that if she broke her vow, God would take her "during the act of marriage." In return for this vow, she asked only one thing of God, that her children would be able to study. Jane encouraged the women in the room saying, "Let us look at our bodies as temples that we are given. Now your body is a temple, so it should build up you and your family." Jane told the women in the room that her decision not to remarry was her own, and should not be followed by everyone. She cited I Corinthians 7:9 to say it is better to marry than burn with passion. For Jane, what was important was that she made a covenant with God, and even when the hard times came, she kept her covenant.

Among the women in the group, Jane had a unique understanding of embodiment. As she talked about her body being a temple that should build up herself and her family, the other women in the room listened. As one of the oldest members in the group, she expressed a deep wisdom that was respected by the others in the room. Even though Jane had contracted HIV within her marriage, she still saw her marriage vows as sacred because the vows had been made to God.

Jane's relationship with her husband was also different from the experiences of many of the other women in the group. She said her husband

was a Christian who went to church and made a mistake by going outside of the marriage. When HIV came into the marriage, Jane said her
husband was truly sorry and apologized for bringing the disease home.
We could argue that within her marriage, Jane had a stronger sense of her
bodily rights than many of the other women in the group, which may
have helped shape her sense of bodily integrity after her husband's
death. But even for Jane, marriage was risky.

Marriage will never be safe until both partners treat one another as
embodied agents, worthy of respect. Within marriage in sub-Saharan Africa, women's bodies are simply not valued highly enough. Christian
churches need to understand this and value women's bodies by promoting self-love and by speaking out against limitations on women's agency.
If women are not valued as agents, if they are not perceived as equals,
then men will feel few moral obligations toward them. They will subject
women to the same risks they take when they have unprotected sex outside of their marriages.

Marriage as an Expression of Right Relationship

Once we begin to address the need to create a contextualized theology
of embodiment that valorizes bodily integrity, we can then begin reaching toward the possibility of mutuality in relationships. For the women in
this study, a model of true mutuality in marriage simply did not exist.
When asked about Christian teachings on marriage, the women named
obedience to their husbands as the key Christian teaching they must
follow.

Mama Gasabile, who preaches as a lay leader in the Anglican church
on marriage and leads marriage seminars, described Christian teachings
on marriage by saying: "The most important thing is obedience of the
women towards their husbands and the love of husbands towards their
wives."[93] While she and others believed that husbands loving their wives
was just as important as the wife's obedience, they also believed that in
all but extreme cases (such as domestic violence) obedience was still required on the part of the woman, even when her husband was not living
up to his end of the deal.

As previously mentioned, the women found a real space of freedom in
tying the obedience of wives to the command for husbands to love their
wives as Christ loved the church. Yet as they expressed this belief, it was
still not expressed as a demand a wife could make of her husband, but
something that a good Christian husband should do. In this sense, even
with this freedom, the women were still dependent on their husbands to
do the right thing.

Western feminist theologian Christine Gudorf argues that even
though the Ephesians passage the women cited addresses the roles of
both spouses, little protection is provided for women. In the patriarchal

culture in which this text was written, love of self meant self-discipline, even to the point of mutilation. In expounding on this, Gudorf cites Matthew 18:8-9, where the people were instructed to chop off an offending limb or poke out a wayward eye if it causes you to sin. Self-love in this context meant inflicting pain, and love of others meant keeping them in line.[94] Simply put, husbands were responsible for the actions of their wives. Wives were to obey, but they were not agents in their own right.

Interestingly enough, the women in this study never mentioned other passages of scripture, which would have given them even more freedom within their marital relationships. While they quoted Ephesians 5, citing the link between obedience and love, they were not familiar with verses such as 1 Corinthians 7:3-4, which talks about the importance of mutual conjugal rights. The verse reads:

> The husband should give to his wife her conjugal rights, and likewise the wife to her husband. For the wife does not have authority over her own body, but the husband does; likewise the husband does not have authority over his own body, but the wife does.[95]

Even a simple understanding of wives having some authority over the bodies of their husbands could have given the women more space to negotiate sexual agency. Yet, as we know, within Christian tradition, the equality within this verse in terms of equal sexual rights has been largely ignored.[96]

When we look at the ways in which the women in this study conceptualized Christian teachings on marriage, we quickly realize that much was lacking. If the only word Christian churches can offer women is that good will come if they obey their husbands, then they are responsible for the unsafe space that marriage has become. It is their fault for not giving women anything better. They, along with African culture, are complicit in not challenging structures that prohibit life. Yet even so, when marriages fail, churches find an easy out as they are able to blame women and men for not living up to the standard of obedience and love. Instead, churches must address the real problem, that when patriarchy is not challenged, when it underpins the teachings on Christian marriage, then churches are complicit in marriage unsafe.

Marriage as "Loving the Enemy"

A pandemic such as HIV tends to point out the weaknesses in a society. The way a virus spreads teaches us much about human behavior and societal inequalities. In the midst of this pandemic, HIV and AIDS have much to teach us about the failings of Christian churches. It is pointing out the ways in which our theologies make marriages unsafe and literally jeopardize the lives of the already oppressed. Changing the tide will not be easy. The suggestions made in this book will take generations to implement. But even if a vaccine was discovered tomorrow, there are still lessons we must learn from this pandemic in order to better love God and better protect our neighbor.

Hopefully, Christian churches will chose to walk this long transforming road together. Yet even if we embark on this journey, a provisional ethic is still needed to keep women safe. Here, I suggest a model from Western feminist theology that can be re-contextualized by women in sub-Saharan Africa as a provisional model for expressing Christian love in the midst of a pandemic.

In responding to the link between violence and heterosexual sexuality, Western feminist theologian Karen Lebacqz argues that in creating a sexual ethics, there is a need to take seriously imbalances of power between partners. Lebacqz begins her argument by listening to the lived experiences of women who have been raped both inside and outside of marriage. Writing in 1990, she argues that in the United States, these crimes were not being taken seriously enough and often excused, especially when the rapist was not a stranger to the victim. Lebacqz believes that these experiences show us that sexuality and violence are linked in the US context, which is problematic for the formulation of any sexual ethics. Lebacqz argues that this imbalance of power must be taken seriously.[97] She says:

> The power of men in a sexist culture is morally relevant in determining an appropriate sexual ethic for men and women. If sexual contact between people is ethically problematic when one has more power than the other, then all heterosexual sexual contact is ethically problematic in a sexist society.[98]

Lebacqz argues that male power has become eroticized and that women have been socialized to accept this.[99] While Lebacqz's argument is set in the US context, her words are relevant for our sisters in sub-Saharan Africa as well. According to the women who participated in this fieldwork, a strong link exists between violence and sexuality in the East African context as well. Violence was the expected outcome for their refusing sex, and sex was rarely pleasurable for women.

Lebacqz proposes that in response to the link between violence and sexuality, we should think about the Christian ethic of "love of enemy." In this context, it means seeing men in a representative role as the "enemy." It means recognizing that because society accepts the link between violence and sexuality, men represent a threat to women. Lebacqz argues that even when an individual man seeks to not be oppressive, the category of "love of enemy" is still important in a representative sense.[100]

The concept of loving the enemy might be a better provisional model for marital love in an unequal pandemic. It forces us to take seriously the danger of patriarchy and think realistically about marriage as an unsafe space. It gives women a way to process the pain of having made vows to another person who turns out to be the enemy either through intimate violence or unfaithfulness. This concept also provides a way to balance out the loves present in a relationship, to separate love of self and love of neighbor, until equality exists.

The idea of loving the enemy also provides space for transformation. Christianity compels us to pray for our enemies and hold them accountable, to seek out change as a prerequisite for reconciliation. While this idea would need to be recontexualized within African Christian theology, it provides a hopeful space for rethinking marriage while marriage is still unequal and unsafe.

WHEN MARRIAGE SHOULD END: ALLOWING FOR DIVORCE

Within both Christian and African traditions, separation and divorce have not often been seen as morally acceptable options. Even today, many Christian churches still do not allow or do not approve of divorce. For example, in the Roman Catholic Church a civil divorce is permitted as a last resort, but even in this case the moral (though not legal) obligations to a living spouse end only in the event of spousal death. Likewise, even in some Protestant churches in sub-Saharan Africa, those who are divorced are often not allowed to remarry or can even be completely expelled from the church. As previously mentioned, this is connected not only with Christian tradition but also with the African conception of the indissolubility of marriage.[101]

Both Agnes and Mama Gasabile talked about the concept of marital separation not existing in most Tanzanian churches. For one PAR exercise, Agnes interviewed a church elder in the Anglican Church who told her, "The church is not allowed to break up a marriage. The couple may separate and go opposite ways if they disagree, but the church's only role is to intervene and try to save the marriage, not to give permission for a divorce." Mama Gasabile added to Agnes' report by saying that, "If it is separation, it goes to the courts. The church does not separate anyone."

While divorce may be the responsibility of civil courts and not of the church, it is of interest that Christian churches in Tanzania have a role in civil divorce. As previously mentioned in chapter 2, when a couple seeks a civil divorce, they must first go to the church where they were married to see if the marriage can be reconciled. In this event, Christian churches have been given an important opportunity in that they can stand against violence and abuse in a marriage by giving a blessing that the marriage should end. This space represents an opportunity to not only end the injustice and structural inequalities present within a bad marriage but to affirm the church's commitment to marriages that are fair and just.

Agnes believed that in an ideal world marriage should last "until death shall part them." She said, "This is because you have already entered into a covenant between you and God." But Agnes elaborated further to say that marriage is a covenant that exists on two levels—first, between you and God, and second, between you and the community. She went on to say:

> But for the human side you think you set a covenant between you and those who are present there. But it is true as they say—I can be taken or that man can be taken. Because even the Bible says that there will be two and one will be taken. Two will be on the farm, one will be taken, two will be in the field one will be taken; two will be sleeping, one will be taken.

The Bible verses Agnes references comes from a passage in Matthew 24 where Jesus is speaking and tells his followers to be watchful and ready for the "coming of the Son of Man." [102] In the passage Agnes quotes from, the stage is set by saying that in the days before the "coming of the Son of Man," people will be "marrying and giving in marriage." [103] By referencing these verses, Agnes seems to differentiate between individual responsibility (a covenant with God) and responsibility to the other (a covenant with one's partner). She suggests that even in the most intimate relationships, a covenant with God takes priority over a covenant with a partner.

Marriage in sub-Saharan Africa is considered to be permanent. Violet Kimani puts it this way: "Culture expects a married woman to remain married so that even the death of the husband is not supposed to alter this status." [104] In this way, cultural attitudes toward marriage and Christian theology on marriage have merged to allow little space for divorce.

For Grace, it was important that the church allow divorce. She said:

> When a church conducts a marriage there should be a law that says if this marriage turns bad, there should be a law to dissolve this marriage. Yes, someone should not just be oppressed just because she got marred. No, definitely not. There should be a law that we dissolve this marriage. A law should be there because getting married should not be like putting a noose around your neck.

Mama Gasabile echoed Grace's concern and said, "Maybe I should just add that the church should have the power to dissolve a marriage just like the government."

In light of the experiences of the women in this study, I would argue that Christian churches should not only permit divorce but, in cases where one partner is in danger, divorce should be encouraged as the best option in a complex, tragic situation. Divorce can offer a liberative possibility for a woman whose partner endangers her life through infidelity or abuse.

I once heard a sermon that described divorce as a proper burial for a relationship that has died. The pastor argued that when a loved one dies, we do not refuse to bury them simply because we wish they were still living. She said we owe the same respect to a relationship. While tragic like a death, divorce is a way of giving a dead relationship a proper burial. [105]

When we think of divorce in this way, we could go even further and argue that the Christian command to care for widows should be extended to all whose relationships have died, whether through death or divorce. Even if divorce were more permissible in sub-Saharan Africa, churches and governments would still need to deal with the vulnerability of women who are single or divorced. More laws are needed to protect women who divorce through providing equal distribution of marital assets and not requiring the return of *mahari*. When divorce is not a moral option, when it presents an excessive burden to women, then we are forcing women to remain married and thereby endangering their lives when their marriages become unsafe.

CONCLUSION

In this chapter, and throughout this book, I have argued that a single-minded focus on sexual ethics, especially one that concentrates primarily on abstinence and faithfulness, is inadequate in light of the complex problems that make marriage an HIV risk factor for women. In response to this, I have attempted to broaden our focus by pointing to issues within social ethics in the sub-Saharan African context that merit our attention, such as dowry/*mahari*, marriage age, violence against women, and women's property rights. I have further argued that women are vulnerable to HIV in many ways, which include biological, economic, legal, social-cultural, global and relational vulnerabilities. And in making this case, I have also argued that because Christian churches sanction marriage, they must play a role in helping to make marriage safe. I have also looked at key themes that emerged from the fieldwork, such as stigma and self-sacrifice, in order to better articulate both the vulnerabilities women face and the obstacles in making marriage a safe space.

As the women in this study said time and time again, "It's better to be single." Yet even as they made this statement, they still looked with hope toward the future of Christian marriage, believing it to be a liberating practice. I believe their hope is not misplaced. Within Christian scriptures and Christian tradition there are immense resources for creating a contextualized theology of marriage that values both justice and love. But the discipline of Christian ethics reminds us that in addition to scripture and tradition, reason and experience are also key components to the moral life. My hope is that as churches seek to address the injustices of this pandemic, they will move beyond scripture and tradition and listen to the experience and reasoning of women. Because African women carry the burdens of this pandemic, they have much to offer the global church, but the church must be willing to listen.

NOTES

1. Three similar ethnographic studies also support these findings. See Fuller, *African Women's Unique Vulnerabilities to HIV/AIDS*, 61–90. See, Aylward Shorter and Edwin Onyancha, *The Church and AIDS in Africa*, 116. And also, Britta Thege, *Women's Agency in Intimate Partnerships: A case study in a rural South African community in the context of the HIV/AIDS pandemic*, (Saarbrücken, Germany: Suedwestdeutscher Verlag fuer Hochschulschriften, 2009). Male infidelity is also problematized by relief and development agencies as well as African theologians. For examples by relief and development agencies, see Avert.org, "Women, HIV and AIDS," http://www.avert.org/women-hiv-aids.htm (accessed March 3, 2011). See also, Bertil Lindblad, "Men and Boys Can Make a Difference in the Response to the HIV/AIDS Epidemic," UNAIDS Expert Group Meeting on "The role of men and boys in achieving gender equality," Oct 21–24, 2003, Brasilia, Brazil, www.un.org/womenwatch/daw/egm/men-boys2003/WP4-UNAIDS.pdf (accessed March 3, 2011). For examples from African theologians, see J.N. Amanze, F. Nkomazana, and O.N. Kealotswe, *Christian Ethics and HIV/AIDS in Africa*, (Gaborone, Botswana: Bay Publishing, 2007), esp. chapters 2, 4, 6, and 15. See also, Daniela Gennrich, ed. KwaZulu-Natal Church AIDS Network, *The Church in an HIV+ World*, (Pietermaritzburg, SA: Cluster Publications, 2007), 14–17. See also, Dube, "Let Us Change Gears! Ethical Considerations in the HIV&AIDS Struggle," in *The HIV & AIDS Bible*, ed. Musa Wenkosi Dube, (Scranton: University of Scranton Press, 2008), 174.

2. UNDP & UNAIDS, "Fact Sheets: Global Crisis, Global Action," (Geneva: UNDP&UNAIDS, 2001) as cited in Dube, " Let Us Change Gears! Ethical Considerations in the HIV&AIDS Struggle, " 174.

3. This is the general consensus coming from the literature on HIV/AIDS prevention strategies in sub-Saharan Africa. While churches vary on their interpretations of whether or not to endorse or allow condoms, almost all churches begin with abstinence and fidelity. Irish Jesuit theologian Michael Kelly says that this is the primary message of churches because abstinence and faithfulness have been key teachings in throughout church history, and they provide high ideals that should be promoted, even when they are unachievable. See, Michael J. Kelly, S.J., "Some AIDS-Relevant Teachings of Moral Theology in the Field of Sexuality," in *A Holistic Approach to HIV and AIDS in Africa*, ed. Marco Moerschbacher, Joseph Kato, and Pius Rutechura, (Nairobi, KY: Paulines, 2008), 117–28. See also, J.N. Amanze, F. Nkomazana, and O.N. Kealotswe, *Christian Ethics and HIV/AIDS in Africa*.

4. This is especially seen in popular Christian literature written for Catholic and Protestant congregants. As part of this project, I surveyed ten popular books available at Christian bookstores in Mwanza, Tanzania, and Nairobi, Kenya. All of these books promoted well-defined gender roles to varying degrees and counseled women to obey their husbands. These books were among the more popular books at Christian bookstores and could be considered typical reading for individuals looking for books on Christian marriage. Books written on Catholic marriage emphasized complementarity while books written for Protestants typically centered on Eph. 5:25 where wives are told to submit to their husbands. Books surveyed included, Gilbert Emonyi, *Preparing for Marriage*, (Nairobi: Uzima, 2006); *Today in Africa Answers Your Questions About Sex and Marriage*, (Kijabe, KY: Kesho Publications, 1993); Matondo Kua Nzambi, *Wake Up, Catholic Woman!*, (Nairobi: Paulines, 2003); Peter Oloruntowoju, *Marriage & The Happy Home for Bachelors, Spinsters & the Married*, (Lagos, Nigeria: Arise and Shine Publications, 2003); Bruce and Carol Britten, *Answers for your Marriage*, (Nairobi: Uzima, 2006); Theresia Makau, *A Successful Wife*, (Nairobi: Paulines, 2009); John Burke, *Christian Marriage*, (Nairobi: Paulines, 2007); Steve Ogan, *How to Beat Your Wife*, (Nairobi: Uzima, 2006); Steve Ogan, *How to Beat Your Husband*, (Nairobi: Uzima, 2007); Eliud Okoth Ouma, *How to Be A Good Husband and Father*, (Nairobi: Uzima, 2010).

5. It should be noted that according to Canon Law, both Joyce and Scholastica should have been able to have a church wedding even though their husbands were

not Catholic. The decision to disallow a church wedding would have been decisions made by their local clergy or church leadership and is not in keeping with the Catholic Church's position on this issue. For a summary on interfaith marriage in the Catholic Church, see, Emilie Lemmons, "Church Teachings: Interfaith Marriage," Article prepared for *For Your Marriage,* An initiative of the United States Conference of Catholic Bishops, http://foryourmarriage.org/catholic-marriage/church-teachings/interfaith-marriages/ (accessed March 3, 2011).

   6. See Ephesians 5:21-33.

   7. Obed Kealotswe, Bénézet Bujo, James Amanze, and Laurenti Magesa all argue that African Christianity's normative claims on marriage, family and sexuality have either replaced or severely altered positive aspects within African traditional systems of morality. Kealotswe and Bujo both lament the loss of initiation rituals, which were used in African societies for moral formation. (Though in making their arguments, neither scholar fully sees all aspects of initiation rituals as morally formative). See, Obed Kealotswe, "The Church and AIDS in Africa: An Overview and Ethical Considerations," in *Christian Ethics and HIV/AIDS in Africa,* 14–27. See also Bénézet Bujo, *Plea for Change for Models of Marriage,* (Nairobi: Paulines, 2009), 69–81. Amanze argues, "By and large, most African traditional ethics pertaining to human sexuality have been supplanted by Christian sexual ethics." Amanze believes this has led to a negative theology of sex rather than a positive view of sexuality in Africa. See James N. Amanze, "Stigma: The Greatest Obstacle in the Fight Against HIV/AIDS in Africa," in *Christian Ethics and HIV/AIDS in Africa,* 35–43. Likewise, Magesa argues that Christianity brought a Western worldview that did not relate to the ways in which African peoples interpreted issues such as sexuality and sickness, and that this impacts African communities today in light of HIV/AIDS. See Laurenti Magesa, "Recognizing the Reality of African Religion in Tanzania," in *Catholic Ethicists on HIV/AIDS Prevention,* ed. James F. Keenan, S.J., (New York: Continuum, 2005), 76–83.

   8. Mbiti, *Love and Marriage in Africa,* 39.

   9. According to the 2010 US Census numbers, 49.9 percent of people over fifteen years old in the United States are married and living with their spouse, and 30.7 percent have never married. See US Census Bureau, "America's Families and Living Arrangements: 2010," http://www.census.gov/population/www/socdemo/hh-fam/cps2010.html (accessed March 3, 2010).

   10. Grace Kumchulesi, *An Investigation of Declining Marriages in Post-Apartheid South Africa, 1995-2006,* The Population & Poverty Research Network, 2009, www.poppov.org/Portals/1/documents/papers/50.Kumchulesi.pdf (accessed March 3, 2011).

   11. Campbell, *Letting Them Die: Why HIV/AIDS Prevention Programmes Fail,* 23–35.

   12. Philippe Denis, "Sexuality and AIDS in South Africa," *Journal of Theology for Southern Africa* 115 (March 2003): 63–77.

   13. Reflecting on Joan's statement, it is important to note that African cultures vary widely on responses to children born out of wedlock. In some cultures having a child out of wedlock demands some form of punishment for one or both parents, while in other cultures, this can be interpreted as a symbol of fertility that makes a woman more attractive to potential husbands. In most cases, even if the parents are punished, the children are still accepted into the community and seen as a blessing. See Mbiti, *African Religions and Philosophy,* 110-20 and Magesa, *African Religion: The Moral Traditions of Abundant Life,* 81–92.

   14. It is fair to say that at least culturally and publically, East Africa is a heteronormative context. This does not mean that same-sex relationships or same-sex sexual activity does not exist (as some lawmakers and politicians in East Africa have suggested). However, when these relationships do exist, they tend to be hidden from public view. In many cases, sex between partners of the same gender is not considered sex at all. Signe Arnfred makes the argument that in Africa, no penis means no sex. (See, Signe Arnfred, *Rethinking Sexualities in Africa,* (Uppsala: Nordic Africa Institute, 2004), 21.

15. Mary E. Hunt, "Same-Sex Marriage and Relational Justice," Roundtable Discussion on "Same-Sex Marriage," *Journal of Feminist Studies in Religion* 20, no. 2 (2004): 83–92.

16. Marvin Ellison, "Response to Mary E. Hunt," Roundtable Discussion on "Same-Sex Marriage," *Journal of Feminist Studies in Religion* 20, no. 2 (2004): 96–97.

17. Emilie Townes, "Response to Mary E. Hunt," Roundtable Discussion on "Same-Sex Marriage," *Journal of Feminist Studies in Religion* 20, no. 2 (2004): 100–103.

18. Ibid., 102.

19. Hunt, 89.

20. Arnfred, 21.

21. Ibid., 21–22.

22. Farley, *Just Love,* 248.

23. Magesa, *African Religion,* 111.

24. Ibid.

25. Kealotswe, 21.

26. Oduyoye, "A Coming Home to Myself: The Childless Woman in the West African Space," in *Liberating Eschatology: Essays in Honor of Letty M. Russell,* ed. Serene Jones and Margaret A. Farley, (Louisville: KY: John Knox Press, 1999), 105–20.

27. Ibid.,116.

28. In the Ugandan context, Tinkasiimire refers to this as "bride-wealth." See, Therese Tinkasiimire, DST, "Responses to HIV/AIDS in Hoima Diocese, Uganda," in *Calling for Justice Throughout the World: Catholic Women Theologians on the HIV/AIDS Pandemic,* ed. Mary Jo Iozzio with Mary M. Doyle Roache and Elsie M. Miranda, (New York: Continuum, 2008), 188–89.

29. Ibid.

30. An example of this can be seen in popular Catholic literature on marriage and family. A prime example of this is found in the book *Wake Up, Catholic Woman,* by Matondo Kua Nzambi. In this book the unitive dimension of marriage is confined to male-female complementarity. The book says, "Brethren, the creation of woman is thus marked from the outset by the principle of complementarity. Woman complements man, just as man complements woman: men and women are complementary" (p. 16). While the book goes on to talk about women overcoming oppression, the arguments are based on finding the strengths in women's nature, which are said to be different from and complementary to the strengths of men. See Matondo Kua Nzambi, *Wake Up, Catholic Woman!,* (Nairobi: Paulines, 2003). Another example of this can be seen in the work of Congolese Catholic theologian, Bénézet Bujo who says, "Neither as man nor as woman are human beings complete but rather both together constitute a whole human being." (Bujo, *Plea for Change for Models of Marriage,* 37).

31. Bujo, *Plea for Change for Models of Marriage,* 38-39. See also, Osei-Wusu Brempong, "HIV/AIDS in Africa: Christian Ethics in Ghana," in *Christian Ethics and HIV/AIDS in Africa,* 73.

32. Bujo, *Plea for Change for Models of Marriage,* 39.

33. Mbiti, *African Religions and Philosphy,* 110–20 and Magesa, *African Religion: The Moral Traditions of Abundant Life,* 81–92.

34. Mbiti, *Love and Marriage in Africa,* 39.

35. Francis-Xavier S. Kyewalyanga notes that among many peoples in East Africa, the only reason for a person not marrying would be their having a disease or deformity (such as leprosy) or being thought to be under the influence of witchcraft. (See Francis-Xavier S. Kyewalyanga, *Marriage Customs in East Africa,* 31–32.) Because of this belief, people who do not marry in the East African context are often considered to be witches or thought to have some other sort of deformity or sickness. It should also be noted that while originating from different context, this same stigma of not marrying exists in Western cultures as well.

36. Mbiti, *Love and Marriage in Africa,* 44.

37. Ibid.

38. Bujo, *Plea for Change for Models of Marriage,* 107–9.

39. Bujo, *Plea for Change for Models of Marriage,* 49.
40. Ibid.
41. Peterson, 983–1010.
42. Ibid., 994–95, 999, 1001
43. Ibid., 984–85, 987, 995.
44. Ibid., 996–99.
45. Bujo, *Plea for Change for Models of Marriage,* 48–49.
46. Peterson, 996–99. It should also be noted that early Christians were persecuted for similar anti-social behavior. However, the difference (in my opinion) is that the missionaries, as agents of colonialism, were in a position of power and therefore the decision for new Christians to abandon family in favor of a new Christian family might not have been as voluntary as the decisions of early Christians due to the economic incentives and other advantages provided by living and working at the mission stations.
47. It should be noted that this is a local requirement set by some churches in sub-Saharan Africa—both Catholic and Protestant—in order to protect the individuals in their congregations. Whether or not this is required is a decision made by the individual church and its leadership. It can be compared to a pastor or priest requiring a couple attend pre-marital counseling before being married.
48. This is a euphemism for having sex. Her full statement in Kiswahili was this: *"Kweli wanalinda ile heshima lakini kwa sasa hivi mambo yamebadilika ni kwamba tunaoana mtu ameshatembea mmeshachokana. "*
49. While there are no statistics that I know of citing the participation of women in churches in Tanzania, I can say from experience that in each of the fifteen churches I visited while in Mwanza, women made up about two-thirds of the congregation. In most Mwanza churches—both Catholic and Protestant—the women sit on one side of the aisle and the men sit on the other side. In this way, it is easy to see that the primary attendees are women and not men. Beyond Tanzania, this phenomenon of women as the primary congregants in Christian churches has been cited in other African countries. In South Africa, 70 percent of church members are women but 90 percent of church leaders are men. (Gennrich, 16). Oduyoye also cites this same trend more generally as she reflects on churches across the continent. See Oduyoye, *Beads and Strands,* 99–100.
50. For instance, according to leadership at the Diocese of Victoria Nyanza interviewed in my fieldwork, while the Anglican Communion worldwide ordains women, the Anglican Church of Tanzania does not. However, the Anglican Communion website notes that ten women in Tanzania have been ordained in "Low Church Dioceses." See "The Anglican Church of Tanzania, http://iawn.anglicancommunion.org/world/tanzania.cfm (accessed March 3, 2011). In another example, the ELCA denomination in Tanzania has over 2000 male clergy but has only ordained 116 women. The Diocese East of Lake Victoria (where Mwanza is located) ordained the first women in the diocese in 2011. See The Lowden's Blog, "East African Women Theologians Meet in Arusha," April 14, 2010, http://elcaarusha.blogspot.com/2010/04/east-african-women-theologians-meet-in.html (accessed March 4, 2011).
51. Prior to this activity, the group had discussed understandings of justice and the use of justice as a tool for doing ethics.
52. John Rawls, "Justice as Fairness," *The Philosophical Review* 67, no. 2. (1958): 164–94.
53. Ibid., 193.
54. Bujo, *Plea for Change of Models of Marriage,* 99–107.
55. One issue arising from Grace's idea of a "trial marriage" is whether or not children would be protected under this type of union. While this question was not addressed by the group, I would suggest that in Grace's paradigm, children would have the same protections as those in a traditional marriage since in many African cultures, being born out of wedlock does not make a child "illegitimate." Further, because the African family structure relies on an extended family model rather than a

nuclear family model, it could be argued that the position of the children would not be drastically affected even if the marriage were dissolved.

56. This is not the case in all Christian churches in East Africa. In fact, Bujo suggests that some people are not interested in Christian marriage because their churches do not require *mahari* (or the equivalent in their cultural context). However, Bujo does not make a distinction between churches who require this and those who do not. See Bujo, *Plea for Change for Models of Marriage,* 128–29.

57. Bujo, *Plea for Change for Models of Marriage,* 128.

58. Ibid., 129.

59. Ibid., 129, fn. 419.

60. See chapter 2 of this book under "Legal Vulnerabilities." See also, Sara Cameron, "Tanzania passes landmark Law of the Child," UNICEF, November 6, 2009, http://www.unicef.org/infobycountry/tanzania_51662.html (accessed March 9, 2011).

61. International Planned Parenthood Federation and the Forum on Marriage and the Rights of Women and Girls, *Ending Child Marriage: A guide for global policy action,* (September 2006): 12.

62. I'm grateful to my colleague Emily Reimer-Barry who discovered this through talking with young girls in an IDP (Internally Displaced Person) camps during our 2009 fieldwork project in Kenya.

63. I would like to thank the staff of the International Languages Training Center in Mwanza for the information given on kitchen parties in Tanzania.

64. "Tanzania: What every bride needs to know," *PlusNews,* Dar es Salaam, Nov. 7, 2008, http://www.plusnews.org/Report.aspx?ReportId=81359 (accessed December 30, 2010).

65. Osei-Wusu Brempong, "HIV/AIDS in Africa: Christian Ethics in Ghana," in *Christian Ethics and HIV/AIDS in Africa,* 74.

66. Frederick Wangai, "Home Management," in *Responsible Leadership in Marriage and Family,* ed. Mary N. Getui, (Nairobi: Acton Publishers, 2008), 93.

67. Ibid., 94.

68. Ibid., 94–95.

69. For more on this argument, see Browning, "HIV/AIDS Prevention and Sexed Bodies: Rethinking Abstinence in Light of the African AIDS Epidemic," *Theology and Sexuality,* Vol. 15.1, (2009): 27–46.

70. Shishanya, "The Impact of HIV/AIDS on Women in Kenya," 58.

71. For an example of a culture where virginity is revered, see Mbiti, *African Religions and Philosophy,* 127–31. To the contrary, Francis-Xavier S. Kyewalyanga uses field research with multiple ethnic groups to argue that expectations surrounding virginity involves both levels of tolerance and differing degrees of penalties for children born out of wedlock. See Kyewalyanga, *Marriage Customs in East Africa,* 37–41. In addition, Benezeri Kisembo, et. al, (writing in the 1970s) argue that premarital sex was very common in many African cultures and that it has often been seen as a way to get to know one another or see whether or not the girl can become pregnant. See Kisembo, et. al, *African Christian Marriage,* 149.

72. Bujo, *Plea for Change for Models for Marriage,* 107–20.

73. WHO, "Violence Against Women," Fact sheet N°239, November 2009, http://www.who.int/mediacentre/factsheets/fs239/en/ (accessed March 9, 2011).

74. I am grateful to Patricia Beattie Jung for the idea that fidelity should be seen as a servant virtue.

75. Mbiti, *African Religions and Philosophy,* 142–45.

76. For more on patriarchy and how it affects men, women and children, see Christine E. Gudorf, *Body, Sex and Pleasure: Reconstructing Christian Sexual Ethics,* (Cleveland, OH: Pilgrim Press, 1994).

77. Ibid., 74–80.

78. Oduyoye, *Beads and Strands ,* 90–100; See also, Phiri and Nadar, "Treading Softly but Firmly," in *African Women, Religion and Health,* 1–13.

79. The Christian Council of Churches in Tanzania (CCT), which is comprised of most of the non-Pentecostal protestant churches in the country, has encouraged its churches not to promote condoms but to focus exclusively on abstinence and faithfulness. Their position, which is similar to the position of the Catholic Church in Tanzania, is that condoms will promote promiscuity.

80. For a more thorough explanation of condom promotion and prohibitions throughout sub-Saharan Africa, see Amanze, Nkomazana and Kealotswe, *Christian Ethics and HIV/AIDS in Africa.*

81. For more on African attitudes to condoms, see chapter 2 of this book.

82. Peter Seewald and Pope Benedict XVI. *Light of the World.* (San Francisco: Ignatius Press, 2010), 117–19.

83. Ibid.

84. The Christian Council of Churches in Tanzania (CCCT) is comprised of most non-Pentecostal protestant churches in the country.

85. Dube, "Theological Challenges: Proclaiming the Fullness of Life in the HIV/AIDS & Global Economic Era," 535–49.

86. It is important to note that while female condoms are available (though less available than male condoms) in Tanzania, they do not necessarily provide a woman centered solution because men can generally tell that women are using a barrier device. In this way, they carry the same stigma as a woman asking her husband to use a condom. For a woman centered method to truly protect women, it must be able to be used in a way that is undetectable in a sexual encounter. Because of this, microbicides in the form of a gel or a vaginal ring hold the most promise for creating a woman centered technical solution for prevention.

87. For more on the Tamar Campaign, see their page at the Fellowship of Christian Councils and Churches in the Great Lakes and Horn of Africa (FECCLAHA) website: http://www.fecclaha.org/index.php?page=tamar-campaign (accessed December 10, 2010).

88. Currently there is very little data on reporting marital rape in Tanzania, primarily because it is not criminalized. As mentioned in chapter 2, marital rape in Tanzania is only criminalized if the couple is separated at the time when the rape occurs.

89. The Human Rights Committee (The Female Genital Cutting Education and Networking Project), "Tanzania: Human Rights Committee Considers Report On Tanzania," September 7, 2009, http://www.fgmnetwork.org/go-news.php?subaction=showfull&id=1248106410&archive=&start_from=&ucat=1& (accessed March 9, 2011).

90. As previously mentioned, the idea of two bodies becoming one body is very present in African Christian theology. An example of this can be seen in the work of Congolese Catholic theologian, Bénézet Bujo who says, "Neither as man nor as woman are human beings complete but rather both together constitute a whole human being." (Bujo, *Plea for Change for Models of Marriage,* 37).

91. Bujo, *Plea for Change of Models For Marriage,* 104–7.

92. For an example of this argument see Christine Gudorf, *Body, Sex and Pleasure: Reconstructing Christian Sexual Ethics,* (Cleveland, OH: Pilgrim Press, 1994).

93. Ephesians 5:21-33.

94. Gudorf, 163–65.

95. 1 Cor. 7:3-4, NRSV.

96. Gudorf, 163.

97. Karen Lebacqz, "Love Your Enemy: Sex, Power and Christian Ethics," *Annual of the Society of Christian Ethics* (1990).

98. Ibid., 11.

99. Ibid., 8.

100. Ibid., 12–13.

101. Bujo, *Plea for Change of Models For Marriage,* 104–7.

102. The exact verses she references are Matthew 24: 40-41. The entire passage includes Matthew 24:36-44.

103. Matthew 24:38-39, NRSV.
104. Violet Nyambura Kimani, "Human Sexuality," *Ecumenical Review* 56, no. 4, (2004): 408.
105. I'm grateful to my pastor, Julie Pennington-Russell, for this metaphor that she shared in a sermon on marriage at Calvary Baptist Church in Waco, Texas.

Appendix

Guide to Research Collaborators

The following guide gives some background information on the women who participated in the participatory action research (PAR) portion of this fieldwork study. Each name listed is the name chosen by the participant, which might be their real name or could be a pseudonym. With the exception of the research advocate, participants are listed in alphabetical order. Each participant's age (as recorded during the fieldwork) is listed in parenthesis beside her name. Other participants named in the research, such as those who participated in varying focus group meetings, are introduced in the text but not listed here since background information was not recorded at these events.

Pauline Gasabile—Mama Gasabile was the research advocate and my fieldwork mentor for this project. She is the director of programs related to HIV and AIDS and children at the Diocese of Victoria Nyanza in Mwanza. She attended all the meetings of the PAR group, and she also directs the Anglican HIV/AIDS support group, which I observed. Mama Gasabile is an active lay minister in her church, St. Paul's Anglican Church in Mwanza, and frequently preaches and leads in other ways in this setting. She married and is the mother of five children. She has lived most of her life in Mwanza, but also spent several years as a student in the United States.

Agnes (28)—As the youngest member of the group, Agnes was only twenty-eight years old. She had been married but abandoned by her husband after frequent miscarriages and two children dying from AIDS. Agnes regularly attended a Pentecostal church and was very active in her church. Once during the research, she even lost her voice due to participating in an all-night prayer meeting. Agnes was only seventeen when she first married and believed she contracted HIV from her marriage. She had finished standard seven (7th grade) and had her own small business.

Christine (47)—Christine worked as a counselor/receptionist at a local clinic where she was able to counsel people who were beginning ART drug regimens for the first time. She was twenty-three when she was married and believed she contracted HIV from her marriage. She stayed with her husband until he died of AIDS and then she began to work to take care of her five children. One of Christine's children died of AIDS. She has been HIV-positive since 1998 and, like most of the women in this study, has remained healthy through access to AIDS drugs through Tanzania's government-sponsored health program. Christine grew up Roman Catholic, but after her husband died, she joined the Church of God. She very much believes that she can be healed of HIV and prays that this will one day happen.

Domina (36)—Domina was one of the first women who enrolled in this study because she was actively involved in an income-generating group for HIV-positive women, which met at the Diocese of Victoria Nyanza. Domina was a member of a local Roman Catholic church. During the fieldwork, she was invited to speak at an Anglican church where she gave her testimony about being HIV-positive. Domina was only fourteen when she was married informally. The marriage did not last long, and she later remarried, again informally, and believed she contracted HIV from her second husband. She has two children, both of whom are teenagers.

Esther (37)—Esther was one of the quietest members of the group, who always smiled and encouraged her fellow group members. She was twenty-two when she married her husband in a traditional marriage ceremony. Later, her husband abandoned her for another woman. She has three children and regularly attends the Tanzania Assemblies of God fellowship (which is not connected with the American Assemblies of God church). She was one of only four women in the group who was able to go to secondary school (high school). She completed Form 2 (10th grade). Esther owns a small business in Mwanza.

Grace—Grace married young, at only fourteen years old, to a man who later took a second and third wife without her consent. When Grace could no longer function in a polygamous marriage, she moved to Nairobi, Kenya, to look for work. She found work as a maid, and when her son was no longer able to go to school, she consented to sex with her boss in order to pay his school fees. She contracted HIV as a result of this sacrifice. Grace is an Anglican and regularly attends a local Anglican church. She is very involved in her church and leads through singing and even occasional preaching. She has two grown children and works in a local elementary school.

Jane (49)—As one of the oldest members of the group, Jane was well respected by the other women in the group. She was also only fourteen when she married, and her husband was her only sexual partner. After he died of AIDS, Jane made the commitment to live in celibacy for the rest of her life. Jane is very active in an Anglican church in Mwanza and has seven children. She was married in the Anglican church, and her husband also attended church regularly his whole life. Even though she knows she contracted HIV from her marriage, she remembers her husband as a good man who made a mistake and who asked for her forgiveness.

Jesca (37)—Jesca was the only woman in the PAR group who was still married during the research. She married young, at seventeen, in an informal marriage, but later she and her husband married in the Roman Catholic Church. Growing up, Jesca had an especially hard life. Her parents were divorced, and her stepmother abused her. As a teenager, Jesca was raped. Then once she was married and found out she was HIV positive, her husband publically stigmatized her and then abandoned her. Jesca believed she contracted HIV from her marriage and ended up caring for her husband once he returned home sick with AIDS. Jesca has two children and had one child who died of AIDS.

Joan (45)—Joan was one of the most educated women in the PAR group; she had not only finished secondary school (high school) but had completed a post-secondary course as well. She worked with a NGO she helped to start which provided income-generating opportunities for HIV positive people through selling nutritional foods that were particularly important for those with HIV. Joan was a member of a local Roman Catholic Church and was an officer in the Anglican Church support group. She had never been formally married but lived for some time with the father of her three children. At the end of the research period, Joan was given a scholarship for a women and development certificate course in Canada and was raising money to pay for airfare so she could enroll in the course.

Joyce (39)—Joyce was also a Roman Catholic but she no longer attended church regularly. She married a Muslim in a traditional ceremony when she was eighteen years old and therefore was ostracized from her church. She believed she contracted HIV from this marriage, yet she didn't know her husband's status until after he died from AIDS. Joyce works in a small business in Mwanza sewing clothes for people. She has three children.

Maria (46)—Like many of the women in the group, Maria also married young, at only fourteen. She was not asked whether or not she wanted to be married; the *mahari* was simply exchanged, and she was ordered to marry in a traditional ceremony. Maria is a Roman Catholic and always wished that her marriage had been a Christian marriage instead. She found out her HIV status when her in-laws intervened and told her to be tested because they had seen her husband with a woman who was HIV-positive. Maria has seven children that she is putting through school, even though she never had any formal schooling herself.

Scholastica (38)—Scholastica was one of the few women in the group who had experienced a happy marriage. Her first husband, who was Rwandan, was kind and faithful but died when a ferry boat overturned in Lake Victoria. She remarried informally and contracted HIV from her second marriage. Once she disclosed her status, her husband abandoned her and took all their things while she was out of town. Scholastica works as a fish seller outside of Mwanza. She is a Roman Catholic and attends church regularly. She has three children.

Veronica (33)—Veronica was the second youngest member of the group. She also was the group member who was married the youngest at only thirteen years old. She did not know she was leaving home to be married but thought she was going to work as a maid for a truck driver. One day when the man came home, she was locked in his bedroom and told she was now to become his wife. The marriage was soon formalized when a Catholic Priest forged her birth certificate to allow her to marry this man in the church. Veronica is still a Roman Catholic and attends church regularly, though she laments that the church and her family did not do more to protect her when she was married as a child. Veronica's husband died of AIDS, and now she is raising their four children. She makes her living by sewing clothes in a small shop in Mwanza.

Bibliography

Ackermann, Denise. "From Mere Existence to Tenacious Endurance." In *African Women, Religion and Health,* edited by Isabel Apawo Phiri and Sarojini Nadar, 221–41. Maryknoll, New York: Orbis Books, 2006.

Amanze, J.N., F. Nkomazana, and O.N. Kealotswe. *Christian Ethics and HIV/AIDS in Africa.* Gaborone, Botswana: Bay Publishing, 2007.

Amanze, James N. "Stigma: The Greatest Obstacle in the Fight Against HIV/AIDS in Africa." In *Christian Ethics and HIV/AIDS in Africa,* edited by J.N. Amanze, F. Nkomazana, and O.N. Kealotswe, 35–43. Gaborone, Botswana: Bay Publishing, 2007.

AMFAR. "AMFAR AIDS Research." http://www.amfar.org/abouthiv/article.aspx?id=3594 (accessed Sept. 3, 2010).

_____. "Statistics: Women and AIDS." November 2009. http://www.amfar.org/abouthiv/article.aspx?id=3594 (accessed Sept. 3, 2010).

_____. "Basic Facts About HIV." http://www.amfar.org/abouthiv/article.aspx?id=3352 (accessed Sept. 7, 2010).

Andolsen, Barbara Hilkert. "Agape in Feminist Ethics." *Journal of Religious Ethics* 9 (1981): 69–83.

Arendt, Hannah. "Organized Guilt and Universal Responsibility." In *Collective Responsibility,* edited by Larry May and Stacey Hoffman, 273–83. Savage, Maryland: Rowman & Littlefield, 1991.

Armstrong, Sally. "Marital Rape in Africa: The right to say no." *The Globe and Mail,* June 11, 2010.

Arnfred, Signe. *Rethinking Sexualities in Africa.* Uppsala: Nordic Africa Institute, 2004.

Asaah, Augustine H. "To Speak or Not to Speak with the Whole Mouth: Textualization of Taboo Subjects in Europhone African Literature." *Journal of Black Studies,* 36, no. 4, (2006): 497–514.

Avert.org, "Women, HIV and AIDS," http://www.avert.org/women-hiv-aids.htm (accessed January 20, 2011).

_____. "The ABC of Prevention." www.avert.org/abc-hiv.htm (accessed January 22, 2011).

_____. "Universal access to AIDS treatment: targets and challenges" http://www.avert.org/universal-access.htm (accessed November 28, 2010).

Bahemuka, Judith Mbula. "Social Changes and Women's Attitudes toward Marriage in East Africa." In *The Will to Arise: Women, Tradition and the Church in Africa,* edited by Mercy Amba Oduyoye and Musimbi R.A. Kanyoro, 119–34. Maryknoll, New York: Orbis Books, 1992.

Baird, Karen L. "Globalizing Reproductive Control: Consequences of the 'Global Gag Rule.'" In *Linking Visions: Feminist Bioethics, Human Rights, and the Developing World,* edited by Rosemarie tong, Anne Donchin and Susan Dodds, 133–46. New York: Rowan and Littlefield Publishers, Inc, 2004.

Baylies, Carolyn and Janet Bujra, ed. *AIDS, Sexuality and Gender in Africa: Collective Strategies and Struggles in Tanzania and Zambia.* NY: Routledge, 2000.

Beehler, Don. "True Love Waits to expand anti-AIDS initiative in Africa." *Baptist Press,* April 12, 2007.

Belcher, Stephen. *African Myths of Origin.* Harmondsworth, England: Penguin, 2005.

Benedict XVI and Peter Seewald. *Light of the World: The Pope, The Church and the Signs of the Times.* Ignatius Press, 2010.

Beya, Bernadette Mbuy. "Human Sexuality, Marriage, and Prostitution." In *The Will to Arise: Women, Tradition and the Church in Africa,* edited by Mercy Amba Oduyoye and Musimbi R.A. Kanyoro, 155–79. Maryknoll, New York: Orbis Books, 1992.

Beyrer, Chris. "HIV Epidemiology Update and Transmission Factors: Risks and Risk Contexts—16th International AIDS Conference. Epidemiology Plenary." *Clinical Infectious Diseases,* 44 (2007): 981–87.

Boff, Clodovis. "Methodology of the Theology of Liberation." In *Systematic Theology: Perspectives from Liberation Theology,* edited by J. Sobrino and I. Ellacuría, 1–21. New York: Orbis, 1996.

Bond, Patrick. *Looting Africa: The Economics of Exploitation.* London: ZED Books, 2006.

Bond, Virginia *et al. Kanayaka "The light is on," Understanding HIV/AIDS related stigma in urban and rural Zambia.* Zambia: The Zambart Project, 2003.

Bradley, Candice, Philip L. Kilbride, and Thomas S. Weisner. *African Families and the Crisis of Social Change.* Westport: Bergin & Garvey Publishers, 1997.

Brady, Margaret. "Female Genital Mutilation: Complications and Risk of HIV Transmission." *AIDS Patient Care and STDs,* 13, no 12, (1999): 709–16.

Brempong, Osei-Wusu. "HIV/AIDS in Africa: Christian Ethics in Ghana." In *Christian Ethics and HIV/AIDS in Africa,* edited by J.N. Amanze, F. Nkomazana, and O.N. Kealotswe, 70–85. Gaborone, Botswana: Bay Publishing, 2007.

Britten, Bruce and Carol. *Answers for Your Marriage.* Nairobi: Uzima, 2006.

Brockman, Norbert, *et al.* "Kenya." In *The Continuum Complete International Encyclopedia of Sexuality,* edited by Robert T. Francoeur and Ramond J. Noonan, 2004. http://www.iub.edu/~kinsey/ccies/ke.php (accessed Sept. 20, 2010).

Browning, Melissa. "Epistemological Privilege and Collaborative Research: A Reflection on Researching as an Outsider," *Practical Matters,* Issue 6, May 2013.

_____. "HIV/AIDS Prevention and Sexed Bodies: Rethinking Abstinence in Light of the African AIDS Pandemic." *Theology and Sexuality,* 15.1, (2009): 27–46.

_____. "Listening to the Particular through Action Research on HIV and AIDS," *Feminist Studies in Religion,* Vol. 28, No. 2 (2012).

Bujo, Bénézet. *The Ethical Dimension of Community: The African Model and the Dialogue Between North and South.* Nairobi: Paulines Press Africa, 1998.

_____. *Plea for Change for Models of Marriage.* Nairobi: Paulines, 2009.

Burke, John. *Christian Marriage.* Nairobi: Paulines, 2007.

Cahill, Lisa Sowle. *Theological Bioethics: Participation, Justice, Change.* Washington, DC: Georgetown University Press, 2005.

Cameron, Sara. "Tanzania passes landmark Law of the Child." UNICEF, (November 6, 2009) http://www.unicef.org/infobycountry/tanzania_51662.html (accessed March 9, 2011).

Campbell, Catherine. *Letting Them Die: Why HIV /AIDS Intervention Programmes Fail.* Oxford: International African Institute, 2003.

CATIE (Canadian AIDS Treatment Info Exchange). "Women and the Biology of HIV Transmission." http://www.catie.ca/eng/PreventingHIV/fact-sheets/Women-Biology.shtml (accessed Sept. 7, 2010).

_____. "HIV Transmission: An Overview." http://www.catie.ca/eng/PreventingHIV/fact-sheets/transmission-overview.shtml (accessed Sept. 7, 2010).

Center for Disease Control and Prevention. "HIV among African Americans." http://www.cdc.gov/hiv/topics/aa/ (accessed Sept. 20, 2010).

_____. "Male Circumcision and Risk for HIV Transmission and Other Health Conditions: Implications for the United States." http://www.cdc.gov/hiv/resources/factsheets/circumcision.htm (accessed Sept. 10, 2010).

Chellew-Hodge, Candace. "Ugandan Gay Rights Activist Murdered, US Evangelicals Must Take Responsibility." *Religion Dispatches.* January 27, 2011.

_____. "Gay Rights Activists Condemn 'Spiritual War' in Uganda." *Religion Dispatches.* February 10, 2011.

Chesney, Margaret A. and Ashley W. Smith, "Critical Delays in HIV Testing and Care: The Potential Role of Stigma," *American Behavioral Scientist*, 42, no. 7, (1999): 1162–74.

Chitando, Ezra and M.R. Gunda. "HIV/AIDS, Stigma and Liberation in the Old Testament." *Exchange* 36 (2007): 184–297.

Clarke, Elizabeth A., ed. *St. Augustine on Marriage and Sexuality*, Washington DC: Catholic University of America, 1996.

De Walque, Damien "Who Gets AIDS and How? The Determinants of HIV Infection and Sexual Behaviors in Burkina Faso, Cameroon, Ghana, Kenya, and Tanzania." *World Bank Policy Research Working Paper No. 3844*, 2006.

Denis, Philippe. "Sexuality and AIDS in South Africa." *Journal of Theology for Southern Africa* 115 (March 2003): 63–77.

Dewey, Joanna. "Let Them Renounce Themselves and Take Up Their Cross': A Feminist Reading of Mark 8:34 in Mark's Social and Narrative World." In *A Feminist Companion to Mark*, edited by Amy-Jill Levine, 23–36. Sheffield, England: Sheffield Academic Press, 2001.

Diallo, Assitan. "Paradoxes of female sexuality in Mali. On the practices of Magnonmaka and Bolokoli-kela." In *Re-thinking sexualities in Africa*, edited by Signe Arnfred, 173–94. Uppsala: Nordic Africa Institute: 2004.

Dirie, Waris. *Desert Flower*. New York: Harper Perennial, 1999.

Douglas, Mary. *Purity and Danger: An Analysis of Concepts of Pollution and Taboo*. New York: Routledge, 2003.

Dube, Musa. "Adinkra! Four Hearts Joined Together." In *African Women, Religion, and Health: Essays In Honor Of Mercy Amba Ewudzi Oduyoye*, edited by Isabel Apawo Phiri, Sarojini Nadar, and Mercy Amba Oduyoye, 131–51. Maryknoll: Orbis Books, 2006.

_____. "Consuming a Colonial Cultural Bomb: Translating Badimo into "Demono" in the Setswana Bible (Matthew 8.28-34; 15.22; 10.8)." *Journal for the Study of the New Testament* 73, no. 03 (1999): 33–59.

_____. "Fighting with God: Children and HIV/AIDS in Botswana" *Journal of Theology for Southern Africa* 114 (Nov 2002): 31–42.

_____. "Go Therefore and Make Disciples of All Nations" (Matthew 28:19a): A Postcolonial Perspective on Biblical Criticism and Pedagogy." In *Teaching the Bible: The Discourses and Politics of Biblical Pedagogy*, edited by Fernando F. Segovia and Mary Ann Tolbert, 224–46. Maryknoll, NY: Orbis, 1998.

_____. "Healing Where There is No Healing: Reading the Miracles of Healing in an AIDS Context." In *Reading Communities, Reading Scripture: Essays in Honor of Daniel Patte*, edited by Gary A. Phillips and Nicole Wilkinson Duran, 121–33. Harrisburg, Pa.: Trinity Press, 2002.

_____. *HIV/AIDS in the Curriculum: Methods of Integrating HIV/AIDS into Theological Programmes*, Geneva: World Council of Churches, 2003.

_____. "Jesus, Prophesy and AIDS." In *Reflecting Theologically on AIDS: A Global Challenge*, edited by Robin Gill, 89–99. London: SCM Press, 2007.

_____. "Let Us Change Gears! Ethical Considerations in the HIV&AIDS Struggle." In *The HIV & AIDS Bible*, edited by Musa Wenkosi Dube, 171–88. Scranton: University of Scranton Press, 2008.

_____. *Postcolonial Feminist Interpretation of the Bible*. St Louis: Chalice Press, 2000.

_____. "Rahab is Hanging Out a Red Ribbon: One African Woman's Perspective on the Future of Feminist New Testament Scholarship." In *Feminist New Testament Studies: Global and Future Perspectives*, edited by Kathleen Wicker, 177–202. Basingstoke: Palgrave Macmillan, 2005.

_____. "Theological Challenges: Proclaiming the Fullness of Life in the HIV/ AIDS & Global Economic Era." *International Review of Mission* 91, no. 363 (2002): 535–49.

Dube M. and M. Kanyoro, ed. *Grant Me Justice, HIV/AIDS and Gender Readings of the Bible*. Pietermaritzburg: Cluster Publications, 2004.

East African Community/AMREF Lake Victoria Partnership Programme (EALP) Briefing. www.iucea.org/downloads/BRIEF_Consult12.pdf (accessed April 25, 2010).

Echezona-Johnson, Chinazo. "Sexual taboos and HIV/AIDS in Africa." *Helium.com,* http://www.helium.com/items/805050-sexual-taboos-and-hivaids-in-africa　　(accessed Sept. 20, 2010).

Edet, Rosemary and Bette Ekeya. "Church Women of Africa: A Theological Community." In *With Passion and Compassion: Third World Women Doing Theology,* edited by Virginia Fabella, M.M. and Mercy Amba Oduyoye, 3–13. Maryknoll: Orbis, 1996.

Ellison, Marvin. "Response to Mary E. Hunt," Roundtable Discussion on "Same-Sex Marriage." *Journal of Feminist Studies in Religion* 20, no. 2 (2004): 96–97.

Emonyi, Gilbert. *Preparing for Marriage.* Nairobi: Uzima, 2006.

Epstein, Helen. *The Invisible Cure: Why We Are Losing the Fight Against AIDS in Africa.* NY: Picador, 2008.

Fanusie, Lloyda. "Sexuality and Women in African Culture," In *The Will to Arise: Women, Tradition and the Church in Africa,* edited by Mercy Amba Oduyoye and Musimbi R.A. Kanyoro, 142–51. Maryknoll, New York: Orbis Books, 1992.

FAO, "Women and Food Security," 2011. http://www.fao.org/FOCUS/E/Women/Sustin-e.htm (accessed February 21, 2011).

Farley, Margaret A. *Just Love: A Framework for Christian Sexual Ethics.* New York: Continuum, 2006.

_____. "Partnership in Hope: Gender, Faith and Responses to HIV/AIDS in Africa." *Journal of Feminist Studies in Religion* 20, no. 1 (Spring 2004): 133–48.

Farmer, Paul. *Infections and Inequalities: The Modern Plagues.* Univ. of California Press, 2001.

_____. *Pathologies of Power: Health, Human Rights and the New War on the Poor.* Los Angeles, CA: University of California Press, 2003.

_____. Haun Saussy and Tracy Kidder, ed. *Partner to the Poor: A Paul Farmer Reader.* Berkeley: University of California Press, 2010.

Faus, José Ignacio González. "Sin." In *Systematic Theology: Perspectives from Liberation Theology,* edited by J. Sobrino and I. Ellacuría, 194–204. New York: Orbis, 1996.

Fleischman, Janet. "Beyond 'ABC': Helping Women Fight AIDS." *The Washington Post.* June 29, 2004.

Foster, Claire. "Disease, Suffering, and Sin: One Anglican's Perspective." *Christian Bioethics* 12 (2006): 157–63.

Freire, Paulo. *Pedagogy of the Oppressed.* New York: Continnum, 1997.

Fuller, Linda. *African Women's Unique Vulnerabilities to HIV/AIDS.* Basingstoke: Palgrave Macmillan, 2008.

Gachiri, Ephigenia W., IBVM. *Female Circumcision.* Nairobi: Paulines, 2000.

Gennrich, Daniela, ed. KwaZulu-Natal Church AIDS Network, *The Church in an HIV+ World.* Pietermaritzburg, SA: Cluster Publications, 2007.

Gettleman, Jeffrey. "Ugandan Who Spoke Up for Gays is Beaten to Death." *The New York Times.* January 27, 2011.

Getui, Mary N. and Matthew M. Theuri, ed. *Quests for Abundant Life in Africa.* Nairobi: Acton Publishers, 2002.

Girard, Rene. *Violence and the Sacred.* Baltimore: Johns Hopkins University Press, 1979.

Goffman, Erving. *Stigma: Notes on a Spoiled Identity.* New York: Simon & Schuster, 1963.

Goldstein, Valarie Saiving. "The Human Situation: A Feminine View," *Journal of Religion* 40, no. 2 (1960): 100–112.

Green, Edward C. *Rethinking AIDS Prevention: Learning From Successes in Developing Countries.* Westport, CT: Praeger, 2003.

Gudorf, Christine. *Body, Sex and Pleasure: Reconstructing Christian Sexual Ethics,* Cleveland, OH: Pilgrim Press, 1994.

Gutierrez, Gustavo. *A Theology of Liberation.* Maryknoll, NY: Orbis Books, 1988.

_____. *We Drink from our Own Wells: The Spiritual Journey of a People.* Maryknoll, NY: Orbis Books, 1992.

Haddad, Beverly. "Faith Resources and Sites as Critical to Participatory Learning with Rural South African Women." *Journal of Feminist Studies in Religion* 22, no. 1, (2006): 135-54.

_____. "We Pray But We Cannot Heal": Theological Challenges Posed by the HIV/AIDS Crisis," *Journal of Theology for Southern Africa* 125 (July 2006): 80–90.

Haram, Liv. "'Eyes Have No Curtains': The Moral Economy of Secrecy in Managing Love Affairs among Adolescents in Northern Tanzania in the Time of AIDS." *Africa Today* 51, no. 4 (2005): 57–73.

Harrison, Beverly Wildung and Carol S. Robb, ed. *Making the Connections: Essays in Feminist Social Ethics.* Boston: Beacon Press, 1985.

Hart, Chris. "Why condom use is an uneasy affair." *The Daily Nation* (Nairobi). March 27, 2010.

Harvey, Jennifer, Karen A. Case and Robin Hawley Gorsline, ed. *Disrupting White Supremacy From Within.* Cleveland: Pilgrim Press, 2004.

Heim, Mark S. *Saved from Sacrifice: A Theology of the Cross.* Grand Rapids: William B. Eerdmans Pub. Co., 2006.

Henderson, Patricia C. "Mortality and the ethics of qualitative research in a context of HIV/AIDS." *Anthropology Southern Africa* 28 (2005): 78–90.

Herr, Kathryn and Gary Anderson. *The Action Research Book: A Guide for Students and Faculty.* Thousand Oaks: Sage Publications, 2005.

Hunt, Mary E. "Same-Sex Marriage and Relational Justice," Roundtable Discussion on "Same-Sex Marriage." Journal of Feminist Studies in Religion 20, no. 2 (2004): 83–92.

Iliffe, John. *The African Aids Epidemic: A History.* Athens: Ohio University Press, 2006.

Immigration and Refugee Board of Canada. "Tanzania: Situation of women victims of domestic violence, including legislation and the availability of protection and support services." July 15, 2008. http://www.unhcr.org/refworld/docid/48d2237a23.html (accessed Sept. 7, 2010).

International Planned Parenthood Federation and the Forum on Marriage and the Rights of Women and Girls. *Ending Child Marriage: A guide for global policy action.* September 2006.

Isasi-Díaz, Ada María, "Mujeristas: A Name of Our Own," *Christian Century*, May 24–31, 1989, 560.

_____. "Solidarity: Love of Neighbor in the 1980's." In *Lift Every Voice: Constructing Christian Theologies from the Underside,* edited by Susan Brooks Thistlethwaite and Mary Potter Engel, 31–40. San Francisco: Harper Collins, 1990.

James, Ruth Muthei. "The Promotion of the 'ABC' of Sex in The Prevention of HIV/AIDS in Africa: Implications for Women." In *People of Faith and the Challenge of HIV/AIDS,* edited by Mercy Amba Oduyoye and Elizabeth Amoah, 143–70. Ibadan, Nigeria: Sefer, 2004.

Jonas, Hans. *The Imperative of Responsibility.* Chicago: University of Chicago Press, 1984.

Kalipeni, Ezekiel, ed. *HIV and AIDS in Africa: Beyond Epidemiology.* Malden: Blackwell, 2004.

Kanyoro, Musimbi R.A. "Engendered Communal Theology: African Women's Contribution to Theology in the 21st Century." In *Talitha cum! Theologies of African Women,* edited by Nyambura J. Njoroge and Musa W. Dube, 158–80. Pietermaritzburg, South Africa: Cluster Publications, 2001.

Kaplan, Laura Duhan. "HIV/AIDS Policies: Compromising the Human Rights of Women." In *Linking Visions,* edited by Rosemary Tong, Anne Donchin, and Susan Dodds, 235–46. New York: Rowman and Littlefield, 2004.

Kealotswe, Obed. "The Church and AIDS in Africa: An Overview and Ethical Considerations." In *Christian Ethics and HIV/AIDS in Africa,* edited by J.N. Amanze, F. Nkomazana, and O.N. Kealotswe, 14–27. Gaborone, Botswana: Bay Publishing, 2007.

Keenan, James, ed. *Catholic Ethicists and HIV/AIDS Prevention.* New York: Continuum, 2001.

Kelly, Kevin. *New Directions in Sexual Ethics: Moral Theology and the Challenge of HIV/AIDS*. London: G. Chapman, 1998.

Kelly, Michael J. *Education: For An Africa Without AIDS*. Nairobi: Paulines, 2008.

_____. "Some AIDS-Relevant Teachings of Moral Theology in the Field of Sexuality." In *A Holistic Approach to HIV and AIDS in Africa*, edited by Marco Moerschbacher, Joseph Kato, and Pius Rutechura, 117–28. Nairobi, KY: Paulines, 2008.

"KENYA: Deadly Catch: Lake Victoria's AIDS crisis." *IRIN News*. Nov. 10, 2005. www.irinnews.org/Report.aspx?ReportId=61001 (accessed April 12, 2010).

Kigozi, Joan. "Sexual taboos and HIV/AIDS in Africa." *Helium.com*. http://www.helium.com/items/425552-sexual-taboos-and-hivaids-in-africa (accessed September 20, 2010).

Kimani, Violet Nyambura. "Human Sexuality." *Ecumenical Review* 56, no. 4, (2004): 404–21.

Kisembo, Benezeri, Laurenti Magesa and Aylward Shorter. *African Christian Marriage*. Nairobi: Paulines, 1998.

Kriel, J.D. and Molebatsi M. Mapogole. "To be clogged up by an impure woman: A male malady among the North Sotho." *South African Journal of Ethnology* 21, no 4 (Dec 98): 181–84.

Kumchulesi, Grace. *An Investigation of Declining Marriages in Post-Apartheid South Africa, 1995–2006*. The Population & Poverty Research Network, 2009. www.poppov.org/Portals/1/documents/papers/50.Kumchulesi.pdf (accessed March 3, 2011).

Kwok, Pui-lan. "Mercy Amba Oduyoye and African Women's Theology." *Journal of Feminist Studies in Religion* 20:1 (2004): 7–22.

_____. *Postcolonial Imagination and Feminist Theology*. Louisville: WJK, 2005.

Kyewalyanga, Francis-Xavier S. *Marriage Customs in East Africa*. Hohenschaftlarn: Renner Publication, 1977.

Lacayo, Beverly, MSOLA. "Sisterhoods and Empowerment of Women in Central and East Africa." *SEDOS Bulletin* 26 (1994): 270–75.

Landman, Christina. "Spritual Care-giving to Women Affected by HIV/AIDS." In *African Women, HIV/AIDS and Faith Communities*, edited by Isabel Apawo Phiri, Beverley Haddad, and Madipoane Masenya (ngwana' Mphahlele), 189–208. South Africa: Cluster Publications, 2003.

Law of Marriage Act 1971. United Republic of Tanzania. www.tanzanet.org/.../laws/the_law_of_marriage_act_1971_(5_1971).pdf (accessed Sept. 7, 2010).

Lebacqz, Karen. "Love Your Enemy: Sex, Power, and Christian Ethics." *Annual of the Society of Christian Ethics* 10.01 (1990): 3–23.

Legalbrief Africa. "Customary & Islamic Law and its Future Development in Tanzania." Issue 107, Nov. 28, 2004. http://www.legalbrief.co.za/article.php?story=20041128143334824 (accessed Sept. 7, 2010).

Lemmons, Emilie. "Church Teachings: Interfaith Marriage." http://foryourmarriage.org/catholic-marriage/church-teachings/interfaith-marriages/ (accessed March 3, 2011).

Lindblad, Bertil. "Men and Boys Can Make a Difference in the Response to the HIV/AIDS Epidemic." UNAIDS Expert Group Meeting on "The role of men and boys in achieving gender equality." Brasilia, Brazil, (Oct 21–24, 2003): www.un.org/womenwatch/daw/egm/men-boys2003/WP4-UNAIDS.pdf (accessed March 3, 2011).

Lorde, Audre. *Sister Outsider*. Trumansburg, New York: The Crossing Press Feminist Series, 1984.

Lovin, Robin W. *Christian Ethics: An Essential Guide*. Nashville: Abington Press, 2000.

Lykes, M. Brinton. "Creative Arts and Photography in Participatory Action Research in Guatemala." In *Handbook of Action Research: Participative Inquiry and Practice*, edited by Peter Reason and Hilary Bradbury, 363–71. Thousand Oaks, CA: Sage Publications Ltd., 2001.

Magesa, Laurenti. *African Religion: Moral Traditions of Abundant Life*. Nairobi: Paulines Publications Africa, 1997.

_____. "AIDS and Survival in Africa: A Tentative Reflection." In *Moral and Ethical Issues in African Christianity,* edited by J.N.K. Mugambi and Anne Nasimiyu-Wasike, 197–216. Nairobi: Acton Publishers, 1999.

_____. "Recognizing the Reality of African Religion in Tanzania." In *Catholic Ethicists on HIV/AIDS Prevention,* edited by James F. Keenan, S.J., 76–83. New York: Continuum, 2005.

Makau, Theresia. *A Successful Wife.* Nairobi: Paulines, 2009.

Maryknoll Institute of African Studies. "Witchcraft/Uchawi." *African Cultural Theme* No. 11. Nairobi, Kenya. August 2003.

May, Larry. *Sharing Responsibility.* Chicago: University of Chicago Press, 1992.

Mbiti, John. *African Religions and Philosophy.* Nairobi: East African Educational Publishers, 1969.

_____. *Love and Marriage in Africa.* London: Longman, 1973.

_____. "The Role of Women in African Traditional Religion." *Cahiers des Religions Africaines* 22, (1988): 69–82.

McMahon-Howard, Jennifer, Jody Clay-Warner and Linda Renzulli. "Criminalizing Spousal Rape: The Diffusion of Legal Reforms." *Sociological Perspectives* 52, no. 4 (Winter, 2009): 505–31.

Meyers, Diana Tietjens. *Gender in the Mirror: Cultural Imagery and Women's Agency.* New York: Oxford University Press, 2002.

Mhlanga, Pamela. "Southern Africa: Justice for survivors of marital rape, how far has SADC come?" *Pambazuka News,* Issue 332, Dec. 14, 2007. http://pambazuka.org/en/category/16days/45014 (accessed Sept. 7, 2010).

Miles, Rebekah. *The Bonds of Freedom.* Oxford Oxfordshire: Oxford University Press, 2001.

Morton, Nelle. "The Rising of Women's Consciousness in a Male Language Structure." *Andover Newton Quarterly* 12, no. 4 (March 1972): 177–90.

Muchina, Pauline. *Roundtable Discussion on HIV/AIDS in Africa.* American Academy of Religion Annual Meeting. Nov. 18, 2006.

Mugambi, J.N.K. and Anne Nasimiyu-Wasike, ed. *Moral and Ethical Issues in African Christianity.* Nairobi: Acton Publishers, 1999.

Nadar, Sarojini and Isabel Phiri. "Charting the Paradigm Shifts in HIV Research: The Contribution of Gender and Religion Studies."*Feminist Studies in Religion,* Vol. 28, No. 2 (2012).

Nasimiyu-Wasike, Anne. "Christology and an African Woman's Experience." In *Faces of Jesus in Africa,* edited by Robert J. Schreiter, 70–81. Maryknoll, New York: Orbis, 2005.

Niebuhr, H. Richard. *The Responsible Self.* Louisville: Westminster John Knox Press, 1963.

Niebuhr, Reinhold. *An Interpretation of Christian Ethics.* Cleveland: Meridian Books, 1963.

Niebuhr, Reinhold and Langdon Gilkey. *Moral Man and Immoral Society: a Study of Ethics and Politics.* Louisville: Westminster John Knox Press, 2002.

Niehaus, Isak. "Bodies, Heat and Taboos: Conceptualizing Modern Personhood in the South African Lowveld." *Ethnology* 41, no. 3 (Summer 2002): 189–207.

Nolen, Stephanie. *28: Stories of AIDS in Africa.* New York: Walker, 2007.

Nwachuku, Daisy N. "The Christian Widow in African Culture" in *The Will to Arise: Women, Tradition and the Church in Africa,* edited by Mercy Amba Oduyoye and Musimbi R.A. Kanyoro, 54–73. Maryknoll, NY: Orbis, 1992.

Nygren, Anders. *Agape and Eros.* Philadelphia: Westminster Press, 1953.

Nzambi, Matondo Kua. *Wake Up, Catholic Woman!* Nairobi: Paulines, 2003.

Oduyoye, Mercy Amba. "A Critique of Mbiti's View on Love and Marriage in Africa." In *Religious Plurality in Africa: Essays in Honor of John S. Mbiti,* edited by Jacob K. Olupona and Sulayman S. Nyang, 341–65. New York: Mouton de Gruyter, 1993.

_____. "A Coming Home to Myself: The Childless Woman in the West African Space." In *Liberating Eschatology: Essays in Honor of Letty Russell*, edited by Margaret A. Farley and Serene Jones, 105–20. Louisville: Westminister John Knox Press, 1999.

_____. "Be a Woman and Africa Will Be Strong." In *Inheriting our Mothers' Gardens: Feminist Theology in Third World Perspective*, edited by Letty Russell *et al.*, 35–53. Philadelphia: Westminster Press, 1988.

_____. *Beads and Strands: Reflections of an African Woman on Christianity in Africa.* Maryknoll, NY: Orbis, 2004.

_____. "Church-Women and the Church's Mission in Contemporary Times." *Bulletin de Théologie Africaine* 6, no. 12 (1984): 259–72.

_____. *Daughters Of Anowa: African Women and Patriarchy.* Maryknoll: Orbis, 1995.

_____. *Introducing African Women's Theology.* Cleveland, Ohio: Pilgrim Press, 2001.

Oduyoye, Mercy, Katie Cannon, Musa Dube, Sarojini Nadar, and Letty Russell. "Women Speaking to Religion and Leadership: Honoring the Work of Mercy Oduyoye," American Academy of Religion Annual Meeting, Washington, DC, Nov. 18, 2006.

Oduyoye, Mercy Amba and Musimbi R.A. Kanyoro, ed. *The Will To Arise: Women, Tradition, and the Church in Africa.* Pietermaritzburg: Cluster Publications, 2006.

Ogan, Steve. *How to Beat Your Husband.* Nairobi: Uzima, 2007.

_____. *How to Beat Your Wife.* Nairobi: Uzima, 2006.

Oku-Egbas, Arit. "Peering Through the Keyhole: Marriage, HIV/AIDS and the Implications for Women's Sexual Health." *Sexuality in Africa Magazine* 2:3, (2006).

Okure, Teresa. "Africa: A Martyred Continent: Seed of a New Humanity." *Concilium International Journal of Theology* (2003): 39–46.

Oloruntowoju, Peter. *Marriage & The Happy Home for Bachelors, Spinsters & the Married.* Lagos, Nigeria: Arise and Shine Publications, 2003.

Ortega, Mariana. "Being Lovingly, Knowingly Ignorant: White Feminism and Women of Color." *Hypatia* 21, no. 3 (Summer 2006): 56–74.

Orubuloye, I.O. Pat Caldwell and John C. Caldwell. "Commercial sex workers in Nigeria in the shadow of AIDS." In *Sexual Networking and AIDS in Sub-Saharan Africa: Behavioral Research and the Social Context*, edited by (1994.), I.O. Orubuloye *et al.*, 101–16. Australian National University, Canberra, 1994.

Ouma, Eliud Okoth. *How to Be A Good Husband and Father.* Nairobi: Uzima, 2010.

Overberg, Kenneth. *Ethics and Aids.* Lanham: Rowman & Littlefield Publishers, Inc, 2006.

Oyewumi, Oyeronke. *The Invention of Women.* Minneapolis: University of Minnesota Press, 1997.

Pandemic: Facing AIDS – Uganda, India, Brazil, Thailand, Russia. DVD. Directed by Rory Kennedy. Brooklyn: Moxie Firecracker Films. 2002.

Paterson, Gillian. *Women in the Time of AIDS.* Maryknoll, NY: Orbis, 1996.

PEPFAR Watch. "PEPFAR's Past: 2003–2008." http://www.pepfarwatch.org/about_pepfar/pepfars_past/ (accessed Sept. 20, 2010).

Peterson, Derek. "Morality Plays: Marriage, Church Courts, and Colonial Agency in Central Tanganyika, ca, 1876–1928." *American Historical Review* (October 2006): 983–1010.

Philemon, Lusekelo. "Rise in Women's Incomes has Perpetuated Soaring Domestic Violence." *The Guardian* (Dar es Salaam). Nov. 23, 2007. http://216.69.164.44/ipp/guardian/2007/11/23/102986.html (accessed Sept. 9, 2010).

Phiri, Isabel Apawo. "A Theological Analysis of the Voices of Teenage Girls on 'Men's Role in the Fight Against HIV/AIDS' in Kwa-Zulu Natal, South Africa." *Journal of Theology for Southern Africa* 120 (November 2004): 34–45.

_____. "HIV/AIDS: An African Theological Response in Mission." *The Ecumenical Review* 56 no. 4 (October 2004): 422–31.

Phiri, Isabel Apawo, Beverley Haddad, and Madipoane Masenya, ed. *African Women, HIV/AIDS and Faith Communities.* Pietermaritzburg: Cluster Publications, 2005.

Phiri, Isabel Apawo, Sarojini Nadar, and Mercy Oduyoye, ed. *African Women, Religion, and Health: Essays In Honor Of Mercy Amba Ewudzi Oduyoye*. Maryknoll, NY: Orbis, 2006.

Plaskow, Judith. *Sex, Sin and Grace: Women's Experience and the Theologies of Reinhold Niebuhr and Paul Tillich*. New York: University Press of America, 1980.

PMNCH/Africa Public Health Alliance & 15% Campaign, Press Release: "Countdown to 2015: Small investment could save 11 million African lives." July 21, 2010. http://www.who.int/pmnch/media/membernews/2010/20100721_africanunion_pr/en/index.html (accessed September 20, 2010).

Poku, Nana & Gareth Schott. *Aids in Africa: How the Poor are Dying*. Cambridge: Polity, 2006.

Poku, Nana K. and Alan Whiteside, ed. *The Political Economy of AIDS in Africa*. Burlington, VT: Ashgate, 2004.

Posner, Sarah. "Recounting (Again) The Role of American Religious Activists in Uganda Anti-Gay Violence." *Religion Dispatches*. January 27, 2011.

Quinn, Diane M. "Concealable Verses Conspicuous Stigmatized Identities." In *Stigma and Group Inequality: Social Psychological Perspectives*, edited by Shana Levin and Colette van Laar. 83–103. New Jersey: Lawrence Erlbaum Associates, 2006.

Rajab, Ramadhan. "Kenya: War Against HIV/AIDS Stepped Up." *The Star*, (Nairobi), March 29, 2012, http://allafrica.com/stories/201203300124.html (accessed May 17, 2012).

Rawls, John. "Justice as Fairness." *The Philosophical Review* 67, no. 2 (1958): 164–94.

Reniers, Georges and Rania Tfaily. "Polygamy and HIV in Malawi." *Demographic Research* 19, no. 53 (2008).

Ross, Susan A. and Mary Catherine Hilkert. "Feminist Theology: A Review of Literature." *Theological Studies* 56, no. 2 (1995): 327–52.

Ruellei, Rosemary Radford, "Women's Body and Blood: The Sacred and the Impure." In *Through the Devil's Gateway: Women Ritual and Taboo*, edited by Alison Joseph, 7–21. London: SPCK, 1990.

Schoofs, Mark. "AIDS: The Agony of Africa - Part 5: Death and the Second Sex." *Village Voice*. December 1999. http://www.aegis.com/news/vv/1999/VV991201.html (accessed February 21, 2011).

Schweiker, William. *Responsibility and Christian Ethics*. New York: Cambridge University Press, 1995.

Seewald, Peter and Pope Benedict XVI. *Light of the World*. San Francisco: Ignatius Press, 2010.

Shanthi, K. "Feminist Bioethics and Reproductive Rights of Women in India: Myth and Reality." In *Linking Visions: Feminist Bioethics, Human Rights, and the Developing World*, edited by Rosemarie Tong, Anne Donchin and Susan Dodds, 119–32. New York: Rowan and Littlefield Publishers, Inc, 2004.

Sherwin, Susan. *The Politics of Women's Health: Exploring Agency and Autonomy*. Philadelphia: Temple University Press, 1998.

Shipper, Mineke. *Source of All Evil: African Proverbs and Sayings on Women*. Nairobi: Phoenix Publishers, 1991.

Shisanya, Ambasa C.R. "Socio-cultural Vulnerability of Women to HIV/AIDS: A Theological Strategy to Transform Power." In *People of Faith and the Challenge of HIV/AIDS*, edited by Mercy Amba Oduyoye and Elizabeth Amoah, 244–66. Ibadan, Nigeria: Sefer, 2004.

Shishanya, Constance. "The Impact of HIV/AIDS on Women in Kenya." In *Quests for Abundant Life in Africa*, edited by Mary Getui and Matthew Theuri, 45–61. Nairobi: Acton Publishers, 2002.

Shorter, Aylward and Edwin Onyancha. *The Church and AIDS in Africa*. Nairobi: Paulines Publications Africa, 1998.

Sinclair, Stacey and Jeff Huntsinger. "The Interpersonal Basis of Self-Stereotyping." In *Stigma and Group Inequality: Social Psychological Perspectives*, edited by Shana Levin and Colette van Laar, 235–59. New Jersey: Lawrence Erlbaum Associates, 2006.

Smith, Daniel Jordan. "Romance, Parenthood, and Gender in Modern African Society." *Ethnology* 40:2, (Spring 2001): 129–51.

Smith, David. "Grandmothers' summit to put spotlight on Africa's 'forgotten victims' of Aids." *The Guardian,* May 3, 2010. http://www.guardian.co.uk/world/2010/may/03/grandmothers-summit-aids-africa (accessed January 23, 2011).

Sobrino, Jon. "Systematic Christology: Jesus Christ, the Absolute Mediator of the Reign of God." In *Systematic Theology: Perspectives from Liberation Theology,* edited by J. Sobrino and I. Ellacuría, 124–45. New York: Orbis, 1996.

Somé, Sobonfu. *The Spirit of Intimacy.* New York: Harper Collins, 1997.

Sontag, Susan. *Illness as Metaphor and AIDS and Its Metaphors.* New York: Picador, 1989.

Stefiszyn, Karen. "A Brief Overview of Sexual Offences Legislation in Southern Africa." Prepared for: Expert Group Meeting on good practices in legislation on violence against women. Geneva: UN Office on Drugs and Crime, UN Division for the Advancement of Women, May 26–28, 2008.

Stillwaggon, Eileen. *AIDS and the Ecology of Poverty.* New York: Oxford, 2006.

Swantz, Marja-Liisa, Elizabeth Ndedya and Mwajuma Saiddy Masaiganah. "Participatory Action Research in Southern Tanzania, with Special Reference to Women." In *Handbook of Action Research: Participative Inquiry and Practice,* edited by Peter Reason and Hilary Bradbury, 286–96. Thousand Oaks, CA: Sage Publications Ltd., 2001.

"Tanzania: What every bride needs to know." *PlusNews* (Dar es Salaam). Nov. 7, 2008, http://www.plusnews.org/Report.aspx?ReportId=81359 (accessed December 30, 2010).

Telewa, Muliro. "Kenya's legal same-sex marriages." *BBC News.* Feb. 15, 2012, http://www.bbc.co.uk/news/world-africa-16871435 (accessed May 17, 2012).

ter Haar, Gerrie. "Religion and Development in Africa: Focus on HIV/AIDS." Unpublished paper given at the African Association for the Study of Religion Conference, Gaborone, Botswana, July 11, 2007.

The Body. "Acute HIV Infection." October 14, 2009, http://www.thebody.com/content/art5998.html (accessed Sept. 20, 2010).

The Human Rights Committee (The Female Genital Cutting Education and Networking Project). "Tanzania: Human Rights Committee Considers Report On Tanzania." (September 7, 2009). http://www.fgmnetwork.org/gonews.php?subaction=showfull&id=1248106410&archive=&start_from=&ucat=1& (accessed March 9, 2011).

Thege, Britta. *Women's Agency in Intimate Partnerships: A case study in a rural South African community in the context of the HIV/AIDS pandemic.* Saarbrücken, Germany: Suedwestdeutscher Verlag fuer Hochschulschriften, 2009.

Tinkasiimire, Therese DST. "Responses to HIV/AIDS in Hoima Diocese, Uganda." In *Calling for Justice Throughout the World: Catholic Women Theologians on the HIV/AIDS Pandemic,* edited by Mary Jo Iozzio with Mary M. Doyle Roache and Elsie M. Miranda, 183–91. New York: Continuum, 2008.

Today in Africa Answers Your Questions About Sex and Marriage. Kijabe, KY: Kesho Publications, 1993.

Townes, Emilie. "Response to Mary E. Hunt," Roundtable Discussion on "Same-Sex Marriage." Journal of Feminist Studies in Religion 20, no. 2 (2004): 100–103.

_____. *Womanist Ethics and the Cultural Production of Evil.* Basingstoke: Palgrave Macmillan, 2006.

Trinitapoli, Jenny and Alexander Weinreb. *Religion and AIDS in Africa.* New York: Oxford University Press, 2012.

Turtoe-Sanders, Patience. *African Tradition in Marriage.* Brooklyn Park, MN: Turtoe-Sanders Communications, 1998.

UNAIDS, *AIDS Epidemic Update.* Geneva, November 2002.

_____. *AIDS Epidemic Update.* Geneva, November 2009.

_____. "UNAIDS Report on the Global AIDS Epidemic, 2010." http://www.unaids.org/globalreport/Global_report.htm (accessed Jan. 5, 2011).

_____. "Greater action needed to protect women's inheritance and property rights in the face of HIV." March 13, 2009. http://www.unaids.org/en/Knowledge-Centre/Resources/FeatureStories/archive/2009/20090313_Propertyright.asp (accessed Sept. 7, 2011).

Undie, Chi-Chi and Kabwe Benaya. "The State of Knowledge on Seuxality in sub-Saharan Africa: A Synthesis of the Literature." *JENDA: A Journal of Culture and African Women Studies* 8 (2006).

UNICEF. "Statistics by Country: Tanzania." http://www.unicef.org/infobycountry/tanzania_statistics.html (accessed Sept. 3, 2010).

UNIFEM, *The State of the World Population 2003*. United Nations Population Fund, 2003.

_____. "HIV/AIDS – A Gender Equality and Human Rights Issue." www.unifem.org/gender_issues/hiv_aids/at_a_glance.php (accessed April 30, 2010).

_____. "Women, Poverty and Economics." http://www.unifem.org/gender_issues/women_poverty_economics (accessed Sept 9, 2010).

UNPFA. *The State of the World Population 2003*. United Nations Population Fund, 2003.

_____. *State of the World Population 2005*. http://www.unfpa.org/swp/2005/english/ch5/chap5_page3.htm (accessed Sept. 20, 2010).

US Census Bureau. "America's Families and Living Arrangements: 2010." http://www.census.gov/population/www/socdemo/hh-fam/cps2010.html (accessed March 3, 2010).

Van Niekerk, Anton A. and Loretta M. Kopelman, ed. *Ethics & AIDS in Africa: The Challenge to Our Thinking*. Walnut Creek: Left Coast Press, 2006.

Veal, Yvonnecris Smith. "Women: Choose Your Role." *Journal of the National Medical Association* 88, no. 3 (1996): 143–44.

Vigen, Aana Marie. *Women, Ethics, and Inequality in U.S. Healthcare: "To Count Among the Living."* Basingstoke: Palgrave Macmillan, 2006.

Wangai, Frederick. "Home Management." In *Responsible Leadership in Marriage and Family*, edited by Mary N. Getui. Nairobi: Acton Publishers, 2008.

Wangila, Mary Nyangweso. *Female Circumcision: The Interplay of Religion, Culture and Gender in Kenya*. Maryknoll, NY: Orbis Books, 2007.

Whitmore, Elizabeth and Colette McKee. "Six Street Youth Who Could . . ." *Handbook of Action Research: Participative Inquiry and Practice*, edited by Peter Reason and Hilary Bradbury, 396–402. Thousand Oaks, CA: Sage Publications Ltd., 2001.

Wight, Daniel, *et al.* "Contradictory sexual norms and expectations for young people in rural Northern Tanzania." *Social Science & Medicine* 62, (2006): 987–97.

World Health Organization (WHO). "Violence Against Women." Fact sheet N°239. November 2009. http://www.who.int/mediacentre/factsheets/fs239/en/ (accessed March 9, 2011).

_____. "World Health Statistics 2008." http://www.who.int/whosis/whostat/EN_WHS08_Full.pdf (accessed Sept. 20, 2010).

Index

About the Author

Melissa Browning holds a Ph.D. in Christian Ethics from Loyola University Chicago. Her primary research areas include Feminist theology and ethics, sexual ethics, bioethics, and HIV and AIDS. She is currently an assistant professor at Loyola University Chicago where she directs the MA in Social Justice and Community Development program for the Institute of Pastoral Studies. Melissa attempts to balance her academic work with her commitment to the church and the world. She has worked in relief and development with street children and refugees in Nairobi, Kenya, and has also completed academic fieldwork and study in the East Africa region. Additionally, Melissa has presented numerous papers at academic conferences and has published both academic and popular articles. For more information about her work, or for resources (such as videos and other articles) related to this book, visit her website at www. melissabrowning.com .

Made in the USA
Lexington, KY
10 March 2015